EXTREME
alpinism

Climbing Light, Fast, & High

EXTREME
ALPINISM

Climbing

Light,

Fast,

& High

MARK F. TWIGHT
and James Martin

THE
MOUNTAINEERS

Published by
The Mountaineers
1001 SW Klickitat Way, Suite 201
Seattle, WA 98134

First printing 1999, second printing 2001

Published simultaneously in Great Britain by Cordee, 3a DeMontfort Street, Leicester, England, LE1 7HD

Manufactured in the United States of America

Edited by Don Graydon
Cover and book design by Ani Rucki
Layout by Ani Rucki

Cover photographs: Front: Mark Twight on the Arête des Cosmiques, Chamonix, France. *Photo: © James Martin.* Back: Mark Twight on the Aiguille du Midi, Chamonix, France. *Photo: © James Martin*
Frontispiece: Crampons cooling in the Grivel factory in Courmayeur, Italy. *Photo: © Mark Twight*

Library of Congress Cataloging-in-Publication Data
Twight, Mark, 1961–
   Extreme alpinism : climbing light, fast, and high / Mark Twight and James Martin.
 — 1st ed.
     p.   cm.
   ISBN 0-89886-654-5 (pbk.)
   1. Mountaineering. 2. Mountaineering—Training. 3. Mountaineering—Psychological aspects. I. Martin, James, 1950– II. Title.
  GV200.T95 1999
   796.52'2—dc21   99–6182
                                                   CIP

For my mentors: I owe you everything.

Strategy is beyond the techniques.

Technique is beyond the tools.

One.

Two.

Ten thousand.

CONTENTS

FOREWORD

In June 1977, I had the incredible good fortune to climb in the Alaska Range with two of my personal heroes, Jeff Lowe and George Lowe. Four thousand feet up a new route on the north face of Mount Hunter, Jeff rode a broken cornice for sixty feet, snagged a crampon, and cracked his ankle. Somewhat naive and certainly far less experienced than these titans of the North American alpine climbing scene, I viewed this development with considerable alarm, while my more worldly companions seemingly took it in stride.

In reality, the level of concern Jeff and George had for our predicament equaled or exceeded mine. They simply had so many more miles than I did that they knew exactly how to deal with it. I had the technical skills, but each of them had the head. It was an invaluable lesson, but I would learn a lot more in the coming weeks.

We worked out an efficient system for our retreat and reached the glacier a day and a half later. Jeff flew out to have his ankle treated, and after a few days' rest, George and I returned to the face and completed the Lowe-Kennedy and a descent of the West Ridge in a five-day round trip. Mount Hunter had been a big route, especially for me, but now George and I were faced with a difficult decision. We had originally planned to go for yet another first ascent, but with Jeff, who we both felt was the strongest member of our team, out of action, we struggled with our doubts and fears. What if we came up against something we couldn't climb? What if George or I were injured? Most important, could the two of us, alone, put out the sustained physical and psychological effort needed for our next project, the south face of Mount Foraker?

Unlike Hunter, which was largely a snow-and-ice climb, Foraker would involve mostly technical rock and mixed climbing on a longer route on a higher peak. After reaching the mountain's south summit, we'd have to traverse to the higher north summit, and then descend the treacherous Southeast Ridge. Nothing quite like it had been done alpine-style in Alaska before.

After much discussion, we decided to go to the Cassin Ridge, the classic hard route on Denali. The route had been climbed many times before, and we both felt confident in doing it. But doubts swirled around in my head, and fifteen minutes before leaving, I told George that we should go to Foraker instead. I thought that we'd always question ourselves if we didn't take this step into the unknown.

We made the long approach that night, and spent most of the next day resting and observing the face, guessing at where we'd go, how far we'd get each day, where we might encounter problems. An early-morning dash across the serac-threatened glacier put us onto the route, the line revealing itself as we worked our way up the initial rock pitches.

Scott Backes climbing near the top of the fourth rock band during the first ascent of Deprivation on the North Buttress of Mount Hunter, Alaska. Photo: © Mark Twight

After our second night on the route itself, we knew we didn't have enough gear to rappel down the ground we'd already covered. The only way out was up and over the top. Foraker was the first time I'd experienced this level of commitment, and it was a marvelously liberating experience. We had been apprehensive starting up the route, but as we gained elevation the doubts and fears gradually faded away as we became more and more immersed in the climbing, the details of eating, drinking, and sleeping in this steep, apparently inhospitable world.

On our fifth day, near the end of twenty-four hours of continuous climbing, we came to the hardest part of the route, a steep mixed gully. George suggested that we bivouac so we'd be able to tackle the problem fresh, but I had a second (or third or fourth) wind and went ahead.

What remains is one of my most powerful climbing memories. I recall very little of the actual climbing, the technical details of the moves. What I do remember is looking up and visualizing myself climbing this section—which was probably the hardest climbing of that sort I'd done at the time—and then some time later, looking back down at George as he came up. It is one of the few times I've gone outside my own consciousness, beyond what I thought or knew I could do, a feeling that I've kept looking for since, in climbing, skiing, running, hiking, all the mountain activities we're so fortunate to enjoy. As befits such a rare gift, it has always come unheralded, never when I thought it would or should.

We continued to the top and back down, with a few exciting moments along the way. George and I had spent eleven of the most intense and rewarding days of our lives on the Infinite Spur. Twenty-two years and many mountains later it remains my most influential climb, an experience that opened my eyes to the possibilities in the big mountains of the world. But as much as anything, Foraker awakened in me a deep sense of spirituality and reverence for life that has helped define my life since then.

Like so many who started climbing in the late 1960s and early 1970s, I began as a hiker, soon took up rock climbing, and eventually gravitated toward the mountains. I've never taken a climbing lesson or been to a climbing school. I learned from friends, taught myself a lot, and served a lengthy apprenticeship under the guidance of more accomplished climbers. My education continues, as does my shedding of decades-old bad habits and weaknesses.

There is no shortcut to experience and the hard lessons that only come from making your own mistakes. I've had plenty of both, but how I wish I'd had a resource like *Extreme Alpinism: Climbing Light, Fast, and High* to draw on during those dangerous formative years. Even today, this book inspires and motivates me, forces me to rethink and refine ideas I've long held sacrosanct.

While routes completed and summits attained are a measure of success in alpinism, Mark Twight recognizes that one learns as much or more from failure. He covers, in great detail, the necessary minutiae of taking care of oneself in a cold, vertical environment, climbing technique and training, how to deal with all kinds of terrain, what equipment to bring, and what to leave at home. Of critical importance is the emphasis he places on attitude and character, that vital internal knowledge one gains only through experience and rigorous self-analysis. Follow the advice and you'll eventually develop a sense of how far to push it when the weather gets bad, how to deal with your own inner fears and conflicts, how to be intuitive and aware of every detail, and how to live fully in the present. Mountains are fantastic examples of the power and mystery of nature, and the routes we climb on them are expressions of all that is best in the human spirit. Mountains and routes are only animated by our interaction with them, however, and it is the people we share the mountains with—the relationships we have with them—that are ultimately the most important. Perhaps this is the greatest lesson that Mark has distilled from many years at the edge.

Michael Kennedy
Carbondale, Colorado
March 1999

PREFACE

I first met Mark Twight when he worked at the North Face outdoors shop in Seattle's University District in 1982. He stood out even then—brash, confrontational, passionate, opinionated, theatrical, angry, funny, and driven. I liked him right away, but I had no idea what he would become. I was a climber of long experience but modest accomplishment and less ambition. I valued the times I bumbled into extreme situations. Making life-and-death decisions and willing my way to safety put some steel in my soul, but I never sought to place myself in jeopardy, and I looked toward the next inadvertent test with dread. Mark, on the other hand, needed to push limits all the time. Still, we became friends, and I followed his career through correspondence and in the mountaineering press.

In the next decade Mark focused on transforming himself, forging a new body, mind, and identity. He used alpinism as his crucible. At first his reach often exceeded his grasp, and he would return bitterly disappointed when he fell short, but each failure spurred him to overcome his faults. In a few short years he vaulted to the top of American alpinism, putting up routes in the purest style around the world. Although keen for recognition, Mark cared more about the style of the climb and the quality of the experience than nabbing a summit.

As impressive as his successes were, I was most impressed by his failures because they revealed depths of character that success never taps. I believe that his near-tragic experience on the Rupal Face of Nanga Parbat is one of the great survival stories in mountaineering. While luck played a critical role, the strength, experience, and mental toughness of the team allowed them to fight their way to safety when others might have wilted and died.

As the years passed and Mark told me about his experiences, I noticed that his approach differed from common practices seen in less demanding mountaineering. His attention to every detail and issue seemed almost obsessive, and his knowledge was encyclopedic. I suggested that he and I collaborate on creating a book to document the world of extreme alpinism. It turned out he had already prepared notes for such a project, so we were on our way. I acted as amanuensis and photographer as we created a book that arose from Mark's experience, speaks in his voice, expresses his opinions, and reflects his character.

Mark has climbed with many of the world's best alpinists. During his apprenticeship he learned the open secret that at the edge of the possible, the rules and techniques of climbing become quite different from the nostrums aimed at beginners. Mark and his partners have tested the conventional wisdom and modified it when they found it wanting. This book distills the lessons Mark has learned in almost two decades of pushing his limits.

James Martin

Mark Twight nearing the top of the Frendo Spur on the north face of the Aiguille du Midi, Chamonix, France. Photo: © James Martin

INTRODUCTION

Extreme alpinism can mean different things to different climbers. In this book, we define it simply as alpine climbing near one's limits. We use "extreme" to denote severe, intense, and having serious consequences. To survive in this dangerous environment where ability and difficulty intersect, the climber must visualize the goal and the means to realize it. After training and preparation, the climber tackles the route, moving as swiftly as possible with the least equipment required. For a fully trained and prepared athlete at the top of his or her game, only the hardest routes in the world offer sufficient challenges to qualify as extreme.

The discipline of mountain climbing originated in the French Alps, so the word "alpinism" derives from the French root "alp." Alpine style is mountain climbing reduced to its purest essence, and extreme alpinism takes us to the cutting edge of that style. Alpine style means attempting to climb mountains on the most equitable footing possible, neither applying excessive technology to overcome deficits in skill or courage nor using permanently damaging tactics, and adhering to this ethos from beginning to end. It means being equal to the challenge imposed by the natural state of the mountain.

Back when alpinism first moved to higher ranges like the Andes and Himalayas, the climbing became more logistically complex. The technique of leaving the ground with nothing more than what one could carry, relying only on the skills of each climber and the rope strung between them, disappeared into a mire of fixed ropes, stocked camps, supplemental oxygen, and Sherpa support—a veritable siege of the mountain. The modern variant sees climbers applying big-wall tactics to high mountain walls: fixed ropes, portaledges, and hauling hundreds of pounds of equipment.

Our definition of extreme alpinism follows in the tradition of Bonatti and Messner, with its ethos of climbing the hardest routes with the least gear. Anyone wishing to apply the term to another style is free to do so.

This book is a report on the state of the art of extreme alpinism. It is akin to a manual for using a room full of power tools. Used improperly, the tools will wreak havoc. Although the text reads like a set of instructions, it merely describes how top alpine climbers, with emphasis on Mark Twight's experience, approach the challenge of the world's hardest mountain routes. Other top alpinists may quibble about details, recommending alternative tactics and techniques or advocating other styles, but all will recognize the methods outlined here as common practice among the world's climbing elite. Every climber is free to accept or reject any or all of the book. Personal responsibility is central to climbing.

We look upon both the preparation for climbing and climbing itself as a process of self-transformation, of character building. Character means more than strength or skill. We will belabor this notion because it is the core truth at the heart of hard climbing. Extreme alpinism is a matter of will. We all know this to be true. In every endeavor, people who concentrate and refuse to quit become the elite. "Know thyself" is the first rule, because self-deception kills. If you are not willing to pay the price exacted by edge-of-the-art routes, ratchet your ambition down a notch or two.

Broader knowledge allows a more competent response to danger. Alpinism requires detailed information, and the ability to use it, on many facets of climbing and mountain living. An alpinist needs to acquire facility in rock climbing, ice climbing, weather forecasting, snow safety, approach methods, retreat techniques, bivouacking, energy efficiency, nutrition, strategy and tactics, equipment use, winter survival, navigation, and so forth. The more you know, the safer and more efficient you will be in the mountains.

In a dangerous environment, speed is safety. Climbing routes at the edge of the possible is akin to playing Russian roulette. Each time the cylinder spins, the chance of firing a live cartridge increases. Therefore, "Keep moving" is the mantra of the extreme climber. The idea of speed permeates this book.

Select the techniques that fit your style and ambition. Read, digest, test, adapt, and employ the ideas that work for you. Discard or ignore what you will. Then make sure you and your partner are playing the same game. For some climbers, freeing a climb is everything. Pulling on gear while cleaning a pitch or in a rush will always be out of bounds for them. If you're not quite such a purist, you may want a different partner.

Despite its title, *Extreme Alpinism* has something to say to climbers ranging from beginning mountaineers to experienced alpinists aspiring to move into the first rank. Each reader can decide what is personally useful.

A host of books introduce beginners to techniques for climbing in the mountains, but none describe how elite climbers ascend their toughest routes. Despite the presence of disclaimers warning of climbing's hazards, most of these books tacitly advance the fiction that proper tactics and modern equipment make climbing safe. While common climbing practices are relatively safe and appropriate for most routes, their efficacy can break down in extreme situations. We believe that an understanding of how climbers survive the hardest routes and an appreciation for the severity and omnipresence of alpinism's dangers will benefit all mountaineers, not just aspiring supermen and superwomen.

The popularity of indoor gyms has bred a class of climbers with extraordinary rock climbing ability but paltry experience in the wild. The ability to climb 5.12 in the gym will do little more than allow you to get into deep trouble on a big route. *Extreme Alpinism* alerts gym rats to the skills and preparations needed to apply their ability in the real world. However, we do not cover the basics of mountaineering. For that, consult *Mountaineering: The Freedom of the Hills* (see Appendix 2, Suggested Reading) or any number of other texts. It's also essential to climb with experienced mountaineers. Judgment takes time to acquire. Mentors speed the process and point out pitfalls that could slow your learning or strike you dead.

Experienced alpinists aiming to climb the classics also will find valuable information in the book: tactics for moving quickly, ways to pare down equipment, regimens to increase fitness, unconventional uses for common gear. We discuss how to think about alternative risks. While these alpinists may never apply these techniques on an extreme climb, knowledge of the tricks of the trade will give them ideas for climbing more efficiently and could rescue them from dangerous situations.

Finally, the book is a guide, a source of ideas, for alpinists ready to elevate their art to the highest level. We hope to help shorten the period of trial and error most climbers endure when first pushing their limits after learning the basics and paying their dues.

We organized *Extreme Alpinism* into four main parts, starting with the all-important subject of an alpinist's character and attitude. Bear with our hectoring. Experience shows that the difference between success and failure is in the mind. Most botched attempts were doomed before the climbers arrived at the base of the route.

The next part details how to prepare for the demands of hard climbing through training for psychological fitness, strength, cardiovascular conditioning, and good nutrition.

Then we review favored equipment, including clothing and a range of devices for climbing protection.

The final chapters, on climbing technique, are the heart of the text. We've included discussion of equipment in these chapters as well, because the use and choice of gear is inextricably intertwined. For example, it makes no sense to discuss stoves outside the context of bivouacking. The technique chapters take you up the route and back down again, along with information on safety, communication, and bivouacs.

Throughout the book you'll find climbing stories illustrating aspects of hard alpine climbing. Mark lived most of them. Acquaintances and friends related the others. Consider *Extreme Alpinism* a report from the edge.

PART 1
approach

aTTITUDe aND CHaRaCTeR 1

Climbing is a mental game. Your attitude and emotions act as allies or enemies when attempting a difficult route at the edge of your ability. The best climbers aren't necessarily the fittest or the most skilled. Instead, elite climbers share a passion for climbing combined with the ability to exert their will and to pay attention to both internal and external conditions.

Great climbers remake themselves. They pare away impedimenta from life on the ground and cast a new character suited for the challenges ahead. Although born with an internal fire, they temper that fire with the recognition that only an unsentimental view of themselves will show where they need to improve and learn. Once they see the path to their goals, they adhere to it despite setbacks and difficulty.

It makes sense to emulate the great, but don't look at their accomplishments. Instead, learn from their preparation. Focus on the mental over the physical. At some point on a climb that stretches the limits, the only strength that matters is in the mind.

First, understand who you are, what you want, and what drives you. Self-understanding is the first step toward building self-control. Practicing self-discipline while climbing constructs habits of mind that begin to kick in automatically as experience grows. With experience comes self-confidence, a prerequisite for tackling extreme climbs in the great ranges.

Self-knowledge

Assess your personality before starting on the road to extreme alpinism. Are you an engineer or are you an artist? Some people approach climbing like an engineering problem, solvable step by step. These climbers train in a quantifiable way, investigating calorie consumption and planning meals accordingly, painstakingly weighing and organizing gear, researching weather patterns, and interviewing others to discover the best time to try the climb. They map the route on a photograph, planning each pitch, each night's sleep, each climber's responsibilities.

Other climbers behave like artists. They look at a route and intuitively know where it will go. They *believe* it will go. They load a pack with what they think they'll need, and upon shouldering it, they know whether that weight means success or failure. They plan casually. They know the season when conditions may be best, and they sense how little food and fuel they can get by with. They train just enough. They act flexibly, often probing with tentative forays to the mountain before committing to an all-out push.

Most climbers possess some of both traits, one more dominant than the other. Learn which speaks loudest within you, and obey it.

Pages 18–19: **Barry Blanchard climbing an overhanging serac at 22,500 feet on the Merkl Icefield of Nanga Parbat's Rupal Face in Pakistan. We climbed the serac to avoid a huge windslab on a lower angled slope.** *Photo: © Mark Twight*

Assess your strengths, weaknesses, experience, and ability. Don't attempt the southwest face of Everest in alpine style after climbing the Cassin Ridge on Denali in eight days. The leap isn't rational. Experience at 20,000 feet, lower than the starting altitude for climbing Everest, is insufficient. Of course, dreams are important. Dreams lead toward the great routes of the future. Recognize them as goals and march toward them, *running* toward them every now and then. Still, they belong to the future.

Beware of accidentally succeeding on a route above your ability. Success tends to breed ambition. The next time, a route of similar difficulty and danger may deliver the hard lesson that a single success at a high level may represent luck and not skill. Learn to recognize when you lucked out and when you met the challenge. Without this understanding, such a victory will feed contempt for easy routes on forgiving mountains. Contempt leads to a casual attitude, which results in carelessness and ultimate failure on a grand scale. Respect the routes you complete and those that turn you back. Respect for the mountains is a cornerstone of a long and fruitful career.

Understand your temperament. Read studies on temperament types and apply their insights to particular sports and their subdisciplines (read Jonathan Niednagel's *Choose Your Best Sport & Play It,* listed in Appendix 2, Suggested Reading). Understanding your type will help direct you to routes that match your predispositions. If you diagnose your abilities correctly and combine that with knowledge of your temperament type, the choice of a style of climbing within alpinism will be simple.

For example, great aerobic capacity doesn't translate into the ability to climb K2 in under 24 hours if you are not psychologically predisposed to that style of climbing. Many climbers are disinclined to suffer the monotony of moderate terrain. Others shun the risk of climbing without a rope. Some choose harder, more "interesting" routes at lower elevation rather than high-altitude forays. Pure difficulty bores some people: The drudgery of reclining on a portaledge while the leader spends 4 hours on a pitch may frustrate someone who relishes movement and loves to cover as much terrain as possible in a given time.

Look for routes where you can exploit your strong points, and where you'll be psychologically comfortable and satisfied. Experiment with different types of climbing and learn how you perform both physically and emotionally on them. If you just want to do hard routes so you can say you climbed them—that is, if you are climbing for other people—you'll probably have one or two close calls and then quit. Only by knowing yourself can you avoid using other people's yardsticks to measure your own achievements or to decide whether a route is worth doing.

Accepting Fear

Inexperienced climbers hold the grand masters in awe because of their apparent fearlessness. But whatever their actions suggest, no person is immune to fear. Although the great climber feels comfortable in terrifying situations, he or she knows to fear only that which should be feared. Don't imagine the grand master dispassionately contemplating the arrival of a killer storm. This climber is scared but not paralyzed, terrified but able to turn fear into productive action. The mind produces fear, so fear is subject to its control and direction. Acquire the difficult yet essential skill of directing fear, harnessing it as a source of energy. There is no recipe for this skill, because each mind is different, but some concepts may provide direction.

Nobody controls a situation in the mountains. It is vanity to imagine one can. Instead, grow comfortable with giving up control and acting within chaos and uncertainty. Attempting to dominate constantly changing circumstances in the mountains or to fight the loss of control serves only to increase fear and multiply its effects. Embrace the inherent lack of control and focus on applying skills and ideals to the situation.

To climb through fear, to point fear up instead of down, you need to maintain the desire and strength, the will and discipline, to go until the end of the pitch. If you are scared, reinforce your confidence by biting off what you know you can chew. Successfully swallowing it will encourage you to take another bite, another pitch. Try to keep sight of the long view. Any time your mind can accept a bigger bite, go for the top in one big gulp. Preserve your drive. Don't sketch around or get psyched out or consider lowering off to relinquish the lead. Trust in your skill, and give yourself up to the action.

The scared climber often points his fear at the ground, believing retreat will deliver a more comfortable state of mind. This climber has too strong a connection to the ground. An irrational fixation on retreat will impede upward progress when retreat isn't an option. Instead, learn to aim fear at the belay above. My climbing partner Scott Backes once described a climber as "going for the belay." He meant the guy was psyched *up*—that if he hadn't run out of rope, he would have kept going. He didn't just *hit* the target, he punched through it. Anyone who climbs like this will feel fear, greet it, and keep going.

When self-discipline fails and fear runs unchecked, the spiral into panic is not far off. Panic is uncontrolled, undirected fear and as such is unproductive. It takes a huge amount of energy to panic, and you receive little enduring energy in return. Panic is great for lifting a car off of a baby or fleeing a charging mastodon, but it is useless for getting out of a dangerous predicament in the mountains. Panic blocks thought. If you can't think, you die.

A productive response to fear doesn't derive from the simple decision not to panic. I learned that during my formative years when I was climbing a lot of winter routes in the North Cascades of Washington State, where fear caused me to retreat numerous times. My ambition far outstretched my physical and psychological capacities. After a shouting match with Andy Nock on the summit of one of the Twin Sisters—he wanted to descend and climb the other peak while I simply wanted to get out of there—I quit climbing altogether. I wasn't comfortable in the mountain environment. Fear held me hostage.

My mentor, Gary Smith, believed I couldn't learn any more from climbing itself. He had served with Marine reconnaissance in Vietnam, so he was well acquainted with Mr. Fear. Gary suggested I study martial arts and introduced me to a school in Seattle's Chinatown. I trained there three nights a week, three hours each night, for eighteen months.

Mark Twight retreating across the bergschrund after attempting to solo a new route on the north face of Pic Communism in the Pamir mountains of Tadjikistan. *Photo: © Ace Kvale*

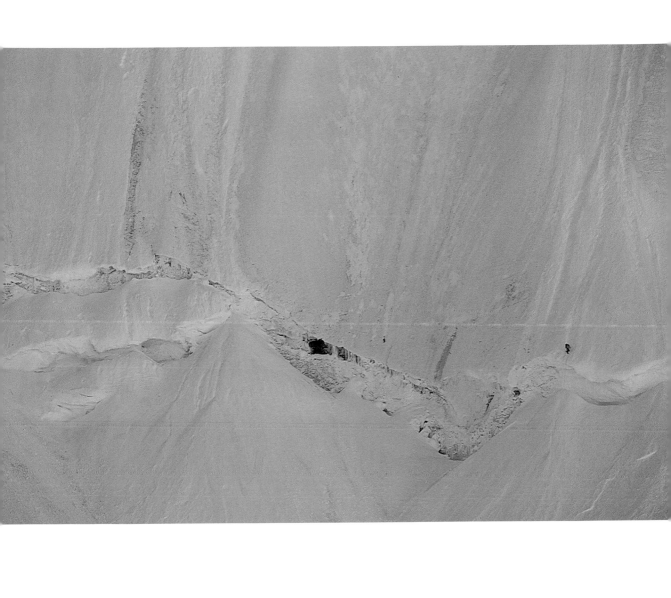

There were no belt ranks, no tournaments, and no bullshit—only discipline, hard work, and slowly emerging self-confidence.

Training with more experienced students, who were capable of really hurting me, taught reasonable responses to fear. The belief in my own strength—developed during my time at the school and during early-morning sessions with Gary learning to play the Japanese strategy game Go—eventually turned me back to the mountains. I said farewell to my mentor and to the school's *sifu*, John Leong, to begin climbing again.

Every martial art and Eastern philosophy has at its heart the "conquest" of fear. Breathing and relaxation techniques learned from the martial arts, meditation, or biofeedback training may be carried everywhere once you learn them. (See Appendix 2, Suggested Reading for works by Krishnamurti, Reinhard Kammer, and Bruce Lee.) These techniques reshape panic into plain old fear or discomfort, thus gaining power over it or releasing it altogether.

Will and Suffering

The difference between a good alpinist and a great one is will. To be a great climber, you must exercise the discipline required to know yourself. You train to be stronger than you think necessary. On a route you eat an energy bar even if it makes you gag, and you drink regularly to stay hydrated. You stop in the middle of a pitch to pull your hood up if the spindrift gets bad, instead of waiting to reach the belay, and you stay dry because of it. You maintain the discipline needed to melt enough ice each night to fill the water bottles, and you sweep snow out of the tent instead of letting it melt. You don't care if your partner's pack weighs less. You wake up and start the stove as soon as the alarm goes off. As a disciplined climber, you recognize when you're having a bad day and admit it to your partner; then you relinquish leads where you might slow the team. You do all the cooking that night. As a strong-willed climber, you fast for a day or two without complaint to wait out bad weather.

Where does this strong will and hardness come from? It derives from recognizing desires and goals and then enduring whatever it takes to fulfill them. A strong will grows from suffering and being rewarded for it. Does a strong will come from years of multihour training runs or do those runs result from a dominating will? There is no right answer because will and action feed one another.

Suffering provides the opportunity to exercise will and to develop toughness. Climb on local crags in weather conditions far worse than any you would intentionally confront in the high mountains. Austrian climber Hermann Buhl carried snowballs in his hands to develop his tolerance (psychological) and to increase capillary capacity (physical). He climbed the local crags all winter long, even in storms, and bicycled for hundreds of kilometers on his way to the mountains. It all paid off when he climbed alone to the summit of Nanga Parbat—history's only solo first-ascent of an 8,000-meter peak.

The mind and body adapt to both comfort and deprivation. The difficult experiences of mountaineering may appear irrational and risky from the comfort of the armchair, but learning to deal with them is essential. Relish the challenge of overcoming difficulties that would crush ordinary men and women.

Michael Gilbert and Scott Backes got soaked to the bone climbing the Waterfall Pitch on the north face of the Eiger. When they stopped for the night at the Brittle Ledges, they discovered their sleeping bags were drenched as well. Michael asked, "What are we going to do now?" Scott replied, "We're going to suffer."

Experience and Learning

Experience acts as a shield against disaster. An experienced climber spots potential problems and takes the right steps to avoid them. Experience provides the raw material for imagining and executing hard routes in the mountains.

But if you don't have the experience, how do you gain it without becoming discouraged or injured in the process? Bite off a little at a time. Choose mountains and routes that fit your ability. Develop a program that promotes progress without getting you thrashed or discouraged. Jumping into the deep end of the pool may be the fastest way to learn to swim, but history abounds with examples of climbers who "swam" too far, too soon, and never came back.

It's easy to look at pictures of skilled climbers on difficult routes and say to yourself, "I want to be there doing that, right now." Instead, move one step at a time. Don't depend on luck instead of skill. You may be cool, you may be talented, and you may have gotten away with some "serious" roadside routes or local alpine test pieces, but don't plan on succeeding on any worthwhile routes your first few times in the Alps, Alaska, or the Himalayas. Don't count on fulfilling your dreams right away. Don't even try. If you are in it for the long run, you have plenty of time—and that's what it takes.

Learn how to learn. Write everything down if there's a risk of forgetting, and refer to these notes whenever a question arises. Read the stories of the grand masters of alpinism. (Books by Reinhold Messner and Hermann Buhl are listed in Appendix 2, Suggested Reading.) These stories aren't intended as instructional, but you'll learn plenty. Ask questions of other climbers; only the unasked question is stupid. And learn from your mistakes. The intelligent climber makes each mistake only once, and he is cured. The burned hand teaches best.

Find mentors with experience relating to your goals and with the willingness to pass it on. If you show dedication and desire, an inclination to learn, and some talent, many climbers will tell you or show you what they know. Even if they refuse to climb with you—and most will decline the honor—a mentor who knows the path you wish to tread can teach far more than any video, book, or school.

Confidence

Confidence makes hardship easier to bear, renders extreme cold less debilitating, and allows you to take long runouts above dubious gear without experiencing a paralyzing fear. Climbing while riddled with fear and doubt conjures worries about the condition of the ropes, the prospect of storms, and whether the "welded" half-inch angle piton will hold. These concerns should prompt attention, not fear.

Most climbers graduating from big-wall climbing, cragging, or sport routes on ice and mixed terrain to major routes done in alpine style allow apprehension and ignorance to degrade their technical ability. This remains true until they adapt to the environment and begin to fully tap their skills. Until then, A2 seems harder than it is. A rating of 5.8 feels like 5.11, and M5 seems as sketchy as M8. All belay anchors look suspect. The awful scale of the mountains seems to transform routine moves into difficult and dangerous ones.

This is a natural reaction. Just remember that nuts have the same holding power at 14,000 feet as they do at sea level, and that 5.8 here equals 5.8 anywhere. If you did it in the lowlands, you can do it here. The consequences of falling are far more serious in the mountains, but performing up to your potential is more important than worrying about falling.

To imagine a difficult new route, to plan it and believe in your ability so strongly that success becomes possible or even probable, demands a powerful ego. Genuine confidence is rare. More often we see a cavalier attitude toward life and death. People with inadequate experience don't understand the consequences of risk and tend to bluster and pose—at least until an accumulation of near misses or the deaths of friends confront even dullards with reality.

The audacity and certitude of youth often have no foundation, yet many routes in the Alps and the Himalayas were realized by pure desire leavened with luck. The young climber who survives his years of boldness will develop into a self-assured, calculating, and mature climber with better chances of both success and survival. Try to live through the learning curve by exercising caution until skill develops.

Talent alone can't get you there. Ambition fueled by ability and vision must be tempered with uncompromising honesty about the limits of your talent, who you are, how much risk is acceptable, and which style of routes fits you best. Belief in your ability is earned. Don't pretend. Understanding your weakness is part of confidence, too. Posturing is fatal.

Failure—and the Tyranny of Success

People usually treat climbing as a goal-oriented sport instead of an experience-oriented sport. However, the lessons and spirit of climbing come from the act of climbing, and their value doesn't depend on reaching a summit. All goal-oriented enterprises contain failure as their antithesis, but turning back on a climb doesn't invalidate the hard work and tough lessons encountered along the way.

Treating climbing as a means to nab a summit or complete a route engenders a fear of failure. Failure then becomes a physical or psychic defect. This is the fate of climbers who value summits over experience, who succumb to the tyranny of success. Unlike other sports disciplines, high-level alpinism becomes more dangerous the more you do it. The drug-like demands of harder, higher, lighter, faster have killed most of the very best climbers the world has ever seen. No one is immune. On the other hand, people who want to learn, who want to live long enough to do a number of good routes and to become climbers that partners and family can trust, learn how to fail and when to fail.

All alpine climbers struggle with learning when to fail. It is one of the most difficult lessons. Every great climber turns back too soon on occasion—or waits too long to retreat, goes past the point of no return, and is forced to "fail upward." No formula determines the correct moment to fail. It can arrive upon shouldering the pack, it can arise fifteen pitches up an eighteen-pitch route, it can bite you after days of toiling upward. Self-knowledge usually solves the problem: You should fail and retreat before completely losing control of yourself.

Learn to turn back before losing all ability to influence what will happen to you. Although no one fully controls a situation in the mountains, you should never voluntarily relinquish control of yourself. Force circumstances to wrestle away your self-control only after a hard fight. Even then, don't allow panic to induce paralysis. Everyone loses it at some point, but those with enough training and experience are able to rely on reflex and their survival instinct to make decisions. Reflex is the result of training, training, training. The will to live is programmed into everyone. Some people's will is stronger than others. Is yours strong, or will you just give up without much of a fight? Know before you go.

Learning *how* to fail is a bit easier. The mechanics of retreat are covered in the final chapter of this book. Besides being physically intricate, retreating safely and efficiently is a state of mind. Depending on the margin of safety, the slightest potential problem with weather or psyche could mandate retreat, or the team could be strong enough to get in really deep before needing to pull the plug. The style of ascent corresponds directly to the style of retreat. Dealing with the possibility of both retreat and of "failing upward" is an integral part of planning for any route in the mountains.

Good and Bad Attitudes

A bad attitude or unsettled mind will destroy focus, guaranteeing failure regardless of training and preparation. You must want (or need) to be where you are. Doing one thing with the body and another with the mind is self-defeating. A mind not giving 100 percent is a liability. If you can't pay attention to the climbing or if you don't want to be on the mountain, don't go.

A bad attitude for a climber bears little resemblance to the usual meaning of the term. Many climbers complete hard routes out of rage or despair—some make a lifestyle out of it. These are attitudes that some people might call "bad." I define a bad attitude as a mental state that prevents you from realizing your desires.

A good attitude consists of a psychological state that allows and spurs you to reach a goal. Both equanimity and rage could qualify. Personal torment has inspired great climbs and great creations. Outsiders may view torment as a negative state of mind or bad attitude. But confusion, questioning, and doubt often act as fountains of creativity, producing grand works of art and action. They meet my definition of good attitudes.

FAILURE

I've retreated from an alarming number of routes during my career. Sometimes I fled storms; other times technical difficulty defeated me. Often I forgot to eat and drink enough, so my strength fizzled, and along with it my confidence. Sometimes I was scared, plain and simple. I've failed in the hut by realizing, the instant my feet hit the cold floor, that I couldn't do what I wanted to do. The hours sleeping in the wake of a decision like that are some of the most refreshing I've had. And I failed at 27,500 feet on Everest after four attempts on a new route in the lightest of styles: no bottled oxygen, no fixed rope, no climbing rope, no sleeping bag—just one partner, my tools, a pad, a stove, and a shovel. I wasn't willing to risk doing "just a little more"—the same "just a little more" that distinguishes the good from the great.

I failed 1,200 feet below the top of the biggest wall in the world—the Rupal Face of Nanga Parbat—after climbing just under 14,000 vertical feet in five days. I failed to climb a new route on the 10,000-vertical-foot north face of Pic Communism because I misinterpreted conditions both on the face and in my head. I wanted to be the guy in the magazine who soloed the hard, new route. Unfortunately my mind wasn't in the mood. I retreated. Twenty-four hours later, I soloed the Czech Route on the same face, a climb more closely corresponding to my state of mind. I knew myself, but it took failure from eight pitches up the virgin line to make me see what I needed.

I've failed on routes because I did not know how to do them, but each attempt was another foray into the classroom. I usually graduated with enough information to complete the climb. The route called Beyond Good and Evil, on the north face of the Aiguille des Pelerins in the French Alps, required three visits to the schoolroom before we figured out how to do it. I retreated twice from the South Pillar of Nuptse, even in the company of a much wiser climber, because for me the route should have been ten years in the future. Blind, foolish ambition coaxed me onto the wall. I'm glad I lived through it.

I have failed a lot. But my attitude toward failing and toward learning keeps me from considering myself a failure. I learn ten times more from every miscarry than from any success. The knowledge I gain gives me the confidence to return to these faces and attempt them again, or to try bigger, harder routes several years down the road. I know how to get down off any mountain, and I can do so in almost any conditions. These skills and this confidence allow me to progress instead of repeating myself, and to imagine the evolutionary routes of my future.

Mark Twight in Kahiltna Base Camp, Alaska. Sometimes after failing the only thing to do is get good and drunk. *Photo: © Michael Kennedy*

PART II
TRAINING

psychological training 2

The mind rules the body. Will, awareness, and understanding all improve through consistent and appropriate psychological training. Although alpinism is more a psychological than a physical challenge, there is no actual separation: it is all psychological and all physical at the same time. Nonetheless, the mental aspects of alpinism are fundamental.

The mind develops in response to day-to-day life. It answers the demands of living in society, in the low-altitude world. Preparing it to exist and thrive in the radically different circumstances of the mountains profits a climber more than any amount of physical training. All your body training depends upon what happens in your mind at the same time. Your performance on the mountain is simply an expression of the ideas and ideals you harbor in your mind.

Awareness

People tend to believe they need to concentrate intensely to attain a goal—that concentration is a benefit by focusing attention forcefully and precisely on the task at hand. Concentrating on one thing, however, excludes many other things. With voluntary blinders, a concentrated mind becomes less attentive and aware.

On the other hand, an aware mind embraces everything. Instead of concentrating on a single task or a single component of a situation, it encompasses every aspect. To do this demands abandonment of oneself to *become* the action. Only in this mindful awareness, without choice, without anxiety, and without conscious direction of attention, is there true perception. Through this perception you can respond correctly to the constantly changing circumstances of the mountain environment and your own place within it.

I define awareness as attention unencumbered by thought or judgment, without memory or speculation, living in the present tense. Awareness strips away the filters of your past experience, allowing an unmediated experience. Awareness of one's condition and the state of one's surroundings permits top-level performance by allowing the mind to apprehend the actual situation and respond to it instantly. The understanding of dangers and opportunities, requirements and personal capacity, become clear in a blink.

The aware climber constantly monitors his own status, asking the questions: Do I need to go faster? Can I? For how long? Are my decisions being degraded by dehydration, lack of food, or sleep deprivation? What is the weather doing? The climber is able to apprehend the world and to react.

Pages 30–31: Steve House leading the eleventh pitch of The Gift That Keeps on Giving on Mount Bradley's south face, Alaska. Steve, Jonny Blitz, and I made the first ascent of this route in March 1998. *Photo: © Mark Twight*

Relaxation

A fear-arousing situation should cue the climber to relax—to let both body and mind go, rather than driving them. But this kind of reaction to fear presupposes a high level of mental training, confidence, and experience. You can only let go, allowing instinctual reaction to prevail instead of conscious reaction, if you believe 100 percent in the ability of the unconscious to direct the action. Reaching such "enlightenment" requires discipline and training beyond most people's imagination. It necessitates an entirely different way of thinking than Western civilization teaches.

Climbing is full of sensory stimuli that, through self-programming, can become cues to relaxation. I prefer to use sound. I automatically relax when I hear and feel an ice tool sink deep into solid ice. I programmed myself to relax upon hearing the ringing sound of the circular adze on an old Stubai ice tool. Like a solid pin placement, it sounded *good* when the tool went in well—and each time it did, I relaxed my grip on the shaft and hung mostly from the leash. When I soloed Slipstream in the Canadian Rockies, I lost myself in this ringing.

Russ Clune told me he uses the sound of a carabiner gate snapping shut as his cue to relax. I began to notice how much comfort I derived from knowing I had clipped the rope to a solid piece, and the sound of the biner was the key. I then attempted to artificially create and hear the "sound" in my head when I'm stressed—and it worked. Today I can induce relaxation virtually at will—except when the world turns to shit, panic looms, and I need to relax the most.

Meditation

Learning to meditate—and there are many forms of it—is a useful tool for climbers. For our purposes, meditation consists of the ability to intentionally realize a state of intense awareness. Quieting the internal dialogue in order to perform a given task without distraction is essential to both physical training and climbing. Without a quiet mind every physical action is hampered by the mind itself.

Many people separate meditation from other activities, scheduling it before training or climbing. The best meditate while they train or climb. This active meditation, while similar to passive meditation, connects thought and action, perception and reaction, instead of segregating components. The interrelation between psychological and physical is total.

Memory and experience are a form of prejudice. While they are appropriate references for conscious thought processes such as preparation or planning, they can block subconscious, intuitive action. Through meditation and development of awareness you may learn to act instantly and intuitively based on what you are perceiving, rather than reacting out of habit in a predetermined manner. Habit-based reactions can kill you.

To learn meditation, begin by reading all you can on the subject. Then move forward on your own. Study a martial art or visit a retreat or meditation training center. Whichever course you take, try to maintain the connection between meditation and mountain climbing. Cast aside what is not useful, nurture anything that proves an asset. Trust that the work you do on your mind will aid your climbing.

Visualization

Visualization is the closed-eye, mental rehearsal of an intended action, such as climbing an intricate pitch. It requires imagination. Visualization presupposes a belief in your ability to achieve a goal. During visualization, mentally rehearse probable moves or routefinding decisions that photographs and topos lead you to expect. Summon a particular state of mind or conjure the awareness necessary while climbing. Run through the entire climb beforehand, or mentally rehearse a particular pitch before making the first move.

In visualization, imagine every detail: how cold it is, whether you are breathing hard, if you had to remove your gloves to place the gear, whether you feel rested or well fed, if the weather is breaking or night is falling. Such details give each imagined piece of thought or action more life and relevance. To increase your familiarity with situations the mountains may toss your way, read books about alpine climbs. Gripping tales, when carefully analyzed and combined with your own imagination, help visualization and rehearsal. They can augment problem-solving skills that otherwise take years of personal experience to acquire.

Beware of building self-defeating traps into your consciousness. Don't visualize failure or poor performance. Once embarked on a session, never stop the procedure until you finish a successful visualization. Each imaginary wrong turn in your mind—grabbing the wrong piece of gear off the rack or limiting your options by predetermining a specific bivouac site— programs those failures or self-imposed limitations into your subconscious. If you catch yourself doing this, stop. Start over from the beginning, and keep practicing until you see yourself making the correct decisions and actions from beginning to end. Rehearse for success.

Don't confuse visualization with planning. Visualization prepares the mind, allowing you to experience in your imagination the feelings, thoughts, and actions you may find on the mountain. Visualization is a creative, right-brain process. Planning is preparation for specific events or actions you will perform or you know will occur; it's a left-brain process. Both are essential.

In his book about soloing Nanga Parbat, Reinhold Messner wrote: "I only plan ahead what is absolutely necessary. I believe in being independent—and that means I do not want to be dependent on my future."

Planning implies that you know what will happen, that you have control over what will happen. Control? No, it is closer to chaos. Only vanity suggests we have control over events in the mountains. If you plan detailed actions based on the assumption of control, you risk becoming a victim of your plan, dependent on your plan. You must be independent of your future. Approach it on the balls of your feet—mentally prepared—knowing that you will take action when action is called for. Keep your mind open to all possibilities. Prepare your mind, your body, and your gear to address the many situations that may present themselves. But do not count on seeing any one thing.

Mark Twight soloing high on the northwest face of Mont Blanc, Chamonix, France. Soloing at this level of difficulty and risk requires a huge reserve of psychological strength and confidence. Photo: © Twight Collection

Brain Synchronization

Elite athletes in all disciplines, like Olympians Picabo Street and Gary Hall Jr., are learning the value of synchronizing the left and right hemispheres of the brain when performing and training. It shortens the time and number of repetitions needed to learn and build specific skills. Thought becomes more coherent. You can more easily learn specific behaviors or direct relaxation, sleep, arousal, focus, and awareness when the brain enters into a synchronized state.

Highly adept practitioners influence which side of their brain controls a particular activity. For example, training is a conscious left-brain modification of specific behavior patterns. The right brain handles competition and performance, the free and creative expression of trained behavior. Unsynchronized brain activity, or the rapid switching back and forth of control from one side of the brain to the other, is suspected to be one of the causes of attention deficit disorder—not the best state for peak performance.

Modern biofeedback techniques permit training to synchronize the two hemispheres. Several companies manufacture synchronization tools that use sound or light frequencies to influence particular brain states. When I began using Hemi-Sync tapes and the Sportslink programs, I wanted to learn to relax, to recover, and to sleep better. (See additional information under "Brain Synchronization Tools," at the end of Appendix 2, Suggested Reading.) Over the course of several months, I reduced insomnia from two nights a week to about two nights per month. Gaining a modicum of control over my brain states helped my training and my climbing.

When I steer myself to the right brain before starting up a pitch, I climb more smoothly and efficiently than I could have imagined possible—right up to the instant when conscious thought crashes the party. Then I'm back to conscious, calculating, less-aware Mark until I can regroup, resynchronize, and ease back "right." Using hemispheric synchronization in conjunction with visualization is one of the best ways to mentally prepare for a difficult route.

Psychological Acclimatization

Coming to terms with the idea of attempting routes at the limit of your ability can be difficult. Making the step from climbing routes that gain 3,000 feet in a relatively civilized environment like the Alps to attempting routes of 7,000 to 9,000 feet in the isolated mountains of the Alaska Range or the Himalayas can overwhelm the brain. I spent three weeks getting used to the idea of cutting loose in a very lightweight style on Mount Hunter in Alaska; it took that long to become comfortable with the mountain.

First, understand the problem. It takes longer to figure out how to climb more difficult and involved routes. Allot more time for adapting to the greater risk and commitment of big, scary mountains compared to smaller, less dangerous ones. Here are some techniques. Visualize at home, or hang out a little longer at the base of the peak. Probe the route's defenses to learn how long it may take to climb to a particular point. Rehearse the descent route to learn how to do it and how long it may take.

Some routes demand several efforts, spread out over days or even years. In 1997 John Bouchard and Mark Richey made an alpine-style attempt on the north ridge of Latok in the

Karakoram. John and Mark joined a list of many suitors for this route, which has refused all comers whether they use capsule, siege, or pure alpine style. Some might consider a failed attempt a wasted trip. But the smart and dedicated climber learns from every failure, assesses what went wrong, tries to change what can be changed, and eventually attempts the route again. After their first attempt, John and Mark became the most qualified climbers to take another shot at the route because they had the most current information. A subsequent attempt one year later was shut down by unseasonably bad weather. If there is a next time, they will possess an unequaled understanding of how to proceed. The use of meditation and visualization in conjunction with on-sight analysis or previous attempts not only increases your psychological security, but also speeds the process of becoming comfortable with the mountain.

Cutting away the psychological ties binding you to the ground can rocket you upward. Become free to explore and express yourself on the mountain, without reservation. Let nothing interfere with commitment. Leave society and the trivia of everyday life so your consciousness becomes lighter and more adaptable, freeing energy for the project.

Use the time that is needed for high-altitude acclimatization to break away from distractions. Actively meditate during the hours of mindless activity. Force yourself to live in the present tense, without the memories of normal life influencing actions in an alien environment. Practice this process at home so you may quickly adapt to the climbing consciousness. Once on the mountain, live in the present.

Performance

On the climb itself maintain an intense level of awareness. Open yourself up to the mountain. Be prepared to see or experience anything. Act and react in total freedom based on what you do see. Do not carry any expectations. (This does not conflict with visualization, which is part of preparation, not performance.)

Conscious thought is vital at times, but at other moments it is simply a waste of time and energy because you already know what to do. Sometimes you will observe or participate in circumstances completely beyond your control. You may think about these events afterward and analyze them, but while they are happening, respond to them spontaneously and naturally as you have trained yourself to do.

The great mistake in climbing (and all things) is to anticipate the outcome of the engagement. Do not consider whether you will succeed or fail. Allow nature to take its course. Your training, preparation, and awareness will allow you to act at the right time to apply the appropriate measures to resolve any problem (and "allow" is the precise word).

Many people habitually program failure into their performance. I used to get under the bench-press bar and tell my spotter to count on my getting three reps, and sure enough that's all I ever got. My mind was comfortable with the idea of failing at three. I said it out loud, and I lived it.

I experience a more insidious, subconscious level of predetermined failure in the mountains. When a route is 500 meters high, I'm tired after 500 meters—but when a route is 2,000 meters high, I'm *not* tired after 500 meters. I subconsciously decide beforehand where

I will become tired. It's difficult to break this habit. Acting and reacting according to what I actually experience is the only way I've found to free myself of this limitation.

Reentry

An alpinist generally spends anywhere from one to five weeks on the physical and psychological acclimatization process before climbing. After climbing, the tendency is to return home quickly. You reenter normal society within one to five days and are quickly immersed in a totally different environment and value system. You are exposed to the close scrutiny of your loved ones and may even return to your job almost immediately.

The dramatic change in surroundings may not match an equal shift in your own consciousness. It takes time and effort to readjust. The process will be more difficult after a high-stress trip involving an accident or death. Those who did not participate in the experience cannot truly understand what you have been through, and you will find it difficult to communicate. You may miss the life-and-death decision-making of the climb, the genuine consequence of your actions.

The problem is internal, and you must learn to handle it. You need to educate your loved ones about this process and allow them to help you through it. Recognizing the problem is the first step. Giving yourself time to acclimatize to society and to the consciousness of lower altitudes is the best gift you can offer yourself. Try not to return to your job right away. Take it easy. Rest. Relax. See some movies. Ride the bus. Get trivial.

Recovery

Set aside time to recover not only physically but psychologically before training again. Let your brain go soft. Watch a lot of television or read trashy spy novels or drink some beer. The shame of the extra fat you'll put on will propel you to train that much harder when you start again. A break from the extreme self-discipline required during training refreshes and prevents burning out and fosters a long and varied alpine climbing career. Time off can also help break the addiction cycle of needing to climb harder, higher, faster, and longer as your mind adapts to the commitment and risk of severe routes.

Time off need not mean forsaking climbing altogether. Cragging and waterfall climbing will maintain muscular tone without involving much commitment. Research and reading will keep the mind active and whet the appetite for future projects. Certain hobbies, like martial arts, practical shooting, or motorcycle racing, hone decision-making skills and self-awareness without burning out the desire to go climbing. Use the time you dedicate to rest and recovery for evolving as a person, without feeling guilt for indulging in a period of relative sloth.

The psychological aspects of alpine climbing are far more difficult to master than the physical. Mental training methods and recipes are specific to each individual. Resources in the form of books, schools, and teachers abound for the climber wishing to delve more deeply into the inner workings of the mind. The future progress of alpine climbing resides in the mind. Improvements in physical fitness and developments in equipment will offer only slow and relatively limited advances, while great strides may result from perfecting the minds of a few gifted climbers.

physical training: a foundation

3

Alpine climbers need maximum power from both mind and body. They train the mind to increase awareness and grit, and the body to augment strength and endurance. The goal of physical training for alpine climbing can be summed up in one phrase: to make yourself as indestructible as possible. The harder you are to kill, the longer you will last in the mountains.

Mountain climbing beats on you with dehydration, inadequate nutrition, debilitating cold, energy- and judgment-sapping high altitude, sleep deprivation, and muscular exhaustion. Training both body and mind to adapt to these combined effects make obvious sense. Climbing up and down several thousand vertical feet of technical terrain in a 24-hour period represents a huge volume of work that most bodies and brains can't tolerate.

While the most specific training for climbing is climbing itself, it is self-limiting. Once the body adapts to climbing's stresses, adaptation ceases. To progress, an athlete needs the ever-increasing workload that the gym affords.

For your physical training, don't simply copy someone else's methods. Mere imitation leads to injury and stagnation. Each body is unique and responds to training differently. Listen to your own body and heed what you hear. Work on your mind at the same time.

In physical training we aim to improve performance in four areas: power; cardiovascular power endurance; cardiovascular extensive endurance; and muscular endurance.

Increased power gives the climber the ability to blast through difficult sections. Cardiovascular power endurance allows the body to recover quickly from these bursts. Cardiovascular extensive endurance optimizes the oxygen uptake of the heart and lungs. And muscular endurance gives the muscles the ability to use oxygen and dispose of waste products efficiently. Training has other benefits as well, but we will focus on these four.

The Training Cycle

Athletes need to vary the intensity of their training to realize maximum benefits. Alpinists should follow a cycle of training with increasing intensity, in order to peak at a specific time for a specific event.

An athlete can peak for a period of one to two weeks and usually no more, and only once per season, or once every six months. Alpine climbers often miss out on the benefits of their peak period because they need favorable weather and snow conditions to proceed. They have to go when conditions permit, not sooner or later. However, it's possible to aim your training toward peaking during a rough window of opportunity.

Here is the chronological sequence of steps in an alpine climber's training cycle (see chart on page 41) that leads to peaking:

1. **Foundation-building:** Creating a base of strength and endurance through a variety of exercises. 4 to 6 weeks. (This foundation work is discussed in this chapter.)

2. **Power training:** Building strength and explosive power through weight training. 4 to 6 weeks. (Described in Chapter 4, on training for strength.)
3. **Cardiovascular power endurance training:** Increasing your aerobic capacity. 4 to 6 weeks. (Described in Chapter 5, on endurance training.)
4. **Cardiovascular extensive endurance training and muscular endurance training:** Building cardiovascular and muscular endurance concurrently. 3 to 4 weeks. (Described in Chapter 5.)
5. **Tapering and rest:** Resting strategically to aid recovery and to prepare for peaking. Taper for 1 to 2 weeks, then rest for 5 to 7 days. (Discussed in Chapter 5.)
6. **Peaking:** Achieving a period of maximum fitness—as long as possible, but usually only 1 or 2 weeks. (Discussed in Chapter 5.)

Some of these steps overlap. For example, training for cardiovascular power endurance begins in the fourth or fifth week of power-training workouts. To avoid digging too deeply into recovery reserves, the program divides workouts into blocks, typically three days of training followed by a rest day.

Foundation-building

If you're starting with little or no foundation of physical fitness specific to alpine climbing, your first training must address the sheer volume of work involved in ascending a mountain. Begin your training program with that magnitude of effort in mind. Ignore all ideas of specialized training for strength or for endurance until you have built a reasonable foundation to train from.

For most people, building this foundation will take six to eight weeks. For those whose bodies respond quickly to training or who already possess a reasonable foundation, this program may take only three to four weeks.

During this phase, address cardiovascular fitness with activities like running, hiking uphill, riding a stationary bike, or using a rowing machine while maintaining an aerobic heart rate. Combine that with some power-endurance sessions on the indoor climbing wall and weight training. This program may be coupled with outdoor activities such as climbing, ski mountaineering, and mountain biking, as long as the aim is training. Climb to punish the body, not to have fun. Every workout in this phase should be based on the desire to increase the maximum volume of work.

Alpine climbing includes hiking or skiing, usually uphill, with a pack to get to the base of a route. A bivouac may follow—an opportunity to recover—or the climbing may start immediately. The unfit start climbing at a deficit. This is no way to attempt a progression of difficult climbs. Building a foundation for further training is the first step toward being ready physically for these climbs. Because each body responds differently to training, specific workout recommendations aren't given here. But during the foundation phase, it will help to observe the following guidelines.

Train long. Building a foundation takes time. Hour-long flat runs or short sessions in the weight room gain nothing (though if time is short, they preserve fitness). Stack different

SAMPLE TRAINING CYCLE

Week	1	2	3	4	5	6	7	8	9	10	11	12	13	14	15	16	17	18	19	20	21	22
Foundation	X	X	X	X	X																	
Power						X	X	X	X	X												
Cardiovascular Power Endurance									X	X	X	X	X									
Cardiovascular Extensive Endurance														X	X	X	X					
Muscular Endurance														X	X	X	X					
Taper																		X	X			
Rest																				X		
Peak																					X	X

types of training on top of each other to
achieve an effect similar to doing an actual
route. Run or bike uphill for an hour, run
down, then do an endurance session on the
indoor climbing wall or, better yet, hit the
weight room. In the weight room, reduce the
usual weight but increase the number of sets
and number of different exercises. A variety
of exercises contributes to overall body fatigue, which is the goal in this phase. Beginners should hire a coach or trainer, determine
their max power, and train at 50 percent of
the heaviest single repetition. Aim for a high

volume of sets (six to eight), keeping the reps around twelve to fifteen.

When the sets become easy, don't increase the weight. Instead, decrease rest intervals
between sets to 30 to 45 seconds. After adapting to the decreasing rest intervals, increase the
amount of weight. Execute each repetition in a slow, controlled motion without bouncing or
cheating by initiating the movement with any other part of your body. Exercise the muscles
you are attempting to train. Don't give them respite through improper form. A foundation
training workout that mixes different types of activity should take from 2 to 3 hours.

Don't dismiss the power of the Stairmaster, especially when used without cheating
(which everyone does). Used properly, it can mimic an uphill workout without stressing
the joints by running downhill. Of course the Stairmaster does nothing to develop the coordination necessary for moving quickly over rough terrain. Stairmaster workouts are appealing when mud or snow makes trails slippery or when you're stuck in the city. Before
climbing Alaska's Mount Hunter, I did not train outdoors while preparing during the winter. I spent an hour a day, three days a week, "running" 4,000 vertical feet on the Stairmaster,
weight-trained, and climbed a couple of waterfalls—that's it. Once in Alaska, the skiing
and pack-hauling quickly forced my muscles to adapt to the specific activity of climbing.

Weight rooms are anathema to outdoor purists, but they offer some advantages. They
provide a place for concentrated, specific training without time lost on driving to and from
the hills or the crag and without the distractions and posturing associated with indoor climbing gyms. Top-level alpine climbers augment climbing itself (as training) with phases of
power training beneath the weight pile. The foundation phase should develop some increased muscle mass, which will be important for the next phase of training.

Once an adequate physical foundation has been developed, it's time to move ahead into
specific training for strength and for endurance in the mountains.

**Mark Twight after seven harrowing days on the Rupal Face of Nanga Parbat.
An alpine-style attempt on this nearly 15,000-foot high wall—the biggest
in the world—almost ended in death for Twight and his partners, Barry
Blanchard, Kevin Doyle, and Ward Robinson.** *Photo: © Mark Twight*

TRAINING: STRENGTH

4

All the fitness in the world is valueless in alpinism without strength. Over time, cycles of strength-building programs will provide a grounding of strength and power. Strength is defined as the ability to exert a given amount of force. Power is strength plus speed.

Few training books or regimens target alpinism, so climbers train unscientifically, inventing programs based on intuition and hearsay. Among conventional athletic events investigated by quantitative training studies, the decathlon comes closest to alpine climbing. Like alpinism, the decathlon—with its combination of running, jumping, and throwing events—incorporates activities requiring both power and endurance. The combination of these events demands a contradictory training program due to the different types of muscle fibers utilized. Every gain made in power costs something in endurance, and vice versa.

This chapter deals mainly with training for strength, power, and power endurance. The next chapter concentrates further on power endurance in addition to extensive endurance training and muscular endurance training. But always keep in mind the close relationship between the types of training. Books and programs designed for decathlon training are valuable resources for information on maintaining the critical balance between maximum power and maximum endurance. (One good source is *High Performance Training for Track and Field* by William Bowerman and William Freeman. See Appendix 2, Suggested Reading.)

Alpine climbing includes steep and overhanging rock and ice, and overcoming these obstacles requires power. These may constitute short bursts of explosive effort, but more often than not, the climber will struggle up to ten minutes at a time between contrived rests. In the case of the ten-minute power-endurance crux, the more personal horsepower at your disposal, the farther below your power threshold—your maximum peak output—you are able to operate. This translates to greater economy of physical resources.

To train for power specific to alpine climbing, decide how strong you need or want to be for a given project. Then train until you become 25 percent stronger in the strength and power exercises than you think necessary. When you stack your endurance training and climbing-specific training on top of this, the conflicting demands on your muscles will result in a loss of 20 to 25 percent of your max power—and you'll end up just where you need to be.

In the Weight Room

Many climbers fear that strength training using weights will make them get bigger, increasing their body size and weight. This is not necessarily so. Besides, size is not an absolute evil. Without a certain amount of muscle mass, there is nothing to train. However, the fear of increased size and weight is justifiable for any athlete whose sport requires the maximum power-to-weight ratio.

Those truly paranoid about gaining size and weight need only take in fewer calories than required to rebuild muscle tissue. But inadequate nutrition translates to an inability to recover and to maintain a useful training intensity. This is a narrow edge to balance, and it requires learning about your body's metabolism and response to stress.

The following guidelines, which apply to athletes with a solid foundation of physical fitness as described in the preceding chapter, show how various weight-training repetitions affect muscle mass (size and weight), strength, and muscular endurance. Of course, exercise affects people differently depending on age, fitness level, gender, and the phase of the training cycle. The total volume of training and its intensity level influence results, too.

The lower repetition ranges indicate that the weights you are using are heavier; the last rep of the set occurs just before positive failure, when you can no longer complete a repetition unaided. Lighter weights, of course, permit more reps before failure.

A total of 1 to 4 repetitions increases pure strength but not muscle mass.

A total of 4 to 9 reps increases both strength and muscle mass.

A total of 9 to 15 reps increases strength, muscular endurance, and muscle mass.

A total of 15 to 30 reps increases muscular endurance with little or no increase in muscle mass or strength.

A total of 30 to 50 reps increases muscular endurance with no effect on muscle mass or strength.

A total of 50 to 100 reps increases muscular endurance and cardio-respiratory endurance, with no increase in strength and a possible loss of muscle mass or fat.

During training for power, use a weight that permits you to perform between two and four reps. Increase the number of sets to a maximum of six while decreasing the number of reps to a minimum of two. Once you can do six sets of three reps, increase the weight so you drop back to two reps.

Many athletes exercise in the weight room to the point not only of positive failure, where they can no longer complete a repetition, but also to negative failure—where another person helps with the positive half of the repetition, moving the weight up, and the athlete tries without success to slow the negative descent of the weight. Negative failure inflicts massive damage to muscle tissue. While this stimulates supercompensation and muscle adaptation, recovery is lengthy and requires many rest days. Furthermore, training to failure coupled with adequate nutrition stimulates an increase in muscle mass.

Muscle recovery and growth after negative failure proceeds like this: For 24 to 48 hours after exercise, traumatized muscle tissue breaks down and is excreted. Then muscle cells rebuild during the following 48 to 72 hours. Maximum strength in that particular exercise will not return for five to nine days after exercising to failure. You need to train with greater frequency to mimic the stresses of climbing, so training to failure is counterproductive.

Some athletes turn to steroids to gain strength. Steroids work by stimulating protein synthesis, thus speeding muscle recovery and allowing the athlete to train more often. However, they do not improve an athlete's power on their own, and the side effects, such as cancer and impotence, can be devastating.

Effective power-training for alpine climbers has less to do with increasing the amount of muscle tissue than with improving the efficiency of existing tissue. Training adds power without adding size by improving muscle recruitment—increasing the number of existing muscle fibers involved in the exercise—and enhancing the efficiency of the neuromuscular pathways affecting recruitment.

Neuromuscular pathways are best trained by using 85 to 95 percent of your one-rep maximum weight, for two to three repetitions. Perform the positive phase of each rep quickly, control the negative, and rest for two to three minutes between sets for a total of four to six sets. This type of training improves neuromuscular efficiency without damaging muscle tissue, so it may be done with greater frequency than if you train to failure. These are heavy weights. Protect yourself with thorough warm-ups.

After several training cycles that culminate in alpine climbs, a 150-pound climber should become strong enough to pull 300 pounds on the pull-down machine. Imagine the climber who can pull 300 in training but only needs to pull 200 while climbing. He will be able to pull 200 all day long because 200 can't overtax his physical capacity. Therein lies the justification for developing power through training.

Muscles used for walking or other frequent activities can be trained more often than less utilized muscle groups. They recover faster because they are accustomed to the work. These include calves and abs. These muscles should be trained using higher reps rather than greater weight, although calves will benefit from some power training.

Larger muscles take longer to recover than smaller muscles. Calves can be trained roughly five times as often as quadriceps. Biceps and pectorals take about equal time to recover. Older athletes take longer to recover than younger ones. If you have little or no aerobic efficiency, you will take longer to recover from weightlifting.

Weight-training Exercises

Exercises in the weight room require good form to produce results and avoid injury. See Appendix 2, Suggested Reading, for some books that describe their proper form and use. For example, Bill Pearl's *Keys to the Inner Universe* illustrates hundreds of exercises. Consult these books or ask in the weight room if you aren't familiar with some of the following exercises.

Warm-up

Among suitable warm-up exercises are the seated dumbbell press, front dumbbell raises, bent-over reverse dumbbell flies, bench press, dips, and triceps press. While none of these exercises have any specific effect on your ability to pull, they will help maintain a semblance of muscle balance. Climbers who overdevelop certain muscle groups suffer injuries when the weaker antagonistic (opposite) muscle groups fail to stabilize the joints and connective tissue. These warm-up exercises strengthen shoulder attachment to help prevent injury. Some, like triceps exercises, directly benefit climbing as well.

Back and abdominals

The muscles of the back and abdominals maintain the integrity of your core and create an essential foundation for movement. Strong abs and back help you transfer force to your feet on overhanging terrain, thereby decreasing the amount of force on your arms and hands. Carrying a pack involves these muscles, too. Exercises to use include the stiff-legged deadlift (dangerous; learn to do it correctly), the Good Morning, back extension, standing sidebend, sit-ups (crunches), hanging leg raises, and Russian twist on a Roman chair.

Pulling

Climbing involves pulling (and pushing) oneself up, so emphasize all pulling-related exercises: chin-ups, upright row, bent-over dumbbell row, seated row, and biceps curl. Do lat pulls, using a pull-down machine when your body weight no longer provides sufficient stress. Do lat pulls with a variety of wide and narrow grips, in front of and behind the neck.

Grip strength

Although nothing works like climbing, doing wrist curls and reverse wrist curls and using a wrist roller will help. The best exercise for

improving grip strength is the standing finger curl with an Olympic bar. The vertical motion mimics the angle that fingers assume in climbing, and the wrist is not propped up on a bench, which prevents hyperextension and injury. Let the bar hang from the fingertips of an almost open hand. Then close the hand in a fist around the bar, thus raising it. Repeat.

Legs

Do squats (the king of exercises), lunges, seated or inclined leg presses and, occasionally, standing calf raises. You may also use seated leg extensions and curls to stabilize the knee.

Explosive power

Although not specific to climbing, doing hang-cleans will teach you to employ many different muscle groups simultaneously in an explosive effort.

Workouts

This is a huge number of exercises. It would be impossible to develop maximum power or train neural pathways in every single exercise mentioned. Concentrate on five power

Mark Twight "posing down" in Bolivia. "Power is not a bad thing to have in excess." Photo: © Scott Backes

exercises, leaving the others for the warm-up period or for doing at maintenance intensity between the power-training sets. For power, focus on lat pulls, standing finger curls, bent-over dumbbell rows, leg presses, and, occasionally, standing calf raises.

Power-training all five exercises during a single workout overtaxes the body's ability to recover. Divide them into two groups and train them on different days. Start by separating the lat pull and bent-over row because they work some of the same muscles; thus a good session of either one will preclude achieving top performance in the other on the same day.

Warming up for the six sets of two to three repetitions is extremely important. Get the blood flowing with 5 to 10 minutes of easy spinning on a stationary bike. Then do three warm-up sets of no more than eight reps of each of the shoulder and pushing exercises. More than eight reps stresses the whole system so much that it will not recover adequately prior to the power-training sets. Take 1 to 2 minutes of rest between warm-up sets.

Then begin to slowly work up to the power-training weight in the specific exercises of the day: for example, lat pulls and finger curls, or leg presses and one-arm rows. Start at low weight and do no more than three sets of eight reps at a time before switching exercises. Adhering to the three-set limit warms up without overtiring the muscles. Increase the weight with each set, by 10 to 20 pounds in the easier sets, but by only 2 to 5 pounds as the weight approaches the two-rep max. With the increase in weight, decrease the number of reps until reaching the power-training weight. Do as many as nine sets of progressive warm-up exercises before reaching the two-rep maximum weight. Counting the six actual training sets, the workout then totals fifteen sets for a particular exercise.

The power-training sets themselves are simple. Following an adequate 2- to 3-minute rest period, prepare your mind and body for an explosive 2- to 3-second effort during which every muscle fiber and brain cell concentrate on one thing: moving the weight. Focus everything you have and are on this single burst of power. Lower the weight under control to avoid overstressing joints and connective tissue.

Begin with the maximum amount of weight you can pull or push for six sets of two reps. Again, do no more than three sets before switching exercises, and rest for 2 to 3 minutes between sets. Done correctly, using the proper amount of weight, you will experience huge gains in strength while adding little muscle mass and inducing virtually no soreness. Such is the beauty of improving the efficiency of your neuromuscular pathways.

These sessions take a fair amount of time. However, the body's capacity for performing at a high level decreases during a session. Get out of the weight room after 90 to 105 minutes. Any longer wastes time and can cause overtraining.

TRAINING: endurance

5

Strong muscles run out of gas when limited by a sub-par cardiovascular system. Specific training will enhance endurance. At the beginning of week 5 of the six-week power-training cycle, begin to stack cardiovascular power endurance training into your workouts.

Many climbers don't understand cardiovascular power endurance and its relation to climbing mountains. They train for endurance by running; some may even run uphill. But for the most part, running doesn't resemble the stress inflicted by climbing hard and fast in the mountains. What's needed is training specific to alpinism—training that develops cardiovascular power endurance, cardiovascular extensive endurance, and muscular endurance. The hows and whys of endurance training are the focus of this chapter.

The strongest cause of muscular fatigue is inefficiency or failure of the circulatory and respiratory systems. Contributing causes are dehydration, changes in body temperature, depletion or blockage of energy sources, and psychological malfunctions. But the bulk of muscular fatigue can be traced to a lack of cardiovascular fitness and to intolerance to lactic acid build-up.

Cardiovascular Power Endurance

The special requirements of alpinism call for power endurance. You need training to gain a high level of cardiovascular power endurance that allows you bursts of huge effort without going so far into energy debt that recovery becomes impossible. Climbers always carry more than their own body weight. Clothes and boots alone can weigh 10 to 15 pounds, and crampons or skis on your feet tack on more poundage. Consider also that conditions in the mountains will rarely meet the ideal. Climbers contend with deep snow or breakable crust, higher altitude than the training elevation, and the need to expend long bursts of high-intensity effort to rush under the threat of a serac or to overcome a difficult pitch.

Alpinism is not your average athletic pursuit, and because the consequences of proving unequal to the task are far more serious than losing by a few points, appropriate training and preparation are critical. You can't rely on the ability to run, hike, or climb a long distance slowly.

Oxygen for the muscles

Cardiovascular training optimizes the body's ability to transport oxygen to the muscles and to transport waste products, including lactic acid, away from the muscles. Cardiovascular training increases the number and elasticity of capillaries throughout your body, which

Steve House on the vertical and overhanging fourteenth pitch of The Gift That Keeps on Giving on Mount Bradley's south face, Alaska. This was a two-hour power-endurance effort, with little opportunity to rest. One of the most amazing leads I have ever witnessed. Photo: © Mark Twight

benefits blood flow, keeping extremities warmer as well as improving oxygen transport. This increase is the result of greater demands by more body tissue for oxygen; capillaries grow and expand to feed those areas.

The effect of power (weight) training on capillaries may be even stronger than that of cardiovascular training because powerful anaerobic effort (power training) constricts blood vessels in the muscles and shuts down blood flow within them while at the same time raising blood pressure. Relaxing the muscles allows blood to flow freely, and the state of pressure forces blood through the vessels, stretching vascular walls and pushing capillaries into new areas. Years of aerobic (cardiovascular) and anaerobic training can induce up to a 30 percent increase in the capillary network.

Two important physical measurements will serve as reference points for virtually all your cardiovascular training. They are your VO_2 max and your anaerobic threshold.

VO_2 max is a measurement of your maximum oxygen uptake per minute per kilogram of body weight (with V being volume, and O_2 being oxygen). The more the better. It appears that a person's VO_2 max is determined genetically. It can be improved noticeably by training an untrained person, but further training of an already fit athlete will not increase oxygen uptake. There is some good news, however. Training increases the percentage of VO_2 max at which you can perform for long periods of time. This is a reflection of the increase in your anaerobic threshold.

The anaerobic threshold is the point at which oxygen demand exceeds your body's ability to supply it. Technically, it is the heart rate at which blood lactate content (lactic acid) reaches more than 4 millimoles per liter of blood. The higher your anaerobic threshold, the greater your aerobic capacity—the ability to generate a given amount of energy without producing debilitating lactate levels in the blood.

Medical tests can determine your VO_2 max and your anaerobic threshold. The VO_2 max text, done on a treadmill or stationary bike, measures oxygen exchange during maximal effort. A trained sports physiologist may infer your anaerobic threshold from this test. But only a blood lactate test that samples lactate levels every 15 to 30 seconds during exercise will precisely determine the anaerobic threshold. For testing, check with a sports medicine clinic or the sports science program at the local college or university. Standard medical insurance may cover these tests. They can be quite expensive otherwise. You can also try a less reliable but reasonably functional self-administered text (see *Training Lactate Pulse Rate* by Peter Janssen in Appendix 2, Suggested Reading).

An athlete whose blood lactate test shows a maximum heart rate, for example, of 185 beats per minute, with the anaerobic threshold occurring at 169 beats per minute, would possess a relatively high threshold. Once you pass your particular threshold—pushing yourself in training or climbing to a higher heart rate—anaerobic energy production supplants aerobic energy production, and lactate concentrations trigger acidosis in and around the muscle cells. Coordination suffers, fat oxidation stagnates (fat no longer acts as an efficient energy source), and the risk of injury increases.

The average athlete cannot perform for very long once past the anaerobic threshold, and recovery may take 24 to 96 hours, depending on the duration and intensity of the period above the threshold. Until recovery occurs, aerobic capacity will remain compromised. That's why having a high anaerobic threshold (that is, superior cardiovascular fitness), knowing where the threshold is, and learning to maintain output just below the threshold is extremely important to an alpine climber.

Cardiovascular training basics

In the next few pages, I'll outline a variety of cardiovascular training activities. Each workout demands a level of effort that corresponds to specific heart rates—rates that are a particular percentage of your anaerobic-threshold heart rate. Once you know your anaerobic threshold (your AT), you can calibrate workout intensity by monitoring effort as a percentage of the threshold heart rate.

You may use any form of cardiovascular-type exercise to accomplish any of these workouts: running uphill, skate skiing, using a treadmill or Stairmaster, riding a mountain bike or stationary bike, rowing on a machine—name your poison.

Buy a heart rate monitor and use it to maintain your workload at the desired heart rate during any given workout. Also use it to monitor your recovery from workouts. Check recovery status by taking your pulse when you wake up each morning. Recovery is incomplete if you are a trained athlete and your heart beats a few times more per minute than normal, or if you are an untrained person and your heart rate is six to eight beats per minute higher than normal. Modify the day's workout accordingly.

An increase in your wake-up pulse also indicates when illness and overtraining loom. Keep a workout log and note your waking pulse each day, as well as how much and how well you sleep each night. Use the log to track training progress and to learn how you respond to hard work without enough sleep. Over time you will learn which specific variations in your pulse are cause for alarm.

Because alpine climbers train for efforts ranging from 12 to 72 hours or more, schedule training in blocks of days to imitate the stress of alpine climbing. As you begin to stack cardiovascular power endurance training onto your power training, three days on and one day off is a reasonable program. Take rest days whenever needed, based on your waking pulse, especially if you are thirty-five or older or coming back from injury or a long break from training and climbing. Pay attention when waking pulse is five or more beats per minute higher than normal. Make the hardest session of the three-day training block the first one, right after a rest day, and make other workouts easier until the next rest day. What is easy and what is hard depends on your place within the training cycle.

These three-day training blocks can also include strength training, with weights (as described in Chapter 4). If the first-day workout is a weight-training day, follow it the next day with high-intensity endurance training (described below), followed by a day of recovery workouts (also described below). If the first-day workout consists of speed-strength intervals (see below), then follow with a day of recovery workouts; you could lift weights with your upper body on the third day. Never follow a day of weight training with a day of speed-strength intervals, or vice versa, because the combined stress on the body would be too great.

Rest days are just that: entire days when you do nothing more than stretch. These days are a good time to eat right, hydrate, and read. Don't think about training or performance or anything that may arouse an adrenal response. Simply rest.

Cardiovascular power endurance workouts

Following are descriptions of the various power endurance workouts.

Speed-strength intervals

Speed-strength intervals (short-interval training) develop speed and strength. They force you to work at levels above your anaerobic threshold (AT) for short periods and then allow full, quick recovery. Train at 105 to 108 percent of your AT heart rate. For example, the athlete with an AT of 169 heart beats per minute would push his heart rate to between 177 and 182 beats.

For speed-strength intervals, warm up for 30 minutes without exceeding 75 to 80 percent of your AT. Rest to recovery—approximately 5 minutes—and then stretch. Now explode into the first interval, hitting it hard for 1 minute. The workload must be intense enough to push you past your AT in somewhere between 30 and 45 seconds. Maintain the effort for 60 seconds. Then rest for 4 minutes. The rest period is lengthy to prevent lactic acid build-up, which decreases performance and maximum output. Repeat the interval and rest until you have done five intervals. With enough intensity, the maximum achievable heart rate decreases with each successive interval, eventually dropping by two to four beats per minute. If a decrease of four beats or more occurs before you reach the fifth interval, the workload is too great. Cool down with a recovery walk or bike ride for 30 minutes, maintaining a comfortable heart rate, 30 to 40 percent of your AT.

High-intensity endurance training

This training develops power endurance just below maximum intensity. It teaches you to sense when you are nearing your AT and trains you to maintain a workload close to but not exceeding it. Train at 97 to 99 percent of your AT. The athlete with an AT of 169 heart beats would work out at a rate between 164 and 167 beats.

Two types of workouts fall into the category of high-intensity endurance training. Both are executed by first warming up for 20 to 30 minutes, never going above 75 to 80 percent of your AT.

The first type is a 60- to 120-minute sustained workout; maintain 97 to 99 percent of your AT the entire time. Pay attention to nutrition and hydration during this workout, because the body can't store enough glycogen to fuel this level and duration of output. Replenishing glucose with quickly metabolized carbohydrate gels is essential (see "Eat to Perform" in Chapter 6). Cool down for 20 to 30 minutes at a heart rate of 30 to 40 percent of your AT.

The second high-intensity endurance workout involves completing three to four sets of 10- to 12-minute intervals that achieve and maintain 97 to 99 percent of your AT. Follow each interval with an active rest period (60 to 65 percent of AT) equal in length to the duration of the interval. When all intervals are complete, cool down at 30 to 40 percent of your AT for 30 minutes.

Recovery workouts

These workouts promote circulation and removal of waste products from the muscles and only minimally stress the aerobic system. Train at 60 to 65 percent of your AT. Recovery workouts should last from 30 minutes to 2 hours, at which point benefits decline as glycogen stores become depleted. Riding stationary bikes or running on smooth roads work well for recovery workouts. Use recovery workouts within the three-day training blocks to recover from debilitating power or cardiovascular power endurance workouts.

Lactate training

Lactate training (hypoxic training) develops lactate tolerance and helps increase your anaerobic threshold. But because this training takes place above your AT, it boosts lactic acid levels and trashes the system. Depending on your fitness and the duration of the work, lactic acid levels in the blood may approach 6 millimoles per liter. This training affects aerobic fitness negatively until you fully recover, which may take from 24 to 96 hours.

Here are two examples of workouts for training lactate tolerance. For the first, after warm-up, do a series of activities with a workload great enough to produce a heart rate that is 101 to 105 percent of your AT. These activity intervals may last from 20 to 180 seconds, depending on your fitness level. Keep recovery periods to a minimum—30 to 60 seconds—to prevent lactic acid levels from decreasing too much. Perform as many intervals as possible without exceeding a total workout time of 60 minutes (excluding warm-up and cool-down).

The second lactate-training workout consists of warm-up followed by a workload period of 20 to 60 minutes, at 101 to 102 percent of your AT for the entire time, without any recovery periods. This workout will produce higher, longer-lasting levels of lactic acid than the interval workout.

Two weeks into the cardiovascular power endurance phase of the training cycle, the power-training phase will end. Maintain the three-day training blocks and increase the intensity of cardiovascular power endurance training for another two to three weeks. At the end of this phase, you will be as strong as you are going to get. It's time to begin the extensive-endurance phase.

Cardiovascular Extensive Endurance

Extensive-endurance training develops long-term endurance at a moderate level of physical output. This training also teaches psychological tolerance for boredom and repetition. Workouts for extensive endurance may be performed using any cardiovascular exercise—running, treadmill, and so on—that maintains a consistent 80 to 85 percent of AT. You can keep a conversation going at this level of effort. These sessions may last from 2 to 4 hours.

This training will bring you relatively quickly to an adequate level of endurance for climbing. Endurance training causes the conversion of some muscle fibers from anaerobic (white) to aerobic (red) in order to improve oxygen distribution efficiency; this reduction of anaerobic fibers causes a decrease in overall power. So look for balance between endurance and power. Maximum conversion would make you a triathlete, while no conversion at all would leave you powerful but unable to maintain moderate effort for long periods.

Extensive-endurance training programs your body to metabolize fat, which is a far more efficient energy source than carbohydrates. Twelve pounds of body fat, which is normal for a 160-pound man to be carrying, equals roughly 42,000 calories, enough energy to run twenty marathons. Accessing fat as an energy source requires you to be operating at a heart rate no higher than 80 percent of your anaerobic threshold. Higher heart-rate values overrun the fat delivery system, and the body switches for energy to carbohydrates, which cannot be usefully stored in the same quantities as fat can, so the energy supply is limited. This is another reason to work to increase your anaerobic threshold: By operating at a lower percentage of your AT, but still expending adequate power for the task, you will be able to burn fat rather than carbs, thus carrying an almost limitless supply of energy.

Depletion days

Depletion days are training days that tap the absolute end of your reserves of food, energy, and water. Go alpine climbing, or train in the gym, then go on a 6-hour bike ride—but don't go so far as to prevent full recovery within two days. A depletion day uses as many muscles as possible. Make these days replicate the stresses caused by alpine climbing as closely as possible. Food and water intake during depletion days will vary between individuals. However, taking in 25 percent of the optimum levels described in Chapter 6, on nutrition, should offer the solace of eating and drinking while still meeting the depletion-day goal of going without adequate calories or hydration.

These days develop knowledge about how the body reacts to extreme effort, lack of adequate food, and other stresses. If you have had the experience of seeing your abilities degrade toward the end of a 24-hour effort, you'll be less likely to make bad judgment calls when you encounter tough times in the mountains. Any surprises regarding your capacities can throw off your emotional balance, harming your chances for a successful climb and even survival.

Depletion days also set up the body for loading carbohydrates (glycogen loading) prior

Ed Pope nearing the summit of Peak 5886 in Nepal after making the first ascent of Money Is Not Our God. We summitted the peak ten days after Ed left his home in Milwaukee, an impressive effort made possible by his dedication to training prior to the trip. *Photo: © Mark Twight*

to a big climb. Carbo loading is difficult to master, but the proper execution results in a profound boost in energy. Dr. Michael Colgan's *Optimum Sports Nutrition,* listed in Appendix 2, Suggested Reading, provides a clear account of the technique.

Muscular Endurance

At the same time that you train for cardio-vascular extensive endurance, it's useful to train muscular endurance. Muscles trained specifically for power will have little endurance. They are a sprinter's muscles, and you want the balance of a decathlete.

You will already have a reasonable level of endurance in the muscles affected by the maintenance and warm-up exercises described in Chapter 4, on training for strength. Only muscles trained by the five core power exercises (lat pull, bent-over dumbbell row, standing finger curl, leg press, and standing calf raise) need be further trained for endurance. Do this by decreasing the weight used to train power and increasing the reps to 16 to 50.

Climbing-specific exercises

You may also train endurance into climbing-specific muscles by getting on the wall at the climbing gym and staying on. If you are not bouldering, you need a sympathetic partner willing to belay for 15 to 20 minutes at a time.

You can transform weight-room muscles into climbing muscles by going climbing. The muscles adapt quickly to the new stresses. If you mimicked climbing motions in the weight room closely, the translation will be quick.

If climbing is out of the question, make up some specific exercises that stress the muscles like climbing. For example, attach a finger board or rock rings to the lat pull machine or chin-up bar to train your grip endurance while pulling. A fat dowel attached to the lat pull machine creates a grip like holding ice tools. Do your standing calf raises while wearing rigid climbing boots to increase the leverage and mimic actual climbing. In the rock gym, climb

Mark Twight training climbing specific muscles and movement on the watertower at Volunteer Park, Seattle. Wearing boots and a pack helps to mimic alpine rock climbing problems. *Photo: © Twight Collection*

in boots and wear a pack or a weight belt. These specific exercises are part of the muscular-endurance phase. Using props such as rock rings or dowels during the power-training phase limits your maximum power output by introducing weak links (fingers and forearms).

Do whatever training it takes to prepare for actual alpine climbing. Aim to become equal to the physical demands of the chosen route, instantly ready to attempt it with a minimum of specific adaptation after reaching the base.

Climbing (cragging or waterfall climbing) belongs in the training schedule; how much will depend on the intensity of the workouts, general fitness, and the climbing itself. Most of the time, the relatively low intensity of recreational climbing will be such that several days of climbing in succession act as recovery training, albeit with short bursts of effort sprinkled in. However, with imagination any climb can become productive, specific training.

Recovery

The key to training frequency is not only smart training but recovery, between sets as well as between workouts. Meditative recovery during the rest periods between sets stimulates greater muscular activation in power sets. Merely resting by sitting still is inefficient compared to the effect a meditative state can have on the body's recovery. Meditation in all forms is beneficial, but there are no quick recipes, and explaining meditation is beyond the scope of this book. Check out specialized books and workshops.

Less ethereal forms of recovery reduce time between workouts. One of the best is the recovery shower. Invented by the French, and used in some form by virtually every elite athlete on the planet, it is often confused with some kind of torture. Right after working out, hop into the shower. First, cook yourself for no more than 5 minutes in hot water, relax, get those blood vessels well dilated. Then slowly add cold water to the mix until it's so cold you can't stand it. Endure it. Focus the water on the back of your head and on the muscles you just worked. Feel the blood vessels constrict. Stay under it for as long as it takes to really cool off—2 to 3 minutes. The time it takes to cool down will increase as you adapt, and the temperature required for cooling will decrease. Then, switch the hot water back on. The blood vessels will dilate, and inrushing blood will flush the lactic acid out. Start the cooking process again. Repeat at least two cycles and finish on cold. This induces a tonic effect and you'll rebound, flushing again as your body warms up in your clothes.

Recovery walks or rides work too. Several hours after training, feeding, and resting, go for a 30-minute walk or a spin on the bike at 60 to 70 percent of your anaerobic-threshold heart rate. This will help flush out waste products lingering in your muscles and create a demand for more glucose. When finished, eat a light snack.

Eating properly right after training also speeds recovery. There are two popular schools of thought on post-workout food intake:

Dr. Michael Colgan, author of *Optimum Sports Nutrition* (see Appendix 2, Suggested Reading), says an intake of 225 grams of liquid carbohydrates within 20 minutes after the end of a workout will start the glycogen replacement process. He says this should be followed by solid food, mostly carbohydrates, within an hour.

On the other hand, Dr. Barry Sears, author of *The Zone* (see Appendix 2), advises a Zone

Favorable snack within an hour after working out of not more than 100 calories, followed within another hour by a Zone Favorable meal of not more than 500 calories. Zone Favorable means 30 percent protein, 30 percent monohydrated fat (such as olive oil), and 40 percent carbohydrate.

My experience indicates that Colgan's theory works better for alpinists. The main benefits from the Sears approach come from the protein in the Zone formula, protein being necessary to fuel muscle regeneration. Taking in carbohydrates using Colgan's model while adding extra protein to the mix results in the right kinds of fuel to initiate the recovery process.

For maximum gains and quick recovery, do whatever it takes to stimulate your body's release of human growth hormone (HGH). Anaerobic exercise, like weightlifting, is the only training activity that releases HGH into the blood. HGH is also released during REM sleep, which is why many athletes take a nap after training. HGH not only repairs traumatized muscles, but also burns body fat. With HGH coursing through your body, you regain the metabolism of a teenager.

Adequate sleep aids recovery. So does deep tissue massage. Treat yourself to a massage every ten to fifteen days. Shun those touchy-feely masseuses. Find someone who can dig, restructure, and strip apart bound-up muscle tissue.

The Training Cycle: A Refresher

At this stage in the training cycle, after working through the phases of strength training and endurance training, you'll be heading into a period of tapering down and resting, in preparation for your peak period of fitness. It's a good point to review the steps in the training cycle that were first introduced back in Chapter 3.

1. **Foundation-building:** Creating a base of strength and endurance through a variety of exercises. 4 to 6 weeks. (This foundation work was discussed in Chapter 3.)
2. **Power training:** Building strength and explosive power through weight training. 4 to 6 weeks. (This training was described in Chapter 4.)
3. **Cardiovascular power endurance training:** Increasing your aerobic capacity. 4 to 6 weeks. (Described in this chapter.)
4. **Cardiovascular extensive endurance training and muscular endurance training:** Building cardiovascular and muscular endurance concurrently. 3 to 4 weeks. (Described in this chapter.)
5. **Tapering and rest:** Resting strategically to aid recovery and to prepare for peaking. Taper for 1 to 2 weeks, then rest for 5 to 7 days. (Discussed in the next section of this chapter.)
6. **Peaking:** Achieving a period of maximum fitness—as long as possible, but usually only 1 or 2 weeks. (Discussed below.)

Tapering and rest

During the tapering phase of the training cycle, the climber gradually decreases training intensity in preparation for a rest period and eventual peak performance. Tapering prior to an expedition promotes recovery and supercompensation at deeper levels than is possible within regular training. Done correctly, tapering allows you to hit the mountain refreshed and able to perform better than during training.

As long as you don't slack off for too long, you won't lose what you worked so hard to attain. Even cutting cardiovascular training back by up to two-thirds still maintains your VO$_2$ max and your anaerobic threshold. Tapering workouts in the weight room maintain your muscles' memory of the movements without stressing them. Easy sessions in the climbing gym and moderate hiking or cycling also fit into the tapering cycle. Taper for seven to fourteen days. Decrease the intensity gradually.

After tapering, rest for five to seven days. This rest period is not the same as the do-absolutely-nothing rest days within the training cycle. Walk or cycle easily to maintain circulation and raise the heart rate to no more than 60 to 70 percent of your AT. Maintain your heart rate at this level for 20 to 30 minutes each day to create a demand for glucose, which permits the storage of glycogen.

On some alpine expeditions, you're forced to "taper and rest" whether you want to or not—during long periods of travel, on the approach to the mountain, and during acclimatization. In these cases, continue your training right up to the day you get on the plane. If, for example, you're planning a quick ascent of a technical route at high altitude in the Alaska Range, it's necessary to allot time for acclimatizing before going for the summit. Breathing thinner air without stressing the metabolic system too much can be considered tapering. Once acclimatized, descend to a lower altitude to fully recover (that is, rest). When you're completely recovered, try to blast the route.

Peaking

As mentioned earlier, an athlete can peak for a period of one to two weeks and usually no more, and only once per season, or roughly once every six months. Alpine climbers trying to peak at the right time need some luck regarding weather, ice and snow conditions, and illness. Also, professional schedules don't permit exclusive attention to training. Therefore, an alpine climber rarely is able to time the period of peak fitness with the actual ascent. But you can get close by working backward from the estimated date of ascent. If you want to hit your peak period for an ascent of an Alaskan mountain on or about June 15, for example, begin training around the middle of January to accommodate a twenty-two-week training cycle, including tapering and rest.

By the time you return from your trip, say at the end of June, you will have lost much of your fitness and perhaps as much as 10 to 15 percent of your body weight. Then start all over. Rest brain and body for two to four weeks, eat properly, and regain some weight. Then, forgoing the five-week foundation phase, a training cycle lasting around seventeen weeks will create another peak for the waterfall ice climbing season, which shouldn't place as much stress on your system as the Alaska trip. Use the waterfall season to develop specific climbing muscles and connective tissue. Then embark on an intense training cycle again after establishing a worthy goal for the following spring or summer.

Other Training Considerations

Maintaining flexibility

The matter of flexibility doesn't concern the alpine climber as much as the sport climber or gymnast, since the alpinist's binding clothing and the weight that must be carried inhibits all but the most basic movements. However, limber and relaxed muscles move more efficiently through a longer ranger of motion than tight ones. Inflexibility can occur through disuse or through strength training and weightlifting, which bind together and shorten muscle fibers.

Mark Twight in Ouray, Colorado. The second peak of the year might coincide with the waterfall climbing season, which will also help train climbing specific muscle and connective tissue. *Photo: © Cathy Beloeil*

A simple stretching program helps maintain muscle pliability and improves circulation. However, stretching does not accomplish the same thing as warming up. Employ stretching as an adjunct to the warm-up or cool-down process if you are stretching in conjunction with strength training or cardiovascular power endurance workouts. Place more emphasis on flexibility during the tapering and resting phases of the training cycle.

Saving your knees

Training for alpine climbing, and alpinism itself, puts a huge amount of stress on the knees. Eliminate as much impact as possible during the training cycle. Judicious use of the Stairmaster and bicycles will help a lot. When hiking uphill, add extra stress by carrying a pack with bladders or jugs of water as ballast; then dump the weight out before descending, relieving a fair amount of pressure. Ski poles help absorb some impact otherwise reserved for the knees by supporting up to 30 percent of body weight on the arms. Ski poles also allow you to exploit and train the strength of your upper body when climbing uphill.

Training at altitude

While essential for acclimatization, training at high altitude has limitations. Follow the maxim "Train high, sleep low" as you try to acclimatize on the mountain. This approach prepares the body for visits to higher altitude while not interrupting the sleep cycle and impeding recovery. Move your sleeping altitude up as adaptation to altitude progresses, and subsequently move the training sessions to higher elevations.

Because maximum heart rate declines at higher altitudes, meaningful power training becomes impossible. A climber who has a maximum heart rate of 185 beats per minute at sea level may find it down to 160 at 18,000 feet. The same climber's anaerobic threshold may drop to a heart rate of 140—and all the cardiovascular activities that base their heart rate on the anaerobic threshold take a corresponding dive. Heart rate for the recovery walk, for example, would drop way down to around 90.

Details vary between individuals, but this general rule about altitude applies to everyone. So if you live at 7,000 to 8,000 feet or above, you should descend to a lower altitude for power training or lactate training. A lower site allows the body to produce meaningful heart rates and to push or pull more weight. Returning to altitude will not compromise recovery as long as you are acclimatized to that altitude.

Staying healthy

Maintaining good health is one of the most difficult yet important goals for an athlete. Staying healthy and free of injury is the best way to maintain a consistent level of training. Improving training frequency and consistency are the only ways for already well-trained athletes to progress.

Although moderate levels of exercise can mildly strengthen a person's immune response, intense training depresses the immune system. In fact, elite athletes are far more susceptible to infection and illness than the general population because high levels of training and performance devastate their body's ability to fight back. If your training for alpine climbing is carefully matched to your capacity for improvement, you will not stress your immune system too badly. But going all-out for 12 to 24 hours, truly maxing out your potential, will leave you more vulnerable to illness than you were the day before. Getting into a cycle of obsessive training will crash your immune system faster than anything else.

If you have been to high altitude and performed at near-maximum levels, you will be far more likely to develop an upper-respiratory infection than if you were at the same altitude doing less work. Hence the necessity to train and increase your strength and endurance so that the actual climbing can be done at a lower percentage of your maximum possible output, placing less stress on your immune system.

Being well rested and healthy is even more important when traveling to an unfamiliar environment. By merely stepping off the plane in Kathmandu, you will be bombed by germs that your body has not developed defenses to. If you are overtrained and in the red from a lack of rest, your whole expedition may be compromised by a common cold before you even see the mountains. Avoid air travel as much as possible when training hard because the recirculated air is carrying germs from all over the world. An airplane is a flying petri dish that can transport illness and infection over incredible distances. A strong immune system in a rested, healthy body is the best defense against travel-related colds and illness.

Proper intake of certain nutrients and supplements improves your immune response. Some of these are discussed in Chapter 6.

Keeping cool

A cool muscle is an efficient muscle. If your internal temperature strays outside of the very narrow range of 98 to 100 degrees, your body will automatically sacrifice muscle function in favor of temperature regulation. This is a survival mechanism based on the primordial theory that even complete immobility is probably not life-threatening as long as proper body temperature is maintained.

The higher your core temperature rises, the more blood is used for cooling the body, which means less blood is available for muscle function. The cooler you remain during exercise—trying to stay within the 98-to-100-degree window—the more efficiently your muscles will function. Above a core temperature of 104 or 105 degrees, you are risking heat stroke—not an issue for alpine climbing, but useful to know if you train hard during the summer.

Whether training or actually climbing, it's vitally important not to overheat. Not only are your muscles more efficient when cool, but you also will not lose as much water through sweat or elevated respiratory rate. Minimize your water loss and improve muscle function by keeping your core temperature cool.

ALPINE SOLO

I asked John Bouchard to contribute this story to the book because he was the mentor who influenced my climbing career the most and because his attitude illustrates how a creative mind adapts easily to the toughest conditions of alpinism. A number of John's climbs were ahead of their time, pushing far beyond the period's accepted standards of difficulty and commitment. The new route he describes here, which became known as the Bouchard Route, is a totally independent line. The 1995 French guidebook grades this route V, 80- to 90-degree ice, 5.10a. John's 1975 solo ascent of the 900-meter route took less than five hours. The second ascent required two bivouacs.

Walter Bonatti wrote that the north face of the Grand Pilier d'Angle represented the greatest challenge in the Western Alps and that the route he put in on the face with Cosimo Zapelli was the most difficult of his life. I first heard of it at the Brasserie Nationale in Chamonix one night during the rainy 1973 season.

"You know, John, you should be more careful about what you say," Porter said as we walked back to camp on cold, wet feet.

"What did I say?"

"You told Roger Baxter Jones we should all solo the Pilier d'Angle when the weather improves. Jesus, John, Roger's one of the best around and they take that stuff quite seriously. I thought he was going to take a swing at you."

"Don't be silly. We were just fooling around."

"Don't fool yourself, kid, I saw him get quiet. You really irked him."

The weather never improved, and I had to go back to college.

The next summer, I soloed the Welzenbach routes on the north faces of the Grossglockner and Charmoz, the north face of Les Courtes, and the Frendo Spur. I got the hang of alpine soloing. You just had to go light, really light, day-hiking light, and then launch yourself onto a thirty- or forty-pitch route. x

That winter, *Mountain* magazine published an article on the last challenges of the Alps, and highlighted the Bonatti-Zapelli route on the Grand Pilier d'Angle. They climbed it in 1962, and it had never been repeated. I wanted to solo the second ascent of it.

To make a breakthrough, you have to do something different. I reckoned that if I were stronger and fitter, I'd have a good chance, so I started lifting weights and running. This sounds obvious, but in 1974 no one trained and certainly no one ran, or admitted to it anyway. After classes I worked out in the dreary weight room packed with football players in smelly sweat clothes. Then I ran around the golf course in canvas sneakers. I ice-climbed all winter, putting in half a dozen first ascents—but everything was a first ascent in those days. In the evening after dinner in the cafeteria, I went to the quarter-mile indoor track and ran laps. I graduated and returned to France for the 1975 season.

Training paid off. I was fit, and the ice routes were in shape. A fantastic gang assembled in Chamonix that summer, including Tut Braithwaite, Aid and Al Burgess, Alex McIntyre, Terry King, and Gordon Smith among the Brits. Voytek Kurtyka shared their illegal camp. The French crew included Jean Afanassief, Nicolas Jaeger, Rene Ghilini, Georges Bettembourg, Jean-Marc Boivin, and Patrick Vallencent. And we all wanted the Bonatti-Zapelli route.

While recovering in camp after completing the second one-day ascent of the Davaille route on Les Droites, I found out that the Burgesses, McIntyre, and Braithwaite had left camp the previous day. In a frenzy, I threw my pack together and ran for the cable car. From the summit of the Midi, I raced down the Vallée Blanche and up to the Col du Trident. Panting and sweaty, I burst into the aluminum bivouac hut.

"Have there been any Britanniques here?"

"But of course! The brothers Burgess have made the Bonatti-Zapelli route today with their friends. They have made the second ascent. Look." This fellow led me outside where we could look through binoculars.

"There. They are making the bivouac now on the ridge. They will make the Mont Blanc tomorrow."

I took a deep breath and went inside and signed the register, noting that the four Brits had been here only 24 hours earlier.

"I'm leaving at midnight," I told the hut guardian. "I'll want tea and a liter of water."

I went back outside to cook dinner. The Trident hut is small, like an old Airstream trailer, and you're packed in with at least fifteen snoring, smelly men on a wet mattress. I placed my gear in the corner, snuggled up in a blanket, and put in my wax earplugs. I was awakened at 11:30 P.M.

The sky was clear, but no moon lit the way. I crossed the Col Moore, traversed the Grand Plateau, and made my way to the bergschrund. The gap was enormous so I traversed to

The 900-meter-high north face of the Grand Pilier d'Angle of Mont Blanc. Bouchard's new route threads through the steep wall below and left of the serac. *Photo: © Mark Twight*

63

the avalanche cone, took a deep breath, and climbed up the debris chute knowing that if anything came down, I would catch it full on. The ice in the chute was polished, and its walls rose a few feet on either side.

I counted one thousand breathless steps and then climbed out left and front-pointed up the slope diagonally to reach what I hoped would be the base of the route. The ice slope constricted into a narrow couloir between the rock ribs I could see in my headlamp. I decided to wait for some daylight so I wouldn't lose my way and end up stuck.

When dawn came I realized I was not on the Bonatti-Zapelli route. I had exited too early and was on mixed ground several hundred feet to the left. To regain the route, I would have to descend maybe a thousand feet and then move right.

"But if I keep going," I told myself, "I'll do a new route. A new route, solo, would make up for not doing the second ascent." It was perfectly logical, so I went for it.

There were some dodgy bits, mostly where the ice barely covered the rock. When my crampons and tools hit these spots, the ice often broke away behind me. I climbed to a near-vertical runnel of ice that ended in the middle of a steep granite wall.

"I have to go for it," I thought.

I launched up the ice, but hesitated at the top where it pulled away from the rock. I finally forced myself to make the moves onto the rock and then climbed a corner to a ledge. It was like climbing in a dream: I was outside myself, watching someone else climb what I shouldn't have dared.

I rested on the ledge, staring at the twenty-foot overhanging corner I had to climb next. I took my 7-millimeter rope from the pack, uncoiled it, and tied it to the pack. I climbed ten feet or so until I couldn't bear the fear, whacked in a peg, looped a sling in it, and rested on it. I forced myself to continue.

The corner ended and I pulled over the top. I then saw a big serac I recognized as part of the north-face route to my right. Above me the final ice field rose to the top of the pillar. About eight hundred feet above I saw movement: It was Tut, Alex, and the Burgesses at their bivouac. I sprinted up the ice field.

Almost immediately, I heard their voices. Elated, I shouted out: "I soloed a new route! I soloed a new route!"

"Make sure you finish it," came the reply, calming me somewhat. I slowed down and by 6:30 A.M. I arrived at their bivouac on the ridge. We made a fabulous unroped ascent of the finale to the Peuterey Ridge, over the summit of Mont Blanc, and down to the valley, where we did all sorts of things to celebrate in the establishment of that jolly old publican Maurice Simond.

John Bouchard

NUTRITION

6

Proper nutrition fuels the body. It increases energy while slowing destructive cell breakdown, and it endows the body with recuperative powers both during training and in the mountains.

Many people, even elite athletes, believe they need eat only three square meals a day to live up to their athletic potential. This is laughable. The body is a precision instrument, and because most people do not feel the effects of the food they eat, they remain unaware of how profoundly food affects performance. Scores of books offer nutrition information, much of it valid—but scientific knowledge accrues daily, so the popular formula of five years ago may prove false next month. This chapter deals with food and water as they relate to fitness for climbing mountains. (For more fundamental or more detailed information, consult books listed in Appendix 2, Suggested Reading.)

Just as one type of climbing suits a particular temperament type more than another and one set of physical talents fits certain styles of ascent over others, each individual's biochemistry responds to nutrients differently from every other person's. Environment and lifestyle affect nutritional needs as well. Never strictly follow any nutritional recipe recommended by a book or an expert. Accept responsibility for learning from your own body. Only *you* can know how you feel.

The Sources of Energy

The immense volume of work required for technical alpine climbing burns vast stores of energy—that is, calories. Each of the three principal food types—carbohydrate, fat, and protein—offers a specific number of calories per gram. Carbohydrate provides 4 calories per gram, fat provides 9 calories, and protein provides 4 calories.

Although the body tends to use each of these food types for distinct functions, each may become an important source of energy at some point. Taken at face value, the numbers suggest that burning 1 gram of fat will provide more energy than 1 gram of protein or carbohydrate. This isn't quite true because during energy production, carbohydrates—in the form of blood glucose or muscle glycogen—convert more easily to energy than fat does. Given enough time, the metabolizing of 1 gram of fat produces 9 calories—but these calories from fat yield only half the power produced from glycogen.

While carbohydrates are the ruling energy source for athletic performance, scientific experiments indicate that an efficient body can store only enough glycogen to run about twenty miles. At the same time, the average athlete carries enough fat to supply energy for running several marathons. So how can you program your body to efficiently access this immense well of potential energy from both fat and carbohydrates?

The answer is a diet, combined with appropriate training and performance, that balances fat and carbohydrate burning. Then, providing your workload (pace and thermal loss) doesn't exceed the ability to fuel yourself, you can "go forever." An alpinist's nutritional strategy should aim for this goal.

Protein

Athletes whose sport demands a maximum power-to-weight ratio often ignore protein; some fear too much protein will cause them to bulk up. But adequate protein intake is essential to improve strength and accelerate recovery. No one really knows how much protein a body requires. The U.S. government's recommended daily allowance has been changed more than ten times since 1943. The current recommendation—eight-tenths of a gram per kilogram (2.2 pounds) of body weight per day—is inadequate for a hard-working athlete, who may need up to two and a half times that amount.

Within the first hour of exercise the body begins breaking down what are known as branched chain amino acids (leucine, isoleucine, and valine) in the blood. Once these amino acids are no longer available freely from the blood, the body begins burning muscle protein in order to get at the acids, which make up roughly 20 percent of muscle protein and are essential to both endurance and power exercise. In short, the body begins eating its own muscles for energy. Ouch.

Any time glucose and fatty acids are in short supply as efficient sources of energy, this protein cannibalism increases, and at some point the body begins getting most of its energy this way. This destructive breaking down of protein to access amino acids contributes to the formation of ammonia, which is highly toxic to the cells. The presence of huge amounts of ammonia in an athlete's body causes a dramatic drop in physical performance and in the ability to reason. And it stinks. Ever wonder why, at the end of a long effort in the mountains, the odor coming up from your climbing suit smells like ammonia? Ammonia is the byproduct of the body consuming its muscles for energy.

Averaging the recommendations of several studies suggests that a typical endurance athlete needs around 1.4 grams of protein per kilogram of body weight per day (roughly 98 grams for a 155-pound athlete). A power athlete would require much more. But simply eating additional protein doesn't improve performance, because the body knows precisely how much protein it needs for any activity level, and any excess is converted into carbohydrates or fats or excreted.

Experts argue about which is used more efficiently by the body: animal or vegetable protein. I say "Take it where you find it"—whether it's from cow, chicken, beans, fish, tofu, or cross-flow micro-filtered whey protein in powdered form. However, milk and egg protein is more efficient than vegetable protein, so the body needs lower quantities to build and maintain muscle. Create a demand for protein through training and performance, and then supply the demand. Balance demand and intake to forestall deficiency.

Carbohydrates and fats

Athletes working in short events like a marathon or in training sessions too brief to totally deplete muscle glycogen rarely concern themselves with fat metabolism, because their muscles can get all the energy they need from the glycogen provided by carbohydrates. For these athletes, fat is a terribly inefficient source of energy. Aerobic exercise at a high percentage of one's anaerobic threshold (see Chapter 5, Training: Endurance) burns mainly carbs. Anaerobic exercise (power activity such as weightlifting) uses carbohydrates for fuel almost exclusively.

However, long-term output at moderate levels—the realm of the alpinist—relies more on stored fat than on stored carbohydrates for energy. This doesn't mean that stored carbohydrates aren't still critically important. Successful fatty acid breakdown requires the continual background support of the glycogen and blood glucose provided by carbohydrates. When glycogen is used up and blood glucose levels dip, fat metabolism slows way down.

The amount of work needed to bring about efficient fat metabolism varies with individuals and with the type of activity. The end of the training cycle, as described in Chapter 5, emphasizes cardiovascular extensive endurance. Up to that point in the cycle, power and power-endurance training take precedence, two types of work that rely heavily on carbohydrate metabolism as a source of energy.

The cardiovascular endurance phase, relying more on fat metabolism for energy, prepares the body for the type of work that lies ahead during peaking, as you move into a climb. Aerobic training at a heart rate less than 75 percent of the anaerobic threshold improves the body's fat metabolism efficiency. This training teaches your body to go after stored fat as an energy source. The percentage of energy derived from fat metabolism during a major endurance effort—like climbing an alpine peak—may reach as much as 70 to 80 percent in a finely tuned endurance athlete.

Brief periods of maximum effort—for example, pulling through an extremely steep section—switches the energy demand back to carbohydrates. The trained body quickly switches between the different energy systems. But beware of glycogen-depleting periods of maximum effort early on a route. Once your muscles' stored glycogen is gone, it's gone until it can be reloaded—which cannot take place during exercise. And you need this glycogen not only for times of maximum effort, but also as a background agent for metabolizing fat. Act accordingly.

A protracted effort in the mountains requires a comprehensive nutritional strategy. First, strive to sustain a workload that allows the best use of fatty acids for energy while preserving stored glycogen by using only enough to fuel fat metabolism. Next, look to specific nutrients. Take in enough readily available carbohydrates to maintain blood glucose levels. Ingest enough of the branched chain amino acids to keep high levels available in the blood, thus preventing any dramatic muscle protein breakdown (see the upcoming sections "Eat to Perform" and "Eat to Recover"). Add an ammonia "scavenger" to spare your muscles and to counteract the performance-destroying effects of ammonia (see the information on ornithine and alpha-ketoglutarate in this chapter, under the section "Supplements for Training and Performance"). Take antioxidant supplements (also discussed under the "Supplements" section) during and after activity to combat cell damage produced during the oxidation process (that is, the conversion of sugar and fat to energy).

Eat to Perform

Eating readily available carbohydrates while climbing has become a lot easier over the past five years. One of America's most prolific alpinists, Jack Tackle, still prefers the Snickers bar for its calorie-to-price ratio, even though there are many superior, nutritious energy bars available today. Most alpine climbers initially discounted energy bars when they first appeared more than a decade ago because they froze solid at relatively benign temperatures and required you to drink at least half a liter of water to accompany the bar in order for absorption to take place. And at more than 200 calories per bar—with 2.5 grams of fat and 10 grams of protein—they overloaded the system, diverting too much blood from the muscles to the digestion process. Certainly one could eat just half, but it still slowed gastric emptying—that is, the transfer of food and fluid into the intestines so that their nutrients can then be taken into the blood.

Bill Vaughan, who helped formulate the original energy bars, then developed carbohydrate gels, which are easily ingested and efficiently utilized during exercise. He came up with a product called GU, a gel that supplies 25 grams of carbohydrate in the form of glucose polymers and fructose. The gel, when combined with a couple of mouthfuls of plain water, achieves the solution of 4 percent to 8 percent carbohydrates ideal for gastric emptying. GU contains leucine and valine, two of the branched chain amino acids that are burned up during exercise but are essential for physical activity and muscle recovery. GU also contains a small amount of caffeine to aid fat metabolism and to help keep your mind alert. Some type of blood thinning agent should be taken to counteract the effect of the caffeine in constricting blood vessels (see the sections later in this chapter on aspirin and garlic). GU also includes antioxidant vitamins—fat-soluble vitamin E and water-soluble vitamin C.

The body cannot absorb more than 400 calories per hour during exercise without inhibiting gastric emptying. Aim for an hourly intake of two or three packages of GU (at 100 calories per package) accompanied by plain water. Supplement the GU at different intervals with a "sports drink" containing maltodextrin and sodium (such as Cytomax, Gookinaid, or Endura) mixed to provide 100 to 200 calories per hour. This combination will provide the maximum number of calories the body can absorb without compromising gastric emptying. This ideal rate of intake ensures that blood glucose levels remain high throughout the climb and the descent. Eating any type of solid food, or food containing protein or fat, during the climbing will compromise your performance by requiring blood to leave the muscles in favor of the digestive system. This will slow you down and make you weaker. Save the solid food for pre-climb and post-climb meals or for overnight breaks during a multiday climb.

Develop the discipline to eat and drink regularly on an extreme alpine climb. Set the alarm on your heart rate monitor to go off every 15 minutes. Drink every time you hear the alarm, and eat a package of GU every second time it beeps. Experiential tests show that eating two GU gels every hour results in a higher blood glucose level at the end of a 100-mile footrace than was present at the beginning. While not scientific double-blind tests, these experiments were conducted on a veteran ultra-runner by qualified people. I find the results very encouraging. But even with high blood glucose levels that indicated adequate potential energy, this runner was fatigued. You can exercise the greatest discipline, but 20 to 40 hours of nonstop effort will waste even the fittest runner or alpine climber. The line between fatigue and exhaustion is thin. Working beyond your training level during the opening stages of any ascent depletes glycogen and leads to exhaustion.

At some point the body becomes reluctant to dip more deeply into its fat stores to provide energy. At this point you've reached "the wall." I've noticed—and ultra-endurance athlete John Stamstead concurs—that eating some fat at that time tells the body that more fat is on the way and causes it to release stored fatty acids into the energy pool. Whether this fat comes from a beef-and-pork meat stick (my favorite) or a Spam sandwich, eating fat boosts energy within 20 minutes. This is far too quickly for the body to digest and absorb it; it's still in the stomach. But the surge of energy manifests itself nonetheless.

Yvon Chouinard told me that at the end of a very long day in the Antarctic climbing Mount Vinson, he couldn't get warm by eating carbohydrates. So he tossed back a shot glass of olive oil. Within 20 minutes he began to feel warm—supporting the theory that once the body knows more fat is on the way, it is willing to part with stored fat to produce energy. Go figure. This action contradicts the advice I just gave against eating solid food on the climb—but when "the wall" looms ahead, all bets are off. Do whatever works, all the way to the straight shot of sweetened condensed milk. Mmm, mmm, good. Although performance will dip for some time, reduced performance is better than none at all.

Eat to Recover

Once the climbing stops on a multiday route, apply all energy and thought to recovering before climbing again the next morning. Fluid replacement is foremost (see "Hydration" later in this chapter). Once you have attended to fluids, begin eating. Carbohydrates are essential to replace muscle glycogen. Protein repairs muscle and replenishes the amino acids burned during energy production. Fat generates warmth and delivers a great number of calories. The menu should contain each of these components.

Salty fats such as feta cheese or sunflower seeds provide a good number of calories, while the salt should stimulate both appetite and water retention. Some people advise against eating fats before going to sleep. They say that because digestion of fat requires more oxygen than the processing of carbohydrates, the fat may not be readily digested during sleep, when respiration and circulation drop off. Experience, however, shows that the body processes fat during the night, and that its presence keeps you warm.

Don't worry about the glycemic index of food eaten after a hard day. Sedentary folks who eat simple sugars experience a detrimental insulin response, causing blood glucose levels to fall—the so-called sugar crash. But after exercise, when muscles scream for glycogen, blood glucose moves to the muscles quickly enough that no insulin instability occurs.

Food for Climbing

Here are suggestions for a meal before a day of concentrated climbing, for nutrition during the climb, and for a meal at the end of the period of intense effort.

Pre-climbing meal. Pick and choose from the following examples:
- Bagel with cream cheese or Nutella (delicious chocolate and nut spread).
- Instant oatmeal with protein powder, powdered milk, and sugar.
- Protein-heavy energy bar.
- Halva (delicious sesame seed confection full of glucose and salt; rich in calories, with an acid-buffering effect).
- Tea or cocoa (may have caffeine; add sweetened condensed milk for extra calories and taste).
- Dried fruit (keeps you regular).

During the climbing:
- GU carbohydrate gel: one package every half hour, taken with a few ounces of plain water.
- Fluid replacement drink: half a liter per hour.
- As a last resort when you hit "the wall": halva, meat sticks, or an energy bar.

Post-climbing meal:
- Bagel with feta cheese.
- Freeze-dried dinner drenched with olive oil (healthier than "squeeze" margarine).
- Landjaeger (beef, pork, or reindeer meat sticks high in protein and fat).
- Sunflower seeds (avoid peanuts and other highly acidic nuts).
- Protein-heavy energy bar or protein drink.
- Halva (for dessert).
- Caffeine-free herbal tea (add sweetened condensed milk for extra calories and taste).
- Instant soup.

Food weighs down the pack, but eating accessories needn't. A water bottle or water bag can serve as a cup. Use the pan only for melting snow. Don't carry any food that requires actual cooking; freeze-dried dinners can be reconstituted in the bag. Pack only a spoon for eating; use your belay knife for slicing cheese. Again, light is right.

Carry only what you know you can get down your throat, whether it's sweet or salty, wet or dry. Eat and drink regularly, because descending into calorie debt is counterproductive, no matter the justification. Failing to maintain calorie intake may translate into hitting the wall. You may fail on a climb without knowing why—and that's stupid. Make sure your partner eats, too, because there's nothing worse than having one guy strong and the other weak. Never test new food on an important route. Test it and know its effects beforehand. This is especially important at high altitude, which can cause a loss of appetite or nausea at the sight of food. Carbohydrate gels and hydration become even more important at high altitude.

In the end, though, climbing is anarchy, so you can do what you want—and that goes for food, too. Colorado climber Glen Porzak ate Pringles potato chips all the way up Makalu, while many British climbers of the previous generation prefer Kendall Mint Cakes. Personally, I can eat anything at any altitude, and I love pepperoni when I can find it. Getting enough calories at high altitude requires a strong will and sometimes a strong stomach.

Supplements for Training and Performance

Carbohydrates, fat, and protein fuel physical activity, but optimum athletic performance occurs only when the body's intake of these foods are properly supplemented with some vitamins, minerals, and herbs beyond the basic recommendations of the U.S. Food and Drug Administration.

Individual athletes respond differently to vitamin and mineral supplements. The recommended daily allowance developed in the United States was meant for sedentary people, not athletes. A 24-hour nonstop athletic effort goes beyond the knowledge of most sports nutritionists. Little data exist. Simply eating "well-balanced" meals won't support the nutritional needs of an endurance athlete—but on the other hand, downing handfuls of supplements often just produces expensive pee. Only personal testing can determine the level of vitamin and mineral supplementation that's right for you; however, I will make a few blanket suggestions.

Basic supplements

Take a reasonably priced multivitamin and mineral supplement twice each day to cover general deficiencies.

Vitamin C

For immune system support, increase vitamin C intake. Nobel Prize winner Linus Pauling recommended doses of several grams per day, and while his detractors were many, he outlived most of them. When training hard or while on a route, I'd recommend 1 to 2 grams twice per day. Opinions differ. Sports nutritionist Michael Colgan suggests from 2 to 12 grams of vitamin C daily for athletes.

Antioxidants

Converting sugar and fat to energy creates free radicals, molecules that damage human cells. To combat this, take supplemental antioxidants, either precombined or separately. Antioxidant supplements should contain vitamin C, vitamin E, L-glutathione, and selenium. It may also help if they contain coenzyme Q-10, n-acetyl cysteine, and beta carotene.

Aspirin

Aspirin is a useful supplement, not only as an analgesic but, according to doctors, for prevention of heart disease. How? By inhibiting formation of a hormone called thromboxane A2, which causes concentration of blood platelets and constriction of blood vessels. While climbing in cold weather, take one 325-milligram tablet every 12 hours to help keep blood thin and flowing, which will aid blood flow to the extremities.

Garlic

Garlic is an essential cold-weather supplement. It's a better anti-clotting agent than aspirin and reduces the stickiness of platelets, which improves overall blood circulation. Look for a garlic supplement with a standardized amount of S-allylcysteine, the strongest-acting pharmacological compound in garlic. Saponins, steroid-like compounds found in garlic, inhibit an enzyme in the muscle cells of the arteries, resulting in arterial dilation and reduced blood pressure, thus better circulation. Reinhold Messner used garlic supplements for high-altitude climbing because physiologists claimed they improved vascular elasticity. Both dry and liquid forms of garlic supplements also increase the number of natural killer cells in the body, improving immunity and reducing the risk of cancer.

Eleutherococcus senticosus

This supplement is among the adaptogens—plant-based chemicals that increase immune and metabolic function. *Eleutherococcus senticosus* is a member of the Aralia family of herbs.

Much of the testing on Eleutherococcus senticosus, often referred to as EC, has been done in the former Soviet Union. These tests, when combined with my four years of personal experience and the testimony of other athletes, suggest that EC can deliver great benefits. Many studies show improved cognitive function, accelerated reflexes, and increased endurance. Double-blind European tests confirm 40 to 45 percent increases in endurance, perhaps based on EC's effect of sparing glycogen while increasing oxidation of fatty acids. Blood tests indicate a more even and consistent glucose metabolism, which results in fewer sugar-related highs or lows. EC's active ingredients are glycosides, closely linked to sugar molecules.

EC's aid in adapting to high altitudes is widely known among Himalayan climbers from Eastern Europe and the former Soviet Union. Its effect at altitude was tested extensively on both laboratory animals and people. Russian scientists subjected laboratory rats to simulated climbs by placing them in pressure chambers calibrated to match extreme altitudes. Rats given prophylactic doses of EC lived as much as 60 percent longer that those who received none. EC has virtually no side effects, although the body may adapt to high doses, indicating the need to take the supplement in cycles.

It is "buyer beware" when shopping for pure, genuine EC, which is frequently and erroneously identified as Siberian ginseng. Although in the same family, Siberian ginseng is a distant, less effective cousin. Genuine, pure, properly harvested EC costs more per ounce than gold. PrimeQuest and Zand are two of the better-known suppliers.

Phosphate

Both power and endurance exercise stimulate the release of muscle phosphates into the blood. Low blood-phosphate levels hinder athletic performance. Higher blood-phosphate levels are found in athletes than in sedentary people because the body responds to training by increasing its phosphate levels. Otherwise, the body doesn't produce phosphates, and intake from food alone is not adequate for athletes.

Phosphate supplements have a beneficial buffering effect, reducing lactic acid levels in the muscles. Several tests showed improvement of 6 to 12 percent in VO_2 max. Supplements improved power performance by up to 17 percent.

During depletion days—those days of training or climbing when you are at the end of your reserves of food, energy, and water—take 1 gram of sodium phosphate every 3 to 4 hours during exercise. Loading of 4 grams per day prior to a climb ensures starting off with high phosphate levels. Never take more than 1.5 grams at once as it may cause stomach upset or diarrhea. Good sources of phosphates include Gulf Performance Group's Stim-o-Stam and TwinLab's Phos Fuel.

Creatine monohydrate

To develop explosive strength and extra muscle mass or to acquire an insulin-independent source of very short-term energy, you can try creatine supplementation.

Creatine phosphate is one chemical substrate necessary for anaerobic power output. Muscle supplies dwindle quickly, but the body resynthesizes it quite rapidly. Within the first second of anaerobic work, 80 percent of the energy used comes from creatine phosphate and 20 percent from glycogen oxidation. At 2.5 seconds into the work, energy production splits 50-50 between the systems. A continuous muscular contraction of more than 6 seconds will consume a muscle's supply of creatine phosphate.

Research shows that supplementing with creatine monohydrate (which contains more creatine than creatine phosphate, and costs less, too) saturates the muscles with creatine. Artificially increasing your muscles' stores of creatine extends the time before reserves are expended, thus improving power endurance. Use creatine monohydrate supplements during the strength training phase of the training cycle if you can afford it. No data support its use for enhancing aerobic performance.

Ornithine and alpha-ketoglutarate

Glutamine, a nonessential amino acid, accounts for 50 percent of all free amino acids in the muscles. During and after hard exercise, muscles release huge amounts of glutamine into the blood. Exercise-induced glutamine loss is countered by using other amino acids

Mark Twight looking forward to chipping his teeth on a Power Bar. It's minus 30 degrees in the Tien Shan mountains of Kazhakstan. "I had to break it with a hammer." *Photo: © Ace Kvale*

to make new glutamine. If these amino acids are not available in the blood, the body breaks down muscle protein to acquire them. This results in the cannibalization of the muscles, along with production of highly toxic ammonia.

Glutamine supplements would appear to be the obvious solution, except that glutamine powder degrades into ammonia when mixed with water. But both ornithine and alpha-ketoglutarate act as ammonia scavengers—molecules that bond with ammonia and carry it out of the system—and the body can make glutamine from both of them. Ornithine alpha-ketoglutarate supplements increase the body's glutamine reserves and strengthen the immune system. And because the supplements allow the body to make glutamine without breaking down muscle protein to acquire the components to make it, they help preserve muscle tissue.

To help preserve muscles during intense exercise or while on a multiday route, take 2 to 4 grams of ornithine alpha-ketoglutarate three times per 24-hour period. Among the acceptable brands available is TwinLab's OKG Fuel.

Caffeine

Here's a trick for making a common supplement, caffeine, work better when you go climbing. Most adults use caffeine in one form or another every day. Frequent use causes the body's caffeine receptors to become accustomed to the drug, and it takes more and more caffeine to feel a similar effect. Discontinuing the use of caffeine for as little as three weeks cleans out these receptors and increases their sensitivity. After the cleansing, any caffeine you use during a climb will be more effective at improving fat mobilization, sharpening your mind, and keeping your attitude positive during the roughest of times.

Hydration

CamelBak hawks its hydration systems with the slogan "Hydrate or Die," and a truer statement could not be made. Dehydration, if taken to extremes, causes death. While few climbers die from dehydration, everyone should take the decline in performance caused by a modest 3 percent drop in the level of hydration very seriously. If a muscle dehydrates by 3 percent, it will suffer a 10 percent loss of contractile strength and an 8 percent reduction in speed.

Scientific tests of athletes suffering the effects of dehydration indicate that 5 percent dehydration causes up to a 30 percent decline in performance. Researchers measured these results during events lasting 35 minutes or less. Longer efforts would show more dramatic results. Exercising for 3 to 5 hours without drinking water will increase the heart rate for a fixed level of output by 30 beats per minute. At high altitude, where humidity is lower (because cold air holds less water), respiratory evaporation increases, causing as much as half a liter to 1.5 liters of water to be lost *per hour*. The body can't keep up with this loss without intense vigilance and self-discipline.

Respiratory evaporation is only one method of water loss. The body controls its temperature through sweat. At rest, evaporation through the skin causes roughly 30 percent of water loss, but heavy exercise can increase the amount of sweating as much as three hundred times.

Dehydration reduces blood volume and increases blood viscosity. This leads to several problems, including decreased flow of oxygen and nutrients to the muscles, decreased efficiency in removal of carbon dioxide and lactic acid by the blood, and reduced circulation to the extremities that may result in cold-related injuries. Symptoms of dehydration include muscle cramping, excessive fatigue for a given level of output, and shortness of breath. Next comes vomiting, a hot, dry skin, and finally a state of coma.

How much do you need?

Thirst doesn't accurately tell you how well your body is hydrated. An athlete needs much more fluid than you would expect. A study at Middle Tennessee State University indicated that 1 hour of hard cycling demands 100 milliliters (3.5 ounces) of fluid every 5 minutes for optimum replacement. A 1996 position paper by the American College of Sports Medicine said an athlete performs best when replacing fluid at the same rate it is being lost through sweat and other means. This amounts to between 600 and 1,200 milliliters per hour, depending on the intensity of the exercise and environmental conditions.

Obviously, alpine climbers cannot carry the quantities of water that are recommended. In fact, most climbers impose a 2.5-quart limit on the amount of water and replacement fluids they pack at any one time. This means they have to carry a stove to use for melting snow when the bottles run dry. A team of two must exert the discipline to stop and use the stove every 12 hours. They should be able to melt enough snow in 2 hours to produce 10 quarts of water. They should be able to drink 5 to 6 quarts each during 12 hours. If their clothing systems don't cause them to overheat and sweat too much, this level of hydration will bring them just shy of 50 percent of ideal hydration for optimum performance. This is a big improvement over the standard amount of 2 to 4 quarts per 24 hours that most climbers consume.

Consistently drinking small amounts promotes better hydration than drinking huge quantities at one time. A hydration bladder carried in the pack, with a hose clipped to the shoulder strap, allows you to drink periodically. Take care to prevent the hose from freezing or becoming entangled in the gear sling and runners. CamelBak and Ultimate Direction make bladder and hose systems that work quite well. The best bladders are the MSR Dromedaries in 2-, 4-, and 10-liter sizes, but these do not include a hose.

Downing the fluids you need is actually the easy part. Once you've taken in the replacement fluids, they have to make their way into the bloodstream. The rate at which the intestines transfer fluids into the blood depends upon the rate of gastric emptying— the speed with which the fluids leave the stomach for the intestines. The rate of gastric emptying varies with the volume, temperature, and composition of the fluid. Obviously you will want to do whatever it takes to speed stomach emptying so that fluids get into the blood as fast as possible. Simply drinking the fluids doesn't guarantee that they will reach your blood efficiently.

To help with gastric emptying, try to maintain about as much fluid in your stomach as you can stand without discomfort. Dehydration slows gastric emptying. Therefore, start drinking early on a climb and keep on drinking, because once you're in the hole on the volume of fluid needed, it's far harder to dig yourself out. As the Tennessee study discovered, drink between 600 and 1,200 milliliters per hour—somewhere between a strong half-quart to more than a quart every hour.

The fluid should stay between 59 and 72 degrees Fahrenheit for palatability and absorption. However, sometimes ice-cold water is more appealing, so use your judgment. Add somewhere between half a gram and seven-tenths of a gram of sodium (the equivalent of 1.25 to 1.75 grams of table salt) per liter of water for palatability and fluid retention.

To prevent liquid from freezing, pour boiling water into your hydration bladders or bottles and stash them in insulated cases made for the purpose or wrap them in your belay coat. Even in the coldest conditions, these procedures should keep water from getting too cold before you drink it all. Stainless steel thermos bottles are fine for roadside routes or base camp but are far too heavy to carry on an alpine route.

Mixing your drink

In order to maintain carbohydrate and salt intake while climbing, mix some type of powdered sports drink with your water. Look for drinks whose glucose comes from glucose polymers (maltodextrins) rather than straight glucose and sucrose. Several big-market sports drinks feature glucose and sucrose as their carbohydrate components, and these should be avoided. However, most people prefer the taste of these drinks, despite the fact they interfere with gastric emptying and tend to distress your stomach on a climb. Glucose polymers are far better carbohydrate components, well tolerated during heavy exercise because they are less sweet. Solutions of glucose polymers have the advantage of passing through the stomach faster than solutions of pure glucose, and they maintain blood glucose levels. Stay away from Kool-Aid and soda pop.

After finding a brand of sports drink your stomach accepts, ask the manufacturer for the glucose percentage when mixed according to directions. Then mix stronger or weaker according to the answer to create a glucose (carbohydrate) concentration between 4 percent and 8 percent.

Ingest carbohydrates at a rate of 30 to 60 grams per hour. Since the body can absorb an absolute maximum of 100 grams of carbohydrates per hour, or about 400 calories, without inhibiting gastric emptying—and since a climber will expend approximately 500 or more calories per hour while climbing—expect to be in a deficit no matter how disciplined you are.

Check the list of ingredients to determine whether the supplemental additives in the sports drink are going to help or hinder your performance. Extra amino acids will help recovery; potassium and sodium will ease cramping; phosphates will increase endurance. However, stimulants often appear in sports drinks. While I'm not against them, they usually act as diuretics or vasoconstrictors and thus interfere with the sleep necessary for overnight recovery. Limited amounts of caffeine are probably OK, depending on personal tolerance and the amount ingested from other sources.

Watch out for the herb Ma Huang with its active ingredient norepinephrine. Norepineph-rine improves fat metabolism, which is why some companies put it in their drink, but it is a vasoconstrictor without peer, narrowing the blood vessels and making cold-weather inju-ries more likely. If you want to keep your toes and fingers, do without it. Test drinks while training before committing to them on a long, hard route. Note that your body will not tol-erate some drinks in the required quantities. Among the drinks that are worth checking out for your use are Cytomax, Hydra Fuel, and Endura.

It's impossible to stay fully hydrated while actually climbing, so rehydrating at the end of the day or during breaks between hard effort is essential. Because of the climbing, your body will be dehydrated, your stomach and your entire system will be highly acidic, your muscles will be holding onto metabolic waste, and your glycogen reserves will be gone. First and foremost, you must drink. Plain water is fine. Once you are a quart ahead, start adding your recovery foods and supplements. Avoid acidic food and drink. Your body already is in an acid state, so look for foods that buffer it. Acidic foods also are more difficult to absorb. Citrus juices, for example, are acidic and the high sugar content will impede gastric emptying.

Trainers and coaches warn against staying immobile during breaks. Movement main-tains the circulation needed to remove metabolic waste from the muscles and to prevent cramping. This isn't possible on a technical route where you tie in to a short leash when you stop. Expect some cramping if the work was stressful enough. Continue drinking con-sistently for as long possible before sleeping. Drink until your urine is straw-colored and copious. Do not fall into a pattern of chronic dehydration that leads to declining abilities with each succeeding day on a route.

Water equals life.

Scott Backes brewing up in the Messner Couloir on Denali, Alaska, during a 10-hour dash to the top. Staying hydrated was the key to moving fast and recovering after the single-push effort. Photo: © Mark Twight

MISTAKE ON MOUNT HUNTINGTON

Bill Belcourt and I climbed light and fast on the west face of Mount Huntington in the Alaska Range in 1998, blasting it in 22 hours round trip. Had conditions been better, we could have shaved 3 hours off the time. Had we disciplined ourselves enough to drink adequate water, we might have trimmed a further 4 hours off of that, according to my sports physiologist. Whatever time we spent melting snow and hydrating would have been regained through improved performance. We certainly would have been safer because our minds would have been sharper and our muscular coordination unimpaired.

Despite what I know about the importance of hydration, I made a huge mistake. I based my calculations on the assumption that we would stay on the face for no more than 15 hours and that the predicted cold temperatures would prevail. They didn't.

I began hydrating the day before the climb, then drank 3 liters of water the next morning, with no caffeine to cause excessive urination. I carried only 2 liters of water on the face—and no stove. Five liters over 22 hours is the liquid consumption of an idiot.

We both paid the price, especially since cloud cover kept temperatures warm. Despite dressing very lightly, we both sweated a lot. We were slow on the route, and it took me almost a week to recover from the damage, even after returning to sea level. My resting pulse did not return to normal for five days after the climb, and my pulse while exercising took an additional two days to drop back to normal. Stupid is as stupid does.

Bill Belcourt on the west face of Mount Huntington, Alaska. Stupidly, we drank too little water during the 22 hours we were on the route and it took many days to recover. *Photo: © Mark Twight*

CLOTHING

7

Clothes are the first line of defense against the elements. The climber must sort out what to wear to respond to likely conditions, but the sometimes conflicting claims and unsound theories of the manufacturers make creating an effective clothing system difficult. One goal of this chapter is to debunk the marketing hype that created a consensual reality called the "layering system"—a reality that doesn't exist in the world of extreme alpinism. In fifteen years of testing, reviewing, and designing clothing within the outdoor industry, I've owned (and wrecked) hundreds of pieces of clothing made by name-brand manufacturers from many different countries and by cutting-edge garage designers working from back alleys. No surprise I've got some opinions based on this experience.

Going fast and light on technical alpine routes requires a clothing system that adapts to varying external conditions and changing levels of body heat and moisture. Appreciating the vastly different conditions in which one system—that's right, one system—must keep you warm represents the dilemma of clothing choice.

Ultimately, you must predict the conditions you may encounter on a given route in any particular season, including the stresses you will impose on your body. Remaining still while belaying your partner for two hours may follow an hour of running up 50-degree ice wearing a pack. The climate can switch from dry to wet in a matter of minutes. Climbing in the dead of an Alaskan night or in the heat of day on a Himalayan south face or in the moderate climate and altitude of the Alps demands different solutions. And the clothing forecast, as well as the weather forecast, is usually derived from incomplete or poorly understood data.

Let's Look at Layering

To address all the variables, the outdoor industry develops materials, systems, and combinations of clothing marketed as the next great miracle fabric or idea, which may or may not work in practice. Miracles aside, no item of clothing or fabric choice will cause failure on a route. Reflect on the difficult climbs undertaken in bad weather by climbers from the former Soviet Union and East Bloc nations using what Westerners consider hopelessly antiquated clothing and gear. More often than not, they succeed. Why do Westerners fail on easy routes up big mountains with all the advantages of the most modern equipment? Simply, success and failure come from within.

Let's examine the universally acclaimed layering system: the combining of several thin layers of clothing to accommodate different levels of heat output, outside temperature and humidity. The layering system as now sold is a lie when it comes to technical alpine

Pages 80–81: Steve House climbing disconcerting "snow-ice" on the first pitch of The Gift That Keeps on Giving on Mount Bradley's south face, Alaska Range. Photo: © Mark Twight

climbing. Imagine moving hard and fast wearing only long underwear beneath an outer shell jacket and pants. You stop. It's zero degrees Fahrenheit. Conventional wisdom would have you remove your harness or leg loops and the shells, unpack the fleece, put it on, put the shells back on, and rebuckle the harness. All the while you and your partner remain stationary and unproductive. Such layering addresses virtually every set of internal and external conditions, but at the cost of spending time and energy to stop and strip before getting too hot or to stop and add a layer when chilled.

To move fast, eliminate the word "stop" from your climbing vocabulary. Stopping slows progress. Virtually every existing insulation system depends on the "stop" concept of layering *under* your shell, which doesn't make sense unless messing with equipment is the goal of your trip. Wearing jacket and pants shells large enough to accommodate the many layers needed under them makes them bulky, heavy, and clumsy. To climb fast and make precise, efficient movements, clothes need to fit closely and flex enough to allow an unimpeded range of motion. If a clothing system costs too much time, if it requires multiple decisions, get rid of it. Clothing systems are tools like anything else. Don't let them get in the way.

Layering on top

Instead of adding or subtracting layers underneath the shells, try layering over the top of them.

Suppose that for your climb you wear clothing components that create a light, flexible "action suit." Depending on conditions, this could include light, stretch fabrics worn as outerwear or simply light shells worn directly over long underwear. The minimal action suit will keep you warm while moving without making you so hot that your muscles become inefficient. (Remember that cool muscles are more efficient than overheated ones.) You won't sweat out moisture that must be replaced with melted snow, costing you time and stove fuel. Likewise, if you don't sweat leading a pitch, you won't supercool due to rapid evaporative heat loss once you stop, nor will you soak your insulation and later curse it for not being warm enough. You climb comfortably.

Once stopped, don a big synthetic belay jacket *over* the shell jacket and put side-zip overpants (also with synthetic insulation) over your legs. Pop the belay device through a panel in the front of the overpants and settle in for the two-hour belay. The moisture built up in your action suit pushes into the belay clothes because the suit is now deep inside the temperature gradient. It dries quickly and completely.

Moisture that builds up in the belay clothes either passes through their totally breathable outer surface right away or dries when you wear them into your sleeping bag that night. The whole system gets wet, but it dries easily. It doesn't matter much, though, because synthetic clothes retain much of their insulating value even when wet. You will get wet up there. Make sure your insulation can take it. When it's time to follow the pitch, strip down to the action suit and get moving—again without having to touch your harness.

Choices

Selecting clothes for alpine climbing boils down to insulating for two sets of circumstances: heat-generating movement or heat-losing stasis. There is no in-between. Without the need to layer underneath your shells, you may buy lighter, more foolproof shells. They are often less expensive because you don't need all the so-called features. Forget about full side-zips on the shell pants or on one-piece suits. Without zippers needing double flaps to protect them from abrasion, wind, and water, pant legs are more flexible. Accurately predicting conditions will preclude the need to ventilate with zippers. If it's warmer than anticipated, either strip or endure. If it's colder than anticipated, move faster. Whether layering over or under shells, don't plan on getting it exactly right. Consider predicting temperatures within 10 degrees Fahrenheit either way a direct hit. Sometimes you'll suffer, which is what alpinism is all about anyway. Enjoy it, it's what you signed on for.

If there is a significant difference between starting altitude and the summit, factor the drastic change in temperatures into the clothing system. Adjust the system if plans call for remaining on the climb for a long time living on a calorie-deficient diet. Expending calories faster than you replace them makes your body temperature fall. Near the end of the ascent, when cold and exhaustion sap warmth and energy, you may wear your belay jacket while moving on the summit day.

Torso and legs

Different parts of the body require different insulation. The body generates more heat and moisture with the torso than with the legs. Managing the moisture and heat of the torso affects core temperature dramatically, so errors are dangerous.

Making a mistake with leg insulation is less serious because they radiate less heat than the torso. Since legs don't produce much moisture, go for shell fabrics with greater impermeability rather than the breathability the torso needs.

The breathability factor

Manufacturers argue that breathable insulation such as fleece and pile should transport perspiration away from the body as fast as possible. This notion clashes with the effect of evaporative cooling: Totally breathable insulation transports moisture at such a high rate that in order to remain warm, you need thicker, heavier insulation. You will sweat in the mountains. Most of this moisture develops from overheating due to movement. And most occurs on your back, where no matter how breathable the shell, the closed-cell foam and pressure of the pack blocks moisture transfer to the outside, so your back gets soaked. What happens after removing the pack and allowing the moisture transfer to proceed? Rapid evaporative cooling, or flash-off—the result of super-efficient fabrics wicking moisture away from the body.

You can slow this chilly process dramatically by wearing a semipermeable vapor barrier (such as a microfiber windshirt or a thin shirt like the Patagonia Zephur or Marmot Dri-Clime Windshirt) over thin synthetic long underwear. Used this way, these pieces

Layer a big, fat belay jacket over your "action suit" to stay warm while stationary. Mark Twight and Nancy Feagin on the north face of the Aiguille du Midi, Chamonix. *Photo: © James Martin*

create a microclimate close to the body, slowing evaporation while still allowing moisture to wick through the semipermeable layer. The shirt acts like a second skin. Once moisture passes beyond this second skin into whatever super-efficient transport fabric is worn over it, moisture can transfer swiftly to the outside without conducting rapid evaporative cooling to the body's core.

For this system to work, the fabrics worn over the second skin layer must be more breathable the farther they are away from your skin. Obviously, a shell jacket that is both waterproof and breathable doesn't breathe well enough to give moisture easy passage. Unless wet snow or rain is falling, don't wear a so-called waterproof/breathable shell. Instead choose a garment made from a durable, stretch woven material that blocks some wind and sheds snow, such as those made by Scholler and Malden Mills. Products are made from these fabrics by companies including Mammut, Patagonia, Arcteryx, and North Face. Alternatively, wear a shell made from microfiber—a tightly woven fabric that is quite windproof and water-repellent as well as breathing far better than Gore-Tex or any of its waterproof/breathable cousins.

Wear light insulation on your torso. With the semipermeable vapor barrier in your system—the thin windshirt—you won't need to wear as much clothing to stay warm. When temperatures rise or while working hard, the windshirt that is your second skin can also be your outer layer. It's wind-resistant, snow won't stick to it, and it's light enough to prevent overheating.

In the end you have to choose which concept works for you. Personally I favor insulation offering as much breathability as possible on my legs while wearing a semipermeable vapor barrier on my torso. I complement these systems with different types of shells.

Materials

To choose the different pieces of your clothing system wisely, learn the performance characteristics of the various materials. Manufacturers, media, and salespeople at the local shop tend to hold contradictory opinions. Understand your specific needs and communicate them clearly. Avoid buying whatever the marketing hype or college-student clerk tries to get you to purchase. Buy in haste; repent at leisure.

First of all, look for 100-percent petroleum-based synthetic materials. No cotton, no wool. Most synthetic fibers are solid and cannot absorb water. When synthetic clothes are wet, water becomes trapped between fibers, coating the outside of them. The fibers themselves do not soak up water. Because synthetic fibers cannot absorb water, they transport or wick moisture away from the body. This is simple physics, the implacable process of equalization, of pressure and temperature in this case. The heat source, your body, pushes moisture toward the cooler exterior clothing layers or air. With enough temperature differential between the heat source and the outside air, and with breathable layers, especially the shell, not impeding moisture transport, moisture will flow through the system. Once moisture production stops, the system will dry out.

The outermost layer of the system has little heat differential compared to the air temperature, so there's no reason for moisture to pass through it. Thus the fabric of the outer layer should be as breathable as possible. If moisture freezes on the inside of the shell before passing through it, it becomes an impermeable barrier.

Insulation material shouldn't try to wick moisture by a circuitous route, either. The Patagonia Infurno jacket, for example, avoids this problem with a particularly straight-fiber pile construction that shoots moisture along quickly and easily.

In short, synthetics keep you warm even when they're wet, which is to say they don't lose much of their insulating value when wet. Virtually every clothing component, from long underwear to bibs to jackets, are made from synthetic materials by every manufacturer. Most of the yarns are made by the same international petrochemical companies and are converted (woven and finished) into fabrics by the same "converters" regardless of the brand name that appears on the label. When you choose a brand, you are really choosing a petrochemical company. Beware the hype.

Some fleece garments feature nylon reinforcement panels, ostensibly to improve durability, but the real effects are to impede moisture transport and your own body movements. Some garments stretch more than others. It's easier to move in these, but several stretch garments worn one atop the other feel like a giant Ace bandage. Some fleece garments feature underarm zips to improve ventilation. Why pay for the extra weight, bulk, and cost of construction? If you become too hot, take the jacket off.

Some fleece jackets and pants incorporate windproof films sandwiched between otherwise breathable layers. Wind Stopper and Windbloc are two brand names that function this way. The problem is that these garments trap too much heat for moving quickly and are too heavy and bulky to carry as belay jackets or pants. However, windproof films in fleece shine in lightweight gloves. You can wear them in more situations than you might imagine. Forget the windproof films for hats, though: Unless you puncture the film with a thousand tiny needle holes around the ears, you won't be able to hear falling stones or shouted belay commands.

Look for maximum loft, warmth, and compressibility, and minimum weight, in a belay jacket. Two types of insulation address these requirements: down, or a synthetic such as Polarguard, Primaloft, and Quallofil. Climbers tend to swear by one or the other. High-quality down lasts longer than any synthetic and is ultimately lighter, warmer, and more compressible for a given temperature rating. Down is, however, more expensive—and it loses all insulating value when wet. Saturated, it's worse than wearing nothing at all. When you know your down jacket or down bag are soaked for the duration of the route, you start fixating on the ground and retreat. On Nanga Parbat I watched my Gore-Tex-shelled down bag get flatter and heavier every day as it refused to dry out each night. High on the route, when I needed to be warmer, my insulation was working less efficiently.

Modern synthetic insulated jackets cost 20 to 30 percent less than their down counterparts, weigh only slightly more, and don't compress quite as well. Synthetics lose some loft after repeated compression and long use. However, a synthetic belay jacket is idiot-proof. It will remain warm when wet. Polarguard 3D is regarded as the best of the current synthetics for belay jackets, pants, and sleeping bags.

Adding waterproof/breathable shells of Gore-Tex or similar material on top of the belay jacket actually increases moisture build-up inside the jacket by reducing overall breathability. Gore-Tex is nowhere near as breathable as an uncoated nylon or microfiber shell. When I attempted Khan Tengri in the Tien Shan range, it was a bitter cold winter, and I quite stupidly wore a shell even less breathable than Gore-Tex because it was all I had. Not only did frost build up inside the shell, but my pile jacket actually froze to the shell and prevented any hope of freedom of movement. A microfiber shell would have proved far more appropriate.

Many manufacturers claim their clothing will keep you warm and dry, but in reality warm and damp is usually the case. Synthetic insulation doesn't need protection from an expensive waterproof/breathable shell. In fact, it works better if it doesn't have one.

With my approach of layering over the top, you can put a synthetic belay jacket (whose shell is totally breathable) over clothes soaked from spindrift without a lot of concern. Stuff wet gloves in the interior mesh pockets of the jacket, and they will dry out without compromising the insulation. Don't worry about moisture coming in from the outside, because if the temperature differential between your body and the outside air is great enough, this moisture won't soak through the whole belay jacket. And if it's raining, it's time to retreat. It's too warm, and rocks will begin falling soon.

If the belay jacket insulation gets wet as you're wearing it, it will dry out overnight while you wear it inside your sleeping bag. Placing the jacket deep inside the temperature gradient—that is, inside the sleeping bag—also will dry a jacket even if moisture has frozen in it due to extremely cold temperatures.

Wear your clothes while sleeping. You carry the insulation anyway, so make it work for you 24 hours a day. Factoring the clothes into the sleeping system permits a lighter sleeping bag. In Alaska during the winter, I carried a bag rated to only 20 degrees Fahrenheit on Mount Bradley and a similar bag on Mount Hunter. For winter routes in the Alps, I carry a bag rated to only 45 degrees. These bags effectively weigh nothing. Sleeping in your clothes dries them overnight. When you wake up, you are dressed and ready, which saves time.

Shell Systems

At some point you'll need to decide between a one-piece or two-piece shell system. Proponents of the one-piece suit claim it is warmer and lighter, while two-piece users cite versatility as their system's advantage. Go with personal preference or, God forbid, style, while keeping in mind the clothing concepts described earlier in this chapter.

One-piece suits

Because of their weight and bulk, and the complexity of putting one on while wearing skis, crampons, or a harness, relegate one-piece suits to routes where you can put one on and leave it on for the duration. The sizing of a one-piece suit is important. If you have big shoulders and a broad back but skinny legs, you'll never find a stock suit to fit you. If it fits your shoulders and the sleeves are long enough, the legs will probably be too long and baggy. If the distance between your crotch and shoulders is unusually long, a stock suit won't fit well enough for easy movement. In either case, only a custom suit will do. That said, most folks fit into the suits available off the rack.

Most one-piece suits provide openings for answering nature's call. Again, personal preference will influence the decision. Both rainbow-shaped zippers and through-the-crotch zippers work. A through-the-crotch zipper doesn't require moving or adjusting the harness leg loops, while a rainbow zip requires dropping them. The through-the-crotch zipper also leaves less area exposed to foul weather and is easier to close in a hurry in case of spindrift or an emergency. Rainbow zippers provide a bigger opening. If you've been eating a lot of freeze-dried or third-world food, the larger aperture will prove a blessing.

One-piece suits feature zippers and flaps and so on. Most are justified by the need for ventilation. Pit zips are standard, but they are no miracle: They don't ventilate or cool the body effectively when you're wearing a pack or moving slowly. Skiing could force enough air through to do some good. Pit zips permit you to turn a jacket into a vest, however. Stuff your arms out of the holes, and you'll cool down fairly well.

Designers justify full side-zips in a one-piece for ventilation because the suit is a bear to take off. Side zips may sound good on a hot day, but does the ability to ventilate, especially if used infrequently, justify the added weight of the zippers and the double storm flaps needed to make them waterproof? Who wants the stiffness at the knee joint that zippers and flaps create? Why fight that stiffness with every upward step? Two solutions are available from different manufacturers: pit zips that continue down past the waist but stop at the knee, or "waterproof" zippers that don't use storm flaps. With a "put on, leave on" one-piece garment, you won't need fully separating zips to put the thing on over boots or skis. But if you want to put your shell on and take it off frequently, select a two-piece system.

Two-piece suits

The two-piece shell system, while not significantly heavier then a one-piece suit, offers more versatility in sizing and use in the field. If you have big shoulders and a broad back but skinny little legs, you can simply buy a large jacket and small pants. If it's too hot, you can remove one or the other or both, easily. You're free to mix or match the weight and thickness of each piece.

If you foresee needing to adapt to a variety of conditions, side zips and pit zips may help. Most standard side-zip pants or bibs don't feature rainbow or through-the-crotch zippers for answering nature's call. Unfortunately, this mandates dropping the side zip to the knee and pulling the back of the pants across your backside, which involves considerable fiddling with your harness. Or you can simply drop your trousers from under the harness after removing the leg loops, exposing beaucoup flesh to the outside world while remaining tied in to the waist belt of your harness. A specific zipper dealing with this issue, available in most bibs, is faster and safer.

Consider replacement cost. Most one-piece suits cost a bundle, often more than both components of their two-piece counterparts. Wearing out part of the suit or tearing it up in a fall means replacing the whole thing. Manufacturers understand that no one wants to buy another $800 suit, so they tend to make one-piece suits out of heavier, more durable material than two-piece systems. With a two-piece suit, you need to replace only one piece if something wears out.

Shell Fabrics

Shell fabrics have long been a battlefield between science, rhetoric, and nonsense. Gore-Tex is the undisputed king of shell fabrics, with name recognition on par with the illustrious Swiss Army knife. Although touted as the greatest shell fabric ever, capable of meeting alpine climbing's tremendous demands, it is no miracle. W. L. Gore and Associates place stringent restrictions on the design of any garments made with their fabric. These restrictions by a fabric producer have hindered development of new designs within the outdoor industry for the past fifteen years. Counterattacks made by alternative fabric manufacturers have almost always been crushed under Gore's marketing juggernaut. Despite the lack of market recognition, many alternative fabrics exist, and one of them may suit your specific needs and climate better than Gore-Tex.

If, for example, you climb in the Pacific Northwest, England, or Scotland where you will routinely be rained on, Lowe Alpine's Triple Point Ceramic fabric may be a good choice. Independent tests conducted by EMPA in Switzerland indicate that Triple Point has better "wet breathability" than does Gore-Tex, although Gore-Tex breathes better when the fabrics are dry. But if it's dry, why are you wearing a "waterproof" garment? Triple Point garments are quite a bit less expensive as well.

Patagonia's H2N0 Storm Fabric is waterproof and relatively breathable, but not breathable enough if you are truly working hard. Remember: Starting from an uncoated or unlaminated piece of nylon or polyester, any treatment or coating added to improve its impermeability will compromise the fabric's breathability, and vice versa. In subzero conditions, moisture will freeze on the inside of all but the most breathable shell fabrics, rendering them impermeable.

In this frigid situation, although Gore's Activent and Patagonia's Pneumatic fabrics function better than heavier materials, the only shell fabric of any real value is microfiber. This fact is well known by climbers and skiers who operate during the dead of winter in Scandinavia. Microfiber is a tightly woven fabric consisting of nearly microscopic fibers. The tightness of the weave creates the fabric's windproof qualities, but since it is uncoated, moisture can pass through the fabric with little restriction.

But perhaps you don't need much of a shell at all. When I climbed the west face of Mount Huntington in Alaska in 1998, I wore Mammut stretch pants over stretch fleece tights. My superlight, full side-zip shell pants remained in the bottom of my pack. On top I wore one thin layer of long underwear, a microfiber windshirt, and a medium-weight fleece vest under a Lowe Lite Flite shell, which is lightly coated and breathes reasonably well. We never stopped moving except to belay. I usually climb in good weather because I like to stack the odds in my favor, so I can wear microfiber shells or stretch-fabric outer garments most of the time.

Bad weather has surprised me during my career, but as I gain experience, it happens less and less. Sometimes I choose to climb in bad weather due to frustration or a limited schedule, and during these climbs, garments that are not only reasonably breathable but also waterproof are useful, though not essential.

How often are waterproof/breathable garments truly necessary? Users of these items lament the cost and weight of jackets whose performance features they rarely need. They wear shells with compromised breathability and then bitch when their insulation gets wet from their own sweat. They refuse to exercise the common sense that counsels retreat in bad weather because they have been seduced by the lofty performance promises of gear and materials manufacturers. But granted, there will be situations where they cannot retreat, where shells must provide protection and where survival is questionable. It is essential to prepare for these situations.

Don't buy into the propaganda that insists only a top-of-the-line, high-performance, expensive, super-durable product will do all of the time. It isn't true. And as far as paying extra for heavily reinforced garments to prevent wearing them out, I answer honestly that I have never worn a jacket out. I confess that I usually end up replacing it when something new comes along or the color or brand goes out of fashion. Professional, hard-core users wear things out—people such as guides, ski patrolmen, mountaineering rangers. I can't and don't.

Avoiding pitfalls along the path of shell fabric choices takes research. Training climbs allow for critical evaluation prior to hanging it out on big-league routes. Fine-tune your clothing system so retreat or suffering will be remembered as "fun."

The aforementioned clothing system does not take into account arctic climbs, or high-altitude giants where conditions often feel colder due to lack of oxygen. A one-piece down suit may be inevitable. However, I have been to 27,500 feet on Everest without oxygen, climbed to 25,000 several times in different ranges, climbed in Russia in winter with the temperature at minus 43 degrees Celsius, climbed Polar Circus in the Canadian Rockies at minus 42, and trudged up and down Denali a couple of times without wearing a down suit. Instead, I climbed in one-piece suits insulated with synthetic fibers, which worked quite well when the shell fabrics were breathable enough. Big, puffy suits are for slow plodding. If you must have one, go for the lightest possible model and blow off the Gore-Tex shell as it will compromise breathability. Keep it light, light, light. Move, move, move.

Scott Backes greets the day on the top of the North Buttress of Mount Hunter, Alaska, after having climbed through the night. Temeperatures were cold enough that, even with our belay jackets layered over our other clothes, movement barely kept us warm enough. *Photo: © Mark Twight*

Hands

Gloves or mittens? There is no right answer. Most climbers wear gloves because they want the added dexterity for handling carabiners, ice screws, and nuts and for tying knots. However, they are not warm enough for when it's genuinely cold. Mittens, while warm, prevent you from tying knots, clipping in, or activating a camming device, although motivated climbers can place ice screws while wearing mittens. Mittens dry out faster overnight than gloves because the big space for the hand allows greater air exchange than the cramped tunnels of a glove's fingers. Again, different gear is appropriate to different situations.

Gloves

Wear gloves if possible. Our brains are accustomed to independently functioning fingers. Choose the thinnest possible gloves for a given situation to improve the speed and security of handling gear or performing any function. Ideally, gloves should be both waterproof and breathable. Removable liners permit drying within a belay jacket or sleeping bag.

The palms of the gloves should be sticky, waterproof, and durable. Gloves from most manufacturers fulfill two of the three requirements. Leather is durable and sticky but not really waterproof, even when treated with a waterproofing agent (although most of these, like Biwell or Sno-Seal, make the palms even stickier). Kevlar can be made waterproof, and it is very durable—but it's quite slippery, a big problem when the braking hand can't control a rappel. Rubber or synthetic rubber is generally waterproof and sticky, but wears quickly when subjected to frequent rappelling. Overall, leather and synthetic rubber are the wisest choices for palm material.

If conditions are too warm for standard climbing gloves, use a pair of leather or pigskin work gloves from the hardware store or the Nuevo Ranchero gloves made by Lowe Alpine. While an imperfect solution, these durable gloves don't cost too much and can be treated with Biwell or Sno-Seal over and over again. These gloves need some breaking in to become flexible but will eventually custom-fit to your hand. Some come with fleece liners; if not, buy them oversize to accommodate after-market liners. Wearing cheap leather gloves for rappels preserves the $125 climbing gloves for real climbing.

Two insulation types reflect different design philosophies. Some glove models feature removable fleece liners, while others rely on fixed liners made from Primaloft and Thinsulate. Fleece liners, being removable, will dry faster. Wet liners can be replaced with spare dry ones during the day. However, Primaloft and Thinsulate are less bulky, so the palms of gloves insulated with these are more supple and take less energy to compress when gripping an ice tool or ski pole. But these insulations can be slippery against themselves, so a truly positive grip on an ice tool becomes difficult to maintain. Although these insulations are quite a bit warmer for the weight, fleece is probably the better choice for use in gloves.

Mittens

When it's too cold for gloves, turn to mittens. There are two categories: lightweight technical mittens for hard climbing, and thick, warm, all-night mittens.

Technical mittens should feature removable, relatively thin fleece or pile liners for insulation. In addition, cut pieces of quarter-inch or three-eighths-inch closed-cell foam (EVA) into the shape of the back side of each mitten and slide them between the liner and the shell. The Velcro holding the liner will secure the foam. Not only will the foam protect knuckles from bashing against the ice, but it will provide significant insulation as well. Technical mittens should fit snugly, but not so tight as to hinder sliding the hand in and out easily.

Wear all-night mittens to prevent frostbite at an unintended bivouac or to keep you warm as you hike the last few thousand feet to the summit of Denali. Also use them when climbing through the night or when moving over easy terrain where your hands plunge in the snow a lot and need only hold onto the ice ax in the cane (*piolet canne*) position. When it comes time to place gear or set up a belay, remove the mittens and manipulate the gear barehanded. It's faster, and you drop less gear. Even when it's very cold, handling gear barehanded doesn't pose much risk of frostbite as long as the hands come out of a warm mitten and return quickly. For extra reassurance in really cold weather or to help dry out a wet mitten liner, put a Shake-n-Warm heat-generating packet in each mitt, which will provide 6 to 8 hours of heat.

Buy all-night mittens huge, and don't expect to do any technical climbing in them. They should be insulated with Primaloft or Polarguard 3D so they are warm, yet light and compressible. The palms needn't be super-durable because, ideally, they will never encounter rappels or mixed climbing.

I never used to wear gloves in the mountains. I carried one pair of technical mittens with spare liners and a pair of all-night mitts (though I did pack a light pair of fleece gloves). New developments in gloves, and the fact that I don't climb at high altitude anymore (due to impossibly high Himalayan peak fees which conspire against lightweight, alpine-style climbing and small teams) caused me to reconsider. I climb in gloves more often these days. But mittens remain the ultimate in warm, idiot-proof alpine climbing handwear.

Feet

Our feet are farther from our hearts than our hands are, and subject to slower blood circulation, yet we still protect them with, at most, an inch and a half of insulation and expect them to be warm. On the other hand, thick warm boots are clunky. There is no right answer, only compromise.

After years of supremacy, plastic boots now face competition from a new breed of leather boots. Some leather boots weigh less than plastic models, but many don't. The new leather boots climb better in some situations than their plastic counterparts. Extremely talented climbers used some models successfully for rapid ascents to 8,000 meters and above. But for the most part, reserve leather single-boots to day routes or for roadside waterfall and mixed climbing. On a multiday route, without careful attention to moisture management, the boots will get wet and won't dry overnight. Wouldn't you rather spend that energy thinking about other problems? Plastic boots may not allow climbing at the highest technical level, but they are idiot-proof, waterproof, and don't demand any attention once on your feet.

To counteract the clunky nature of plastic boots, buy them at least a full size smaller. Keep the outer plastic shell boot, but get rid of the standard liner boot that's inside the shell. Instead buy the thinner closed-cell-foam Alveolite liners that are available or have custom liners "flowed" by a craftsman to custom-fit your feet. Using shorter, more compact boot shells makes them lighter and stiffer on your feet, allowing more precise placement. Replacing the foot beds with custom orthotic insoles makes the boots climb and ski better, too.

Cover bare feet with a thin liner sock so friction occurs between the liner sock and your thicker, insulating sock, instead of between the thick sock and your foot. With Alveolite liners (closed-cell foam), both sets of socks will get soaking wet from sweat. Prevent this by wearing a vapor-barrier liner sock between the thin liner sock and the thick insulating sock. This way only the thin liner sock gets wet, and these dry quickly in your sleeping bag. (The vapor-barrier sock also keeps sweat away from the standard liner boots that come with the plastic boots, if you've chosen to use them. These standard liner boots, insulated with Thinsulate or similar synthetics, are difficult to dry overnight once they get wet.)

I prefer to wear Alveolite liners instead of the standard liner boots in all alpine situations. They are lighter, I can wear smaller plastic shells, and I cannot ruin the performance characteristics of the Alveolite liners except through long use and subsequent compression of the foam. Then I simply replace them.

At the end of the day, remove the vapor-barrier socks and liner socks to dry them inside a jacket or sleeping bag. Dry your feet. U.S. Army studies show that trench foot attacks the feet after just 14 hours in a humid environment. Be vigilant. Don't leave the vapor-barrier socks on for long periods. After removing the wet vapor-barrier socks and liner socks, put on a dry pair of liner socks and put the thick insulating pair over that to keep your feet warm at the bivy.

For particular big-wall or free rock and ice routes, some folks wear rock shoes inside the plastic boot shells instead of the normal warm liners. Don't. You can't walk in the boots, and they possess all the warmth and comfort of a rock shoe, according to a veteran/victim of the practice, Scott Backes.

These routes may suit the new, light leather boots. Or perhaps one climber can wear rock shoes while the other wears boots, with each climber leading the pitches appropriate to the footwear. Eric Perlman and I used this system during a one-day ascent of the Walker Spur on the Grandes Jorasses in 1985. As it turned out, he ended up leading all the cool pitches in his rock shoes while I took the sharp end in my plastic boots only when it was chossy or there was just enough verglas to make it miserable. But his light leather approach boots soaked through on the snowy descent. I can assure you that although we may have gone quickly, both of us got burned in the end.

You may need to use supergaiters or overboots to augment the warmth of either leather or plastic boots. Supergaiters leave boot soles exposed so you are not obliged to wear crampons all the time. You can hike and rock climb in them, too. However, they don't add much warmth in relation to the extra weight. Here's why. Modern supergaiters rely on a wide rubber rand to hold the gaiter on the boot. This rand offers absolutely no insulation, so the only extra warmth is from insulation covering the upper three-quarters of the boot. The bottom of the boots and the crampons conduct most of the cold, so supergaiters are at best a compromise.

To add warmth in very cold temperatures, wear overboots. They greatly extend the range of single leather boots without much additional weight. Overboots suit waterfall climbs in the Canadian Rockies during February, for example. Since overboots also cover the sole of the boot, you always wear crampons over them. Thus they work best on snow and ice routes where the rock is easy enough to use crampons. Most overboots employ neoprene or Cordura fabric and either closed- or open-cell foam insulation. La Sportiva makes an overboot insulated with Thinsulate for their single leather boots.

Make sure your overboot fits as tightly as possibly. It should be a struggle to get it on the boot. Be sure no extra bulk hangs out to catch your crampon points or ski edges. If the neoprene or Cordura tears, patch the hole with Tool Dip (available at hardware stores), or better yet, coat the inside arch area of the overboots with Tool Dip before a tear develops.

Packs

Packs belong in the clothing chapter because pack choice affects clothing system decisions.

Light is right for packs, too. Few packs suitable for a multiday route weigh less than 4 pounds. Sometimes it makes sense to sacrifice durability to reduce weight. Wild Things offered a parachute-cloth version of the Andinista pack. It had a volume of 5,000 cubic inches but weighed a mere 18 ounces—barely more than a pound. Light and fragile can work, and some routes will be worth the sacrifice.

With a minimal amount of gear, fuel, and food, virtually any pack will suffice. Naoe Sakashita carried a tiny summit pack on an alpine-style ascent of the west face of Ama Dablam. Joe Josephson and Steve House each carried minuscule day packs on their new route up King Peak near Mount Logan in the Yukon, accounting for 7,100 vertical feet of elevation gain and loss in 35 hours. I used a day pack to solo the Czech Route on the north face of Pic Communism, 10,000 vertical feet up and down in 36 hours. House dispensed with a pack altogether during his solo first ascent of Beauty is a Rare Thing on the 7,000-foot west face of the West Buttress of Denali. So did Erhard Loretan, Pierre-Alain Steiner, and Jean Troillet on the first winter ascent of the east face of Dhaulagiri. Each of the three men carried several candy bars and a pint of water and split an MSR stove between them in the pockets of their one-piece suits for melting snow. They soloed every foot of the route and were up and off it in a day and a half.

Traveling light is the way to go on routes where you can move quickly. On the other hand, technical lines require more belaying of difficult pitches, a bigger rack, and a slower pace, forcing you to carry more weight and move slower. Some routes require hauling the pack. If so, go for a reasonably durable pack.

The approach pack

Approach packs and climbing packs serve two different purposes. Some routes require a long approach that involves hauling supplies for the approach, climb, and hike out. This demands a big-ass pack. These are available in abundance from all the major manufacturers. Look for relative comfort, although how comfortable can carrying 80 pounds or more really be? Look for one without absurd features or criminally useless weight.

For the approach take a Big Dumb Pack, a huge bag with an adjustable harness, shoulder straps, and a frame to transfer the weight to your skeleton. Skip zippered compartments, access panels, or climbing features like gear loops, special ski attachments, shovel pocket, haul loops, and so on. An approach pack should carry up to 7,000 cubic inches. Carry supplies in the behemoth until it's time to go climbing with the light climbing pack that you've carried along. The only pack I find usable for both the approach and climbing is the Wild Things Andinista. Fully loaded, it holds over 5,000 cubic inches, yet closing two ingenious zippers reduces its size to 1,800 inches.

The climbing pack

Your climbing pack should be light, simple, and functional. It doesn't need a frame because frameless packs work fine for loads up to 35 pounds—and carrying more than 35 pounds usually guarantees failure. John Bouchard and Mark Richey carried a total of 100 pounds of gear between them on their alpine-style ascent of the East Pillar of Shivling, in India—including their boots, clothing, food, fuel, and hardware. With the clothing on and the ropes and rack in use, their climbing packs weighed 30 pounds or less. They climbed the route in six days—which was seven days quicker than the first and only previous ascent. This is an example worth imitating.

The climbing pack should hold roughly 3,200 cubic inches (50 liters) or less, and extend to hold 4,000 cubic inches if necessary. It needs a free-floating, totally removable top pocket that can be opened no matter how the pack hangs against the wall. This requires each of the four attachment straps to open and close with side-release buckles.

The pack needs a waist belt without excessive width or padding. The more cumbersome the waist belt, the more it gets in the way of racking gear on your harness and rope handling. When buckled, a wide belt, although comfortable, will fight you every time you raise your leg when moving uphill. Don't wear the waist belt while climbing, because with the pack worn on shoulders alone, you'll be able to reach behind your neck, grab the haul loop, and pull the pack up to your neck and upper back from rockfall. The pack should feature sturdy haul loops in front and back. The rear loop should be big enough to get a mittened hand through.

Don't buy a climbing pack weighing more than 3.8 pounds, and try to find a lighter one. Modify a heavy model by removing any frame or extraneous features. With an allotment of 30 pounds total, 10 extra ounces of useless features supplant 1,000 calories or a day's worth of stove fuel or an extra pair of dry gloves. Spend the weight wisely. Opt for a heavier pack when a route demands a lot of hauling. Such routes are rare in the mountains. Usually you can plan on carrying the pack for 90 percent of the elevation gained and hauling it for one or two pitches. Even light packs will withstand this type of hauling.

The pack as insulation

The pack acts a vapor barrier, so clothing next to your back will become wet because of it. Manufacturers of garments for climbing generally don't take this factor into account, but you can deal with it in a number of ways. Pearl Izumi manufactures a vest for cycling composed of microfiber in the front and mesh in the back. Worn under a pack, the fabric in front blocks the wind while the pack shields your back. The mesh allows some moisture build-up caused by the impermeable pack to dissipate. Removing the pack allows for rapid drying and cooling (though too rapid at times). Several packs incorporate designs aimed at ventilating the spinal area. These work well if you're wearing little or no clothing under the pack. Bulky high-altitude or winter clothing blocks ventilation and thwarts these designs.

For our attempt on Mount Bradley during the Alaskan winter of 1998, Jonathan Carpenter came up with a way to combat the problem. He cut the sleeves off an old windshirt to create a vest and then sprayed the back of it with three coats of Scotchguard waterproofing. Worn underneath his insulating jacket, this homemade vest prevented sweat from soaking the insulation when the pack blocked moisture transport. Sweat couldn't get to the insulation, so it stayed dry.

Joel Attaway at Forty Below also experimented with this approach by making vests composed of fleece in the front and neoprene across the back. I wore one for twenty days on Denali and it worked perfectly, with the neoprene serving as a vapor barrier under my insulation to keep sweat away from it. Radical approaches to insulation such as this are not marketable yet, but they are the future, and ultimately perhaps intelligence will win over marketing.

The Future

Some time in the future, we will be able to regulate the insulating value of clothes to respond to heat and moisture output and to external conditions. Who knows how this will be done or who will do it? Probably the U.S. National Aeronautics and Space Administration (NASA). The outdoor industry lacks both the financing and ambition required to make great technological leaps. There is greater return on investment for finding the next cool color.

Face it, all the specialty clothing out there works well enough, and there is little difference between the competing brands in function and features. Most of the advertising, and virtually all supposedly independent gear reviews of clothing, are full of hype. No one has demonstrated clear-cut differences in the function of different brands of fleece jacket, for example. With designers and manufacturers all doing essentially the same thing, it will be a while before someone builds a line based on the layering-over-the-top system I described at the start of this chapter.

Meanwhile, it's up to you to decide what works best in your own climbing. Every piece in your clothing and equipment system either complements or compromises the other pieces. They are interrelated and interdependent. Choose carefully and try to imagine all the different ways each component in the system affects the others.

DEPRIVATION ON MOUNT HUNTER

My first attempt to make my lightweight action suit/belay coat theory work was on Mount Hunter in the Alaska Range in May of 1994. Scott Backes and I sought maximal energy efficiency for this climb. We applied this concept to nutrition, energy and moisture loss, the stove/fuel equation, and all our gear. After stripping every component down to what we rationally considered the minimum, we subtracted more.

I knew that staying hydrated would be difficult. The dry air and huge oxygen exchange would suck us dry; we would sweat and lose even more water. It would take time and energy to replace it. I knew I was willing to carry only two liters in my pack at any one time, so we would need to stop and melt snow frequently to maintain our goal of drinking 7 liters every 24 hours. Even this is a marginal intake.

I decided to combat fluid loss through sweat by wearing as little clothing as possible while moving, to the point of being chilled at times. Cool muscles are more efficient than overheated muscles anyway.

We started up the route around midnight when the temperature hovered below zero degrees Fahrenheit. I wore lightweight polyester long underwear and stretch fleece tights under my Gore-Tex shell pants, opting for a bit of extra warmth on my legs since I wouldn't add or remove any layers once we crossed the bergschrund. Under the Gore-Tex shell jacket I wore while climbing were two of the thinnest layers of Capilene (polyester) available. Any time we stopped, I immediately layered my belay jacket over the top of the shell. I barely sweated on the entire route. My urine remained straw-colored for the whole 72 hours; dark urine would have been a sign of dehydration.

Scott and I forced ourselves to stop and brew up when needed, drinking up to 3 liters of Cytomax at a sitting in order to stay hydrated. We also used the carbohydrate gel GU in place of Power Bars because GU metabolizes more readily and requires less liquid to do so. Two mouthfuls of water will turn the 100 calories worth of gel into the 4 to 8 percent glucose solution that will accelerate gastric emptying, while it takes at least 16 ounces of water to metabolize a Power Bar. GU doesn't freeze either, even at minus 35 degrees Fahrenheit. Because of our bodies' greater efficiency with water, we could carry less fuel to melt snow—a scant 32 ounces, enough for two comfortable bivouacs and one rough night, living on the ragged edge.

The relative thinness of my action suit compelled me to wear my belay jacket when we climbed through the second night and temperatures dropped to minus 20. Even when ice froze in the cores of the ice screws and several carabiners froze shut, my belay jacket, all-night mittens, and Shake-n-Warms kept me from getting too cold. When the sun rose, we used its warmth and that of our light sleeping bags (mine was rated to 20 degrees Fahrenheit

and weighed just over 2 pounds) to allow us to comfortably relax for 3 hours, eat, hydrate, and nap before continuing.

We climbed up Deprivation, our new route on the North Buttress of Mount Hunter, and back down in 72 hours. By the time we reached base camp at 11 P.M., we'd been on the move for 43 hours straight. I know now that better hydration (12 liters per 24 hours) and intelligent nutritional supplementation would have allowed us to go much faster and with less risk due to improved mental alertness. But our 1994 ascent still halved the time of the previous fastest ascent of the North Buttress.

Scott Backes late on the first day during the first ascent of Deprivation on the North Buttress of Mount Hunter, Alaska. Our packs weighed 27 pounds each without rope or rack in them when we left the ground. *Photo © Mark Twight*

LIGHT AND FAST

Scott Backes, Mike Vanderbeek, and I were in the base camp on the southeast fork of the Kahiltna Glacier in Alaska in May of 1994 when the radio call came in about a climbing party hit by an avalanche. The climbers were still mobile, barely, and needed help. The fading light and lack of detailed knowledge of the area by the National Park Service prevented an immediate helicopter rescue.

Scott, Mike, and I were the only ones in camp with skis. We roped up and sprinted toward the site in the northwest basin near the west ridge of Mount Hunter. Scott and I carried the minimum amount of gear we could foresee needing to remain autonomous. We didn't want to rely on anyone else even if forced to spend the night out. We took a stove and 22 ounces of fuel, two foam pads, a sleeping bag to share between us, some GU, coffee and cocoa mix, and some energy bars. Our packs were light. In contrast, Mike went heavier, prepared for a protracted effort, and could not maintain the pace Scott and I set for ourselves.

Scott and I wanted to get to the injured climbers as quickly as possible, stabilize them, bundle them up, and drag them down to a site where the helicopter could get them in the morning. We applied a climber's rather than a rescuer's perspective to the rescue: light, fast, flexible.

Unfortunately, neither the victims nor the other rescuers appreciated our approach. After reaching their previous night's camp, the victims—two injured and three unscathed—were too tired to continue down, and the proximity of a well-supplied first aid kit persuaded them to stop for the night. When the rescuers on snowshoes arrived several hours later, they wanted to sleep. Scott and I huddled together under our one light bag, anger keeping us warm. Snowfall woke us, and everyone suddenly realized the northwest basin is an avalanche-threatened death trap after new snow. We began moving the injured climbers. Later in the day, both of them were flown to a hospital in Anchorage by light plane.

Mike seemed to understand the lightweight tactics Scott and I had used, understanding how much faster and more flexible they were. The following year, while Scott and I were working for the National Park Service at the 14,000-foot camp on Denali, Mike turned up after climbing the Cassin Ridge. He and his partner applied light, fast tactics to the route, carrying three days of food and fuel, a tent, and one sleeping bag between them. The risks and imperatives of this type of climbing became quite clear when a storm trapped the pair high on the mountain. After a difficult descent down the West Buttress, they used gear from the Park Service rescue cache at the 17,000-foot camp to survive the storm.

I don't think Mike understood at the time the "single-push consciousness" required to safely apply the light, fast climbing style to big routes. You have to go all the way up, or

else retreat at the first sign of any little thing going wrong. Light and fast as a style results in the ultimate autonomy and self-determination—but any time you decide to pare food, fuel, and gear down to a marginal level, you accept great risk and must therefore accept great responsibility. If your style is too light, or you drop a crucial piece of gear, or the weather turns bad, you must retreat. Or if you are too high on the mountain, then you have to fail upward as quickly as possible. You must keep moving at all costs. Movement is your only safe haven.

If you can't fulfill your commitment to autonomy, and instead rely on the actions or material of others in order to succeed or survive, you have to consider it failure. You have to fully realize the risk you impose on others when you require their help. And you have to understand they will believe you were foolish and showed poor judgment in the application of the marginal tactics you chose.

Mike learned a great deal from his ascent of the Cassin and would have gone on to do many more big routes in light and fast style had he not been killed while attempting to rescue another climber on the West Buttress of Denali in 1998. He is deeply missed.

The awesome north face of Mount Hunter, Alaska. *Photo: © Mark Twight*

A SIMPLE MISTAKE

In 1988 I traveled to Pakistan to attempt an alpine-style ascent of the Rupal Face of Nanga Parbat—the biggest wall in the world—with Barry Blanchard, Kevin Doyle, and Ward Robinson. We made several small ascents to acclimatize. I usually undertook mine alone, while the other three climbed as a team.

They set out to climb the north face of Shgiri, which the map indicated was 18,500 feet high, the face being 3,500 feet and easily climbable in a day. Well, maps being what they are in poorly studied parts of the world, the face turned out to be over 7,000 feet high. The team suffered through one bivouac on the face in fine style, sharing one foam pad and a stove between them, and then another bivouac after descending the south face into an unknown valley. Unfortunately, although they were safe, the valley into which they descended was 25 miles away from our base camp. So began the long march.

By the time they arrived back in base camp late on the third night, Ward's feet were destroyed. He had handmade the liners for his plastic boots out of closed-cell foam which was too sticky to allow relatively frictionless movement inside. The liners rubbed his feet raw, then rubbed some more, turning his arches into hamburger. He was out of commission for ten days. Meanwhile, the rest of us climbed up the Schell Route on Nanga Parbat to acclimatize and cache some food and fuel in case we should descend that way. We spent a night at 6,200 meters and another at 7,000.

After resting a few days, we took advantage of good weather and Ward's healed feet to attempt the Rupal Face. We didn't realize how essential acclimatizing on the Schell Route had been until Ward began showing signs of altitude illness on the fourth day. Day five saw us reach our high point of 7,850 meters with a team that needed to be stronger if we were to succeed. Ward's condition didn't allow him to share as much of the work needed for us to move fast enough. It was a blessing in disguise in some ways, though, because we got hammered by a storm that forced us to retreat. We were out of food and fuel, and there was no option but to descend all the way to base camp, which was fine by us when the storm lasted twelve days.

In his decision on footwear, Ward made a simple mistake on one day of a ten-week trip that affected the outcome of our combined efforts. It is ludicrous to lay blame. I have made mistakes like that and sometimes suffered from them and sometimes gotten away with them. I use this story simply to illustrate that one moment of inattention or poor judgment, even your choice of clothes or gear, can change the outcome of a long, well-planned expedition. Be careful you don't outsmart yourself.

Ward Robinson (aka The Suffer Machine) near the top of the Merkl Icefield of Nanga Parbat's Rupal Face in Pakistan. By the time we reached this point at about 24,500 feet he was really digging deep in order to keep up with us. *Photo: © Mark Twight*

gear

8

It's easy to become wrapped up in concerns over technical paraphernalia. Most climbers focus too much on trying to decide which gear is the best, most fashionable, newest, or lightest. A certain period of learning and experimentation is essential for an alpine climber new to the game. But once you know the basics, don't believe that more or better gear will make you a better climber. This chapter will cover the basics.

Harnesses

You'll need a harness to tie the rope into. Gone are the days of a bowline on a coil or a 2-inch swami belt. Modern routes are steep, falls not uncommon, and hanging belays frequent.

Two types of harness configuration are commonly used in the mountains: independent waist belt and leg loops; or a Whillans-type harness, in which the leg loops are formed by two straps that are attached to the back of the waist belt, pulled between the legs, and fastened to the front of the belt. Black Diamond's Bod Harness is an example of this design. Both configurations allow you to remain tied in while evacuating bladder or bowels, both are equally "comfortable" at hanging belays, both get the job done. However, buying separate waist belt and leg loops allows you to mix sizes to get the perfect fit.

First, an alpine harness must be easy to put on and take off. This means the leg loops must open fully so you can put the harness on while wearing crampons or skis. Adjustable leg loops also allow you to add and subtract leg insulation while remaining tied in to the waist belt. Secondly, the harness has to be comfortable to hang in—more comfortable than most cragging harnesses, because you'll hang in it with the extra weight of your gear and pack. Comfort is not a question of more padding—your clothes offer plenty of that—but of fit. Test as many brands and styles as feasible.

Make sure the waist belt has a full-strength tie-in loop in the back. At some point you may want to clip in to the belay anchor while facing out to belay the second or to allow him to jug on a rope fixed to your harness. This situation can occur when an adequate belay anchor is absent, but your stance can support the second's weight.

Gear loops are convenient and essential. Some are stitched to the top of the belt, some to the bottom—they both work. Make sure they don't interfere with placement of your ice-tool holster; cut off the ones that do.

Never use a gear loop as a hammer holster. They're usually large enough that the small head of a hammer can wiggle its way through and disappear. A holster should be big enough for two tools so you can carry both there when they aren't strapped to your pack. Pick a semiflexible holster that won't gouge holes in you when you bivouac.

Some continuously steep routes with numerous hanging belays necessitate a belay seat or butt bag. A butt bag with three points of suspension is more comfortable than a two-point bag. Made from superlight nylon, it should be relatively light and compact. A butt bag can prevent hours of squirming and shifting, numb legs, and sore ribs.

Belay Devices

The mountains are no place for a heavy Grigri belay device. Although a Grigri can be rigged for use as a solo self-belay device that will catch an upside-down fall, feed automatically, and work on an 8.5-millimeter rope, the manufacturer won't tell you how, and neither will I. If you need to know, you'll figure it out.

A belay device should be simple and light and work well for both belaying and rappelling. Pick a device that can remain attached to the locking biner while putting it on or taking it off the rope so you don't drop it. A Bachli Seilbremse fits the bill, but these are only available in Switzerland now. Yates makes a similarly shaped device called the Belay Slave. Neither has to be removed from the locking biner for rappels or belays. A figure-8 device can be made "drop proof" by keeping it clipped to the biner through the big hole. When you want to belay or rappel, pull the ropes through the big hole and wrap them around the stem of the device. It is now held by the ropes so you can unclip it without fear of dropping it and then reclip it through the little hole. Reverse the process to remove it.

Manufacturers and climbers all say that some belay/rappel devices put kinks in the rope more than others. To avoid kinking, try to keep the ropes separated during each rappel and pay attention to the ropes generally.

For three-member climbing teams, a single self-locking belay plate is indispensable for the team. (New Alp calls theirs the Plaquette; the one made by Kong is called the GiGi.) When hung from the "power point" of an equalized anchor, these devices allow you to belay each climber independently as they follow a pitch. Because it self-locks, you can take your hands off the rope to eat or shoot pictures. You can lock off each climber anywhere on the pitch. Belaying the leader with them is tough, however, so carry other belay devices for that.

Mark Twight belayed by Nancy Feagin on the north face of the Aiguille du Midi, Chamonix, France. Feagin belays through a self-locking New Alp Plaquette, which is suitable for belaying one or two climbers who are following a pitch. The self-locking feature allows the belayer to remove his hands from the ropes, to eat or take photos, without fear of dropping the second. *Photo: © James Martin*

The lightest of all belay devices is a knot. Using the Italian or Munter hitch to belay requires nothing but a locking carabiner. It works better for belaying the second, as it is difficult to pay out slack to the leader, especially when using Twin-rope or Double-rope technique. Of course if you're using the Munter hitch to belay, you'll have to use a carabiner brake system to rappel.

Ice Tools

More than any other gear in the alpine climber's arsenal, ice tools and crampons affect a climb's outcome. They are an extension of the climber's muscles and his mind, the filters through which he experiences the medium and the means by which he expresses his will and achieves his goals. Choose these tools carefully, not simply for their technical merit but for aesthetic value and appropriateness to both terrain and your specific style of climbing.

What features make a good technical ice tool for mountains and waterfalls? Consider the physics. There are two ways a tool can function during the swing. A heavy tool takes more starting power to initiate the swing; once moving, it's difficult to alter the tool's trajectory. The momentum creates great penetrating power. For some climbers a heavier tool may be considered efficient, because they feel it "swings itself."

On the other hand, a light tool, with all the weight concentrated in the head, takes less power to initiate the swing. Its path is more easily correctable mid-swing. Rather than the force of weight and mass controlling penetration, pure speed becomes the deciding factor.

A light tool is swung fast, a heavy tool moves more slowly. It is more energy-efficient to swing a light tool fast enough to penetrate than it is to swing the heavier tool. Light, fast tools are more precise, destroy the ice less, and even weak climbers can hold them above their heads and swing them all day long. If you encounter really dense, hard ice, you can always add a head weight to increase the tool's penetrating power. But weight cannot be removed from the head of a heavy tool without compromising the tool's function. There is a direct mathematical correlation between how much (or little) the tool's shaft (lever) must weigh in order for the head (weight and mass) to rotate around the hand (axis) efficiently. A smart guy could figure out the exact equation. You can tell when you feel it.

Look for a small-circumference shaft. It will be easier to grip, more efficient to swing, fit a wider variety of hands, and penetrate hard snow more easily in the *piolet canne* (cane) position. Be aware that molded rubber grips prevent good penetration into hard snow.

Your modular ice tool should accommodate two or three different types of picks:

- A thin waterfall-specific pick, reverse-curved, 2.7 to 3.5 millimeters thick at the tip. Examples include the Grivel Evolution and Black Diamond Stinger.
- A thicker reverse-curve pick for mixed climbing or high mountains where a pick mustn't break. This pick is 4 millimeters thick, taller top-to-bottom than the waterfall pick, and with a longer front tooth, so it can hit rock and be refiled frequently without needing replacement. Examples include the Grivel Goulotte, Simond Pirahna, and Black Diamond Stinger (less appropriate).
- A straight pick with a 29-degree angle like the old Hummingbirds, Stubai FKWs circa 1986-88, or the Black Diamond Alaska pick instead of the classically curved

pick. This angle allows a natural, ball-throw type of swing, which is more efficient on slopes up to 60 degrees than the wrist-flick a reverse curve demands. It also allows better penetration of hard, black ice because the trajectory is not modified mid-swing.

Make sure that any rubber used to improve the grip on the tool covers only an area one hand-width wide at the bottom of the shaft. Extra rubber along the length of the shaft adds enough weight to modify the tool's swing, and will hinder easily stashing the tool in a holster.

Ice-tool shafts

The shaft of the tool should be 50 to 55 centimeters long. Fifty-five centimeters will give you a little extra reach, but will be more awkward to swing in steep, tight places. Fifty centimeters appears to be the length on which most manufacturers base their head-to-shaft weight ratio, so these tools tend to swing the most naturally in any given brand.

Tools 45 centimeters long are available and formerly were quite popular. In fact, Simond Chacals were 43 centimeters, Terradactyls were much shorter, and climbers put up many hard routes with them. These days, 45-centimeter tools are used by climbers who can't swing the weight of a longer tool or who want a third tool or an ice tool that also serves as a piton hammer.

Shaft materials vary widely. Virtually all European-made tools feature extruded 7075 aluminum alloy, a tough and light material with reasonable vibration-damping characteristics. Black Diamond's carbon-fiber tools are the only option if you want a light, vibration-damping American-made tool. They are light, fast, and solid. Expect to see new high-performance designs from a variety of manufacturers.

All ice tools have to pass UIAA and European Community tests if they are to be sold in Europe, so ostensibly none of them are going to fail you in most situations. But beware of any tool you think might have too many holes in the shaft, no matter how sexy the grip looks or how ergonomic the design is touted to be. Ice-tool shafts are easy to break under certain conditions.

Both curved and straight shafts are available, with a couple of different types of curves adapted to specific terrain. Shafts that feature a curve near the head of the tool to reach over bulges and ice mushrooms are not useful for alpine climbing. This tool is usually heavier, you can't turn it around and chop or hammer efficiently.

Tools with a curve near the base of the shaft, originally conceived to modify the angle of the wrist on vertical terrain and mistakenly sold as a feature to save the climber's knuckles, have a place in the mountains. On truly steep ice the curved shaft feels more positive and energy-efficient, which is important when you're 40 hours up a climb and starting to tire. One of your two tools can be shaped like this; which one—hammer or adze—will depend on the type of route you choose.

If you'll hammer a lot of pins but climb little snow and don't plan on chopping a bivy ledge from hard ice, then put the hammer on the straight tool. It will be easier to control when hammering. But for most alpine routes that involve approximately equal amounts of ice, snow, and rock climbing, it will be most efficient to keep an adze on the straight tool. It will act as your primary snow-climbing tool, and an adze is more comfortable to grip than a hammer when jamming the shaft into snow. A comfortable grip is essential when repeatedly driving the tool deep into snow. A bruised hand on an uncomfortable grip discourages driving the shaft deeply enough to provide a secure self-belay. Hammering pitons with a curved shaft is a bit unwieldy, but you can always choke up on the shaft to where it's straight.

Don't get in the habit of climbing with the adze always in one hand and the hammer solely in the other. Analyze each pitch beforehand for as far as you can see and place the tools in the correct hands. Grip the hammer in the dominant hand if it looks like you'll be driving a lot of pins.

Ice-tool leashes

Ice tool leashes end up being a matter of personal preference, but some considerations apply. To choose rationally, you have to know a few things: How do you want the tool to hang when you let go of it to grab rock? How will the leash close around your wrist; how easily can you get in and out of your tools; how comfortable does the leash need to be; and so on.

When you let go of the tool and your leash is attached to the head, the tool will hang spike-down and be difficult to get back into your hand when you wish to continue on ice. Many tools whose leashes are attached to the shaft at the factory (Charlet Moser Quasars and Pulsars, Simond Najas, and Grivel Super Courmayeur and Rambo) have the leash fixed to the balance point, meaning the tool hangs almost horizontally when you drop it. This presents you with another intriguing problem when you want it back in your hand.

The Black Diamond Twist leash and the Grivel Alpine leash both attach to the head of the tool, but feature a loop of webbing that wraps around the shaft close to the wrist loop. Not only does this keep your hand pinned to the shaft on vertical and overhanging terrain, but when you drop the tool, it can hang either head-down but with the shaft close to your hand or head-up with the head only a wrist-loop-length away. This is a great system, and the twisting closure means infinite adjustment without buckles. Plus, when you get scared, you can take an extra wrap in the leash; psychologically it's like chalking up. Buckles and Velcro may feel positive in the store, but when Velcro ices over, it won't close, and when webbing freezes, buckles don't slide as easily. Getting your hand in and out of such a leash becomes problematic.

The new fashion for hard mixed climbing is to use a leash that remains cuffed securely to your wrist, but detaches from the tool via a ball and socket (Charlet), a mini-biner and cable (Grivel), or a spring-loaded clip over a stud (Simond). When a prominent technical adviser was testing the prototypes of the Charlet system, he was overheard telling friends that he'd "dropped tools all over the Alps." The systems have been improved since then. But a climber dropped a Grivel Machine in the 1998 X-Games and a climber in the Canadian Rockies lost control of his tool and it dropped 400 feet. Is this supposed convenience worth the risk of losing your means of climbing both up and down? Not at all.

Leashes presumably need to be comfortable, and many are offered with padded, 2-inch-wide cuffs. These are OK for roadside antics, but too heavy, bulky, and absorbent for the mountains. Besides, take a look at the crook in your wrist when hanging on a tool placed in vertical ice. Does a 2-inch-wide cuff really fit there? Never use anything wider than about an inch of unpadded webbing for the wrist loop. Pick a simple, light, and compact leash. Consider comfort, but don't make a lifestyle out of it. The leash should be made from polyester, which doesn't stretch (nylon stretches when wet), so that once the length is adjusted, it stays that way.

Rules of thumb for ice tools

Determining how many tools to carry on a route isn't as puzzling as it may appear. If going up alone, carry three or four full-size, fully functional tools. Keep a spare easily accessible in a holster. Benoit Grison was caught out while soloing the Boivin-Vallencent route on the Aiguille Sans Nom above Chamonix. He snapped a pick on 80-degree ice only to realize that his third tool was strapped firmly to his pack. He found the next few minutes quite invigorating.

No matter how convenient it may be to change picks on the ground, you won't be doing it while hanging from the other tool on a route, so carrying spare picks instead of spare tools isn't an option if you're soloing. When climbing as a team of two, you can get away with one spare pick between you if both use the same tools. Consider taking no spares at all, since you have four tools between you—and if you've got jumars, the leader is the only one who needs functional tools. Don't bother carrying spare hammers or adzes because they rarely break, and they're heavy. Bring a wrench to tighten loose picks and a little file to keep pick and crampon points sharp. Do not save weight by leaving the file behind. Sacrifice 4 ounces of food instead. Sharp points mean efficient, secure climbing.

Crampons

Without crampons you can't move in the mountains, not safely or quickly anyway. Just ask Jack Tackle. He dropped a crampon 4,000 feet up the north face of Mount Kennedy in the Yukon. He hopped up another 2,000 feet and descended 6,000 without it, probably taking at least twice as long as he might have otherwise. Most parties would have retreated, but Jack's head is very hard.

It's easy to become mired in assessing the many styles of crampons available these days. The evolution of specific types of climbing dictates equipment targeted for each subdiscipline. Crampons like the Grivel Rambo or Simond Pit Bull, whose vertically oriented rails make them ultra-rigid to perform well on vertical ice, are dangerous when walking on snow because they ball up with snow worse than any other crampons. Models that feature aluminum plates under the foot end up skating and rolling on ice mushrooms or rock flakes. Their anodizing works well to prevent snow from sticking to the aluminum until it is scratched, and then they ball up badly as well.

Look for crampons that perform well on snow, ice, and rock; that are light but will absolutely not break; and that provide a secure, user-friendly binding system that doesn't

compress the boots and cut off circulation. The steel must be hard enough that mixed climbing doesn't blunt them immediately, but soft enough not to be brittle. Brittle steel will break, and it doesn't offer as much friction on rock. The front points should be oriented horizontally to offer maximum shear resistance in hard snow. The vertical front points of Grivel Rambos, Lowe Footfangs, Charlet Grade 8s, and others shear easily. Monopoints work well on steep ice and mixed routes, but are not versatile enough for use in the alpine environment.

Climbers of the 1980s recommended rigid crampons for technical ice climbing because no energy dissipated through a flexing crampon, and they didn't vibrate much on impact. In those days everyone was kicking their points into the ice. But now, climbers have learned to be more delicate, "placing" their feet on ice features, using them much like footholds on rock. Because of this, flexible crampons are more prevalent today.

Rigid crampons have a place in the mountains. You won't want to climb multiple pitches of 50- to 60-degree smooth, hard Alaskan ice without them. A flexible crampon locked on to a rigid-sole boot won't provide the performance of a rigid crampon on the same boot. But rigid crampons ball up with snow more and tend to be heavier than flexible models. Unfortunately, no single crampon will work optimally on every route. The terrain and

Scott Backes in Doug Geeting's bunkhouse in Talkeetna, Alaska, before flying in to Mount Hunter. He is surrounded by 400 pounds of the lightest climbing gear known to man. Photo: © Mark Twight

your style of climbing determine which model fits your climbing best.

On cold routes you may wear supergaiters over your boots (see "Feet," in Chapter 7). These usually won't interfere with crampon bindings, although you'll have to be careful not to let the rubber rands cover the welt of your boot. If you find the rands slipping up or down, glue them in place with Coll-Tex glue (made for climbing skins). It will hold them, but is easy to remove when the time comes.

Overboots can compromise the security of "speed bindings" by covering the welts of your boots. If you're up high, oxygen deprived, and tired, you may not notice until it's too late. The Brooks Rangers overboots by Outdoor Research and the Purple Haze overboots by Forty Below are designed for use with speed bindings, which have wire bales in the front and a flip lever in the rear. (For more on overboots, see "Feet," in Chapter 7.)

Other overboots require that you use strap-on bindings, or at least a binding like the Grivel New-Matic, which features a harness made of Zytel (the same plastic that alpine ski bindings are made from) combined with two steel posts in the front and a flip lever in the rear. These bindings are quick to secure and remove and won't cut off circulation like pure strap bindings. Of course, if you wear plastic boots, compression isn't an issue.

Speed bindings for crampons are so common these days that no one thinks twice about their security or durability. But at least one accident has occurred in the past ten years. A front bale separated from the crampon frame and sent Joe Simpson and Mal Duff 1,500 feet before they managed to stop. Make sure the bales fit the radius of your boot's welt closely, and check them now and again to make sure they aren't cracked. Bales are made of extremely durable spring steel, and they rarely break. But they can come out of the crampon frame, especially if they are adjustable and not permanently fixed in one set of holes. Check how much lateral force you put on them when using French technique on 50-degree ice. If there's any movement and it freaks you out, switch to a Grivel New-Matic binding or a Charlet Moser Rapid Fix with straps.

Shovels

If you need a shovel, nothing works as well as the real thing. Try digging a snow cave with your ice ax. It can be done, and it will provide hours of harmless entertainment, but it's hardly energy efficient. A shovel can also help you dig your partner out of an avalanche or shape a tent platform or give you something to set your stove on so it won't melt into the snow. In certain snow conditions, a shovel will even work better than ice tools—but you should dread the very thought of encountering conditions like these. (Also see the discussion on shovels in Chapter 13, Bivouacs.)

Helmets

Rock and ice fall is so common in the mountains that only a fool climbs without a helmet. This is one instance in which a piece of gear has finally been made too light. Several companies offer brain buckets based on bike helmet designs. These are lined with foam that deforms upon impact to absorb shock. Unfortunately, the helmet is useless once it has sustained an impact great enough to deform it. You simply toss it away and buy a new one. That won't be possible in the mountains, and where one rock falls, many usually follow. Just because you fell once on a route and whacked your head doesn't mean you won't knock it on something hard again.

These frighteningly light helmets have been known to break in duffel bags on the plane ride to the mountains. Avoid them, no matter how sleek they appear. They've been designed to be comfortable and unobtrusive to the user so that more climbers will wear helmets. They belong on roadside day routes. They have no place in the mountains where only the real thing will do. Look for a hard plastic or carbon fiber shell with a web harness inside. Statistics show that these work, and work well. Some helmets like the Petzl Ecrin Roc have size adjustment systems you can activate while wearing the helmet. This is especially useful for alpine climbing, where you may add and subtract hats or balaclavas several times during the day.

Goggles

Often overlooked, goggles are an irreplaceable accessory. With them, you can look straight up when you're ice climbing without fear of falling debris, and they're absolutely essential for climbing through spindrift or a howling snowstorm. A yellow lens improves contrast on days of flat light and won't be so dark that you have to switch to a clear lens when climbing by headlamp. Choose flexible lenses and frames so they don't break in your pack.

Headlamps

A headlamp, with spare bulbs and batteries, is a critical piece of equipment for a 24-hour route or late descent. You can't do without it. If caught by darkness with no light, you will bivouac, simple as that. If the weight worries you, you can try to get away with one headlamp for two people, but you'll only do it once. (See Chapter 13, Bivouacs, for a discussion of headlamp models and energy sources.)

Skis

On snow between base camp and the start of the climbing, skis and snowshoes can make travel more efficient. Ski poles can also be very helpful even if you're traveling on foot.

One or more collapsible ski poles give you more stability when hauling big loads during the approach. They also help by involving the muscles of the upper body. Using one or two poles on a route permits a more upright, energy-efficient stance on low angle terrain. Hunching over 50-centimeter ice tools on a 45-degree slope compresses the diaphragm and compromises oxygen exchange. Using only ski poles, or a combination of one pole and one ice ax, Scott Backes, Alex Lowe, Colin Grissom, and I climbed from the 14,000-foot camp to the top of Denali via the Upper West Rib and descended via the West Buttress in 10 hours round-trip. The moderate angle of the terrain did not merit a short tool, or even two tools. They may look cool, but they decrease speed on moderately angled slopes.

A pair of short skis will make travel on snow less tiring and much faster than on foot. Learn to ski in climbing boots while carrying a pack. Steve House and I skied from the 14,000-foot camp on Denali's West Buttress to the 7,200-foot camp on the southeast fork of the Kahiltna Glacier in just over 3 hours. The same 11 miles in the evil snow conditions we encountered would have taken 12 to 16 hours on foot. With cable car access during winter in the Alps, it's possible to ski downhill to the base of routes like the north face of Les Droites or the Super Couloir. In other cases, carrying short skis (130 to 140 centimeters) on your pack up a route allows you to ski down from the summit, terrain and talent permitting. Skis let you cover far more ground in a given amount of time, facilitating "day climbs" of routes with approaches or descents that might require two days to complete in summer conditions.

Find the lightest ski and binding combination possible. Don't fret over safety release features, because skis this short cause less torque in a twisting fall. There's no need to go fast and out of control, anyway. In the United States, Silveretta 300s are the lightest available mountaineering bindings—ones that leave the heel free or clamped down, as you choose. Skialp still markets the Ultralight Mountaineering binding in Europe. It provides no release features and offers limited size adjustments once mounted, but it weighs 40 percent less than the Silveretta 300. A good, wide pair of climbing skins is essential for efficient uphill travel.

Snowshoes don't equal the efficiency of skis by any stretch of the imagination, but for those lacking skiing skills, snowshoes beat boot soles. On extremely technical climbs where packs require hauling and the descent doesn't follow the route of approach, tiny snowshoes are an option for anyone. No larger than the business end of a tennis racket, light and compact snowshoes fit in a pack and offer about four times the flotation of boots alone. Andy Parkin and I used these to quickly approach and descend from the north face of the Aiguille des Pelerins.

Navigation Gear

For determining your position and for routefinding, the best bet is still the combination of a pertinent topographic map along with a compass and altimeter. Global Positioning System (GPS) units are increasingly being used in addition to the classic navigational tools.

Topographic maps

Many countries have been surveyed quite accurately, and the maps are available from hiking and climbing shops, the local tourist office, or the government. Third-world countries are problematic. Some countries, like Bolivia and Nepal, have been mapped by surveyors from other nations. In such cases, maps are available from either the mapped or the mapping country.

Compasses

Compasses all work the same; some are more durable than others. Some feature convenient adjustable declination. It's worth your while to study books about orienteering or map-and-compass travel before counting on being able to find your way off a mountain in a whiteout. The confidence earned from study and practice will keep you from freaking when the shit hits, and it may allow you to risk a few extra hours of climbing to get to the top in the face of an approaching storm since you know you can get off the mountain guided by instruments only.

Altimeters

Altimeters are more affordable than they once were. Digital wristwatch altimeters have served climbers quite well since the early '90s. Some wrist altimeters are notoriously inaccurate, and most of them measure up to only 14,000 feet or to 20,000 feet. The most accurate altimeter of any kind—both for climbing and for forecasting the weather when it's used as a barometer—is the Swiss-made Thommen, which unfortunately is also the heaviest. You may not be able to afford the weight on a route, but it's worth having one in base camp in a remote range, where it can serve as a barometer, since an altimeter functions by measuring barometric pressure.

Global Positioning System units

GPS units become lighter every year. The beauty of the GPS is that it works through cloud cover. Whiteout? If you've diligently marked your waypoints in clear weather, you can follow a return path no matter how dark or how poor the visibility. You can locate your tent or food cache. And the GPS will confirm or deny the accuracy of your altimeter because it depends on satellite triangulation to determine altitude, rather than barometric pressure.

Climbers' topos

Laying your eyes on a topo sketch drawn by a climber who has done the route will save a lot of uncertainty. It will help with rack and rope-system selection, give an idea how long the climb might take, show where the potential bivy sites are, and so on. For a new route, where topos don't exist, try to find a black-and-white photograph. The shadows and textures of a black-and-white photo often tell more about a face than a color picture can.

Traveling Light

The goal in selecting equipment is to carry as little as possible but no less, including climbing hardware, bivy gear, clothing, and transportation (skis, snowshoes, sleds). John Bouchard's dictum "Light is right" is gospel for the products of his company, Wild Things, and applies for all alpine gear. Go light and smart, with just enough gear for the task and no more.

It's easy to say you understand what Bouchard means, but try a simple test to confirm it.

First, fire off as many pull-ups as you can. Rest to full recovery. Let's assume you weigh 150 pounds and can do fifteen pull-ups.

Now do as many pull-ups as you can while wearing a 25-pound weight belt—equivalent to a sixth of your body weight. Rest to full recovery. Were you able to do just one-sixth fewer pull-ups (roughly twelve in this example)?

Now do as many pull-ups as possible while wearing a 50-pound weight belt, which is

one-third of your body weight. Did you do just one-third fewer pull-ups (a total of ten)?

Probably not. Your power does not decrease proportionately in relation to additional weight, especially when the extra pounds approach 35 to 40 percent of your body weight. Again, say you weigh 150 pounds and can pull your body weight up fifteen times. If you add an extra 50 percent—or 75 pounds—to the weight, you probably won't complete *three* pull-ups, much less seven. Performance declines disproportionately with additional weight.

Now you may have a better feel for Bouchard's gospel.

On a multiday, cold-weather technical climb, personal gear will weigh close to 50 pounds, more if the route requires a big rack. In figuring the weight you're carrying, count all the gear, including the boots and clothes you wear. Happily you won't have to pull your body weight plus all the gear with just your arms. Legs take the brunt of the load. When it's too steep, haul the pack. To combat the effects of the load, train yourself to be stronger, and choose gear wisely. Take less, and lighten everything you elect to carry. You'll move faster and live longer.

To reduce the weight of any piece of equipment, simply determine how much it weighs, then find out if anything that will serve the same purpose is lighter.

The rack: The rack seems an obvious place to find weight savings, but most cams, wired nuts, pitons, and ice screws weigh the same from brand to brand. Simply carrying less and being slightly underprotected on some pitches may translate to more speed on moderate terrain, but the climb will slow on technical ground. Your comfort level will decline, and you'll spend a lot of time inventing placements. Belay stations often present few options, so you need a range of sizes at the end of a pitch. And a small rack won't supply many rappel anchors for an unplanned, urgent retreat. Don't carry a huge rack on every route, but a few extra pieces may prove more efficient in the end. Shave weight elsewhere.

To reduce weight from your rack, replace every 50- to 57-gram standard carabiner with a 45-gram wire gate carabiner. For the average alpine rack with thirty carabiners, a savings of 8 grams per carabiner equals a total weight loss of about half a pound. Limit the weight of your harness to 15 ounces; some models weigh as little as 11ounces. A standard figure-8 belay device weighs 130 grams, while a light model weighs only 85. Other belay devices weigh even less: a Black Diamond ATC or Blue Water Airbrake are lighter than 50 grams. Or how about adding zero grams to your pack: Tying a Munter hitch on a locking carabiner adds nothing.

Ropes: You can also save weight with your choice of ropes, depending on requirements of your route. Leading on a light Single rope naturally saves weight over a heavier Single rope or over the pair of light ropes used in Twin-rope or Double-rope techniques (discussed in Chapter 12, Going Up). If the route calls for rappels, stash an equal length of 6-millimeter static line in your pack. A 9.1-millimeter, 60-meter Single rope plus the extra rappel line weighs a total of only 10.4 pounds.

In comparison, two 8.6-millimeter ropes, as used in Double-rope technique, weigh a total of 12.8 pounds. Two 8-millimeter ropes, for use in Twin-rope technique, weigh 10.8 pounds (see chart below). You can see that the lightest Single-rope system including the rappel line shaves more than 2 pounds from the weight of the Double ropes. The savings compared with the Twin ropes is small, but the real advantage shows in the simplicity of rope management and the consequent increase in speed.

Rope Weight Comparison

Single Rope	9.1-mm (53g/m) + 6-mm (26g/m) x 60 m = 10.4 lbs
Single Rope	9.4–9.6-mm (57g/m) + 6-mm (26g/m) x 60 m = 11 lbs
Twin Rope	(2) 8.0-mm (40.5g/m) x 60 m – 10.8 lbs
Half Rope*	(2) 8.6-mm (48g/m) x 60 m = 12.8 lbs

*proper term for rope used in Double-rope technique

Ice tools: Choose the lightest ice tools available that can stand up to the abuse of alpine climbing. To be sure, the DMM Predator, at 31 ounces, and the Charlet Moser Quasar, at 30.5 ounces, are extremely durable tools, but they are neither light nor designed with alpinism in mind. On the other hand, a Simond Naja, extremely light (25 ounces) and designed for pure waterfall climbing, breaks too easily for hard-core alpine use. Instead pick a pair of Grivel Geronimos or Rambo 2s or Black Diamond carbon-fiber Black Prophets, which weigh just over 24 ounces each, and put the lightest leash you can find on them.

Crampons: Crampons suffer the same problem as ice tools: the best technical performers are usually the heaviest and least appropriate for alpinism. Look for a pair weighing no more than 32 ounces.

Boots: Replacing standard plastic boot liners with Alveolites or custom liners can save as much as a pound and a half on a pair of boots.

Clothing: Clothing need not be heavy or especially durable for alpine climbing. Rain or wet snow is not a factor at high altitude or in winter, so you may dispense with the Gore-Tex clothing that boasts "Raingear Without Compromise." Settle for an Activent or microfiber shell system, which is more breathable at less than half the weight (see Chapter 7, Clothing, for suggestions).

Packs: The pack itself may be lightened and simplified to shave off as much as 3 pounds.

Bivy sacks: Obviously a bivy sack will be lighter than a tent and will be better for some routes. But on a route with plenty of tent sites, the tent may result in a lighter load overall because you can carry a lighter sleeping bag. And if you cook inside the tent, stove fuel consumption is reduced.

You can cut weight from a bivy sack if you are reasonably confident you won't be hit with rain or wet snow. Go for a Gore Dryloft bivy sack; Outdoor Research makes a 13-ounce model. Compare that to even the lightest Gore-Tex model, weighing in at 18 ounces. Single-wall tents are about 30 percent lighter than those with a rain fly and are faster to set up.

WHY HELMETS ARE A GOOD IDEA

In November 1991, I was alone in the Khumbu area of Nepal after having acclimatized with Ed Pope on a new route up Peak 5886 (a subsidiary summit of Kongma Tse). I camped at the base of the north face of Kusum Kanguru (6,300 meters) for a few days and waited for things to feel right. Barry Blanchard had soloed the face in the spring and told me what a great route it was. I crossed the bergschrund about 7 A.M. and, once on the ice, I started running, planning to get up and down the 5,000-foot face in a day.

About a thousand feet up I heard a deep whining above the music in my headphones and instinctively sank a tool and made myself small. The rock hit me anyway, driving me to my knees with a loud crack. When I recovered my senses, I scurried to the shelter of a short rock wall and checked for injury. Nothing. My helmet had taken the stone.

I breathed for a few minutes and listened to the mountain and to my internal dialogue. It was a great day for climbing, and I felt strong and right, so I continued. I climbed to within 80 or 100 feet of the summit before funky vertical snow stopped me—it took the entire length of my ice tools and my arms to the shoulder without offering any sense of security. I downclimbed to good ice, looked back up, and wondered how Barry had gotten through it. Bigger balls, I guess. Besides, he had decided beforehand to go up and over the top while I had intended to downclimb and rap the route—a clear psychological difference.

I reached the bottom of the face after 9 hours on the climb. As I strapped my tools to the pack, I checked my helmet and discovered a 3-by-3-inch hole right through the shell. I was using a light helmet designed for hang gliding. The thin fiberglass shell and foam wasn't intended to stop falling stones, but rather to absorb the blunt impact of a pilot hitting the ground. But it served me a whole lot better than a hat. I hiked back to base camp thanking the man who gave it to me, while resolving to wear a "real" helmet in the future.

The 5,000-foot-high north face of Kusum Kanguru in Nepal. *Photo: © Mark Twight*

Mark Twight and Barry Blanchard below Mount Rundle in the Canadian Rockies after Barry snapped a free-hanging icicle, which fell and hit Mark. The helmet saved him. *Photo: © Mark Twight*

WHEN MAPS LIE

Barry Blanchard, Kevin Doyle, Ward Robinson, and I were in Pakistan to attempt the Rupal Face of Nanga Parbat. To acclimatize we planned to do a new route on the north face of Shgiri, a summit that the map indicated was 18,500 feet high. At our bivouac beneath it, the altimeters read 15,000 feet. When the alarm went off at 2:30 A.M., I rolled over and went back to sleep. I could smell an epic in the offing.

The trio persisted and left for the face by 4:30, carrying a minimum of gear: their tools, some food, water, one stove, and one foam pad. They planned to flash the 3,500-foot route in a day. By 7:30 that evening they were nowhere near the summit. As darkness fell I watched their headlamps grind to a halt.

At first light I saw them start climbing again, eager to get moving, no doubt, after a long, cold night. They crested the ridge at around 2:30 in the afternoon, so I hiked to the bottom of the proposed descent route and waited. They didn't show that night or the next morning, so I wandered down to our base camp below Nanga Parbat.

My partners finally strode into camp at 10 the following night, hungry and hammered. On the summit ridge, their altimeters read almost 22,500 feet—a map discrepancy of 4,000 feet. So much for believing the Pakistani Geologic Survey. The ridge that led to an easy descent looked casual from the bivy but turned out to be a double-corniced horror show that they skirted by dropping off the south face into another drainage and, after a second bivouac, hiking 25 miles back to base camp.

The 7,000-foot-high north face of Shgiri in Pakistan, climbed by Barry Blanchard, Kevin Doyle, and Ward Robinson in 1988. The round-trip took two days longer than planned due to an error on the map that indicated the face was only 3,000 feet tall. *Photo: © Mark Twight*

pROTeCTION

9

Even after years of experience, climbers find that determining what to carry on the hardware rack always sparks fretting and debate. The more you know about a route, the better decisions you'll make on just what to include.

If the route's been climbed before, look for a topo and gear list. Check guidebooks, alpine journals, magazine articles, and the Web. Areas with a huge concentration of routes may have an office that houses records. The Office de la Haute Montagne in Chamonix, France, keeps topos and info for virtually every new route done in the area in the past thirty years. The National Park Service ranger station in Talkeetna, Alaska, has topos and information for both the Alaska Range and Kitchatna Spires. In some locales look for the best info in climbing shops or a bar. Finding correct or current data for remote areas like parts of the former Soviet Union, the South American ranges, and the Himalayas is more problematic. But the truth is out there. Check out foreign-language sources, too. Most grades are universal, and a poor belay from tied-off knifeblades sucks in any language. Eventually, experience will give you a general sense of the rack required for a given grade in a given mountain range. Depend on research until experience takes over.

A new route demands imagination. You've seen the route in a photo or on a reconnaissance trip, so you know how much ice, rock, and steep terrain to expect. Rock type influences the size of the rack and which pieces to carry (see Chapter 12, Going Up). In general, limestone requires more gear than granite. Limestone is loose. When fractured, it leaves smooth, parallel-sided cracks where passive nuts don't work well; only cams and pitons will serve. Rough, solid granite takes any kind of gear and often fights you for it when you try to remove it.

Some manufacturers test their climbing gear extensively before releasing it to the public. Others use the public to test their theories. Don't trust anything without seeing specifications for it. Most manufacturers test their equipment according to norms established by the UIAA (Union Internationale des Associations D'Alpinisme), the group responsible for establishing strength and durability standards for climbing equipment. Some of the UIAA tests and norms apply to climbing in the real world, but sometimes they allow weak gear to enter the market. This is especially true with ice-tool shafts. The radical torque encountered on a hard mixed route will break some UIAA-approved shafts. On the other hand, even the best gear breaks from the stress of hard climbing, extreme cold temperatures, and real-world abuse. Get used to it.

Nuts

A horde of manufacturers make passive nuts with only infinitesimal differences in weight, function, and price. Some of these chocks feature straight sides, some curved. Curved nuts offer no greater holding power, but set better in slightly parallel cracks. The inside of the curve will wrap around small rugosities, too. Carry a set of at least five nuts (Wild Country or DMM Nos. 3-7, or equivalent) for moderate routes.

For placements too small for a No. 3, switch brands and shapes. Use brass nuts for soft rock (limestone) and steel/copper-blend nuts for hard rock (granite). The strength and confidence that steel nuts deliver when climbing hard rock make them well worth the premium price. In soft rock, more malleable brass is a better choice than steel. Because the steel won't deform under stress, it can shatter limestone in a hard fall. Brass, on the other hand, deforms in the rock instead of breaking out. Place a piton in any crack that's too small for a No. 3 steel nut. (Note that a No. 3 steel or brass nut is much smaller than a No. 3 DMM or Wild Country nut.) Don't pack steel or brass nuts smaller than No. 3.

For placements too large for a No. 7 Wild Country or DMM nut, turn to spring-loaded cams (discussed next). Each variable-size cam covers a wider range of sizes than a passive nut. Although heavier than nuts, they offer more options.

Rules of thumb for nuts

A well-placed nut holds as solidly as any anchor. To keep rope movement from flipping a nut out, always set it with a good tug and clip a long sling or quickdraw to it. The sling may add several feet to a fall, but most falls in the mountains are so long that those extra feet won't make a difference. At least you can take comfort while airborne, knowing that the rope's whipping won't snap the protection out.

When nuts won't set with a tug, tap them into place with the pick of an ice tool. This ruins nuts because the pick invariably hits the nut's cable a few times, cutting strands in the process, but when you need a good placement, it's worth the wear and tear. In larger sizes, some climbers sling nuts with 5.5-millimeter Kevlar or Spectra cord to save weight. Unfortunately this cord is more susceptible to damage from ice-tool picks than the heavier cable, so I prefer to avoid it. Tapping on nuts hollowed out to save weight is a chore because they don't present a striking surface. Stick with solid nuts.

Practice your nutcraft. Use them normally, but also place them sideways, try stacking them, learn to place them in opposition, and so on. A handful of nuts provides cheap and light anchors for rapping off a big face if need be. And on granite, extra nuts on the rack may obviate the need for additional cams.

Cams

Spring-loaded camming devices are quick and easy to place. With their multiple rotating cams, they cover a wide variety of crack sizes, and they work effectively in parallel-sided cracks. They weigh what they weigh, and they cost what they cost.

Virtually all of these devices work well. Mechanically speaking, no brand is any better than any other. Quality of materials and manufacture varies, however, so stay away from unknown, untested brands, even if less expensive. Usually you get what you pay for. In application, the relevant questions are those of weight and size range.

Double-axle cams (only the Black Diamond Camalots use this design) cover a greater range of sizes than single-axle cams, but they are heavier. Two camps developed here. One side prefers carrying the extra weight of the double-axle cams in order to gain more options when placing each piece. Thus placement is faster and more efficient. The other camp would rather carry a greater number of the lighter cams. Imagine a technical route where nine cams seem about right. Nine Friends or TCUs are lighter than nine Camalots. One group argues that twelve Friends weigh the same as nine Camalots but offer three additional placements. The other group counters that every time you grab a Camalot, it will probably fit the crack in question because each

Camalot covers a greater range—plus they can be used passively as nuts with the cams fully open because the double-axle design is so strong. Both sides have good points. One compromise: carry a set of each to make a total of nine, and enjoy a bit of weight savings.

To save even more weight, for the second set you could use passive camming chocks—Hexentrics or Tri Cams—instead of the heavy spring loaded cams. This approach will cost some time, however, since placing hexes or Tri Cams requires more thought and patience. The Tri Cams are quite heavy in the middle sizes but become acceptably light again at No. 5 and up.

Good choices abound among the smallest-size of spring-loaded cams. TCUs, for example, possess three cams each on a very strong cable stem. Aliens feature four cams on a flexible cable stem, but because the cam springs are inside each cam instead of on the axle beside them, they are roughly no wider than a comparable TCU, and four cams provide greater holding power.

Rules of thumb for spring-loaded cams

Add a quickdraw or runner to every placement so rope movement doesn't cause the cams to walk into the crack and become stuck permanently. The flexible cable on some camming devices also helps to minimize walking.

Avoid jamming one of these devices into a crack that's too small for it. Don't try to place a No. 2 cam into a No. 1-size crack, for instance, because without play in the individual cams, it may be impossible to remove once it's set.

Don't place solid-stem camming devices in horizontal cracks, where a moderate impact can break the stem.

Always orient the piece in line with the predicted load. Don't ask the cam to rotate under the force of a fall until it's in line to absorb the impact.

Avoid rapping off spring-loaded camming devices, except in dire circumstances, because the cam gives no feedback regarding the quality of its placement. I crave the reassuring "ping" of a well-placed piton or the visual confirmation that a nut cannot slip past a constriction in the crack.

Camalots or spring loaded camming devices to be generic. Photo: © Mark Twight

Be aware that spring-loaded camming devices do fail. They can rotate and tear out, break the rock, skid down parallel-sided cracks, or wiggle into a place where they eventually fall out and slide down the rope. Be vigilant.

Pitons

Take pitons on every route. They don't cost much, and in many situations only a pin will do. Knifeblades are a luxury; the skillful application of a hammer can force a Bugaboo into a knifeblade crack. Emphasize longer Bugaboos. They require tying off in shallow cracks, but they endow you with confidence if the crack swallows it to the eye.

Avoid carrying Lost Arrow-style pitons; they're too heavy for the mountains. Shallow angles and Z-shaped pitons cover almost every Lost Arrow size and are lighter. Z pitons hold better, too, although they damage the rock more than a Lost Arrow during removal. Nuts or cams cover cracks larger than a five-eighths angle piton. If a crack is icy and wider than five-eighths of an inch, remove the ice with a tool before placing the nut or cam. Throwing a three-quarters angle into the pack for a big limestone route is prudent, but when weight-shaving begins, it will be one of the first things to go.

To save weight on the pin rack, I often carry some titanium pitons. They're extremely light—but the soft metal precludes planting and removing them as often as steel, and multiple placements eventually wreck them. I won't carry knifeblade-thin titanium pins because I've folded too many, and titanium angle pitons flatten out too easily. But a couple titanium pins of No. 3 or No. 4 Lost Arrow thickness and shaped like a knifeblade or Bugaboo weigh virtually nothing and could be the difference between getting up, getting back down, or failing at both.

Rules of thumb for pitons

Search for a horizontal crack because it will provide the most solid placement. If you must make do with a vertical crack, look for a constriction and place the pin above it. An accumulation of moss or dirt often signifies a constriction in the crack.

Since pitons take more time to place and remove than nuts and cams, the lost time must be repaid in security. Hand-place the piton as deeply as you can and then start hammering. Listen for the ringing tone the piton makes as it goes in, rising in pitch each time it sinks deeper. If you hit the pin and it makes the same tone a second time, you are done. If the tone drops suddenly or thuds when you hit it, something broke inside the crack or the pin hit bottom. The placement is now officially untrustworthy. Remove it and start over with a larger pin, or try a different part of the crack.

To test a driven piton, tap the side of it or simply drop the hammer onto it. If it rings and does not move, consider it good. More hammering won't help. Pitons can be tested more reliably than nuts or cams, and they are less expensive than cams, so it makes sense to carry some for rappel anchors.

Perfect placements exist in a perfect world where all rock is excellent and the climber never gets scared. But for the most part you'll over-drive every piton. In limestone this can degrade the only available placement, so try to be gentle.

Bolts

Not in my book.

Almost any wall can be climbed by unfair means. With a drill, you can "climb" anything. Reinhold Messner called this "the murder of the impossible."

Ice Screws

Again, you get what you pay for. Cheaper used to be better back when all screws were impossible to place, but today the expensive screws work better than most cheaper ones. They certainly last longer. Witness the durability of the plating on Black Diamond screws versus their offshore-produced copies, for example.

Penurious climbers cite cost as justification for buying inadequate gear. I've seen people willing to trade their lives to save a buck. If you can't afford the good stuff, borrow it or wait. Don't scrimp. Your life and your partner's life may hang from a suspect 15-dollar screw instead of from a dependable 42-dollar name brand. If the screw fails a long way off the deck, you'll have ample time to snivel about the failings of your cost/benefit analysis before you ground out.

If lightweight gear is good, how light is too light? Something is too light when you wonder if it will fail. Titanium ice screws come to mind. Titanium is light but not miraculous. Steel holds up better than titanium when the screw teeth hit rock; steel hangers don't strip, and the tubes aren't brittle. Titanium alloys are fickle, and most titanium screws come from former Soviet or East Bloc countries. Who knows whether the metal was appropriated from the aircraft factory and not the teapot factory?

Choose steel screws with a comfortable, efficient hanger. Some hangers will tear up your gloves over the course of a season; some give you a mechanical advantage when placing them (such as the Black Diamond Express); others are plain weird. After stabbing the screw in, you give it a twist and let go to twist again. But watch out: The heavier the hanger, the more likely it is to lever the screw out accidentally. Black Diamond's Express hanger is heavier than a standard hanger but not quite as heavy as the hanger on the Grivel ice screw. The Grivel hanger feels more comfortable, does less damage to the palms of your gloves, and requires less fine-motor coordination to place a screw than the Express lever, an important consideration when your forearms are on fire. Fine-motor skills evaporate first when taxed by fatigue. On the other hand, the Black Diamond plating is more durable than Grivel's; the mirror sheen on the Italian screws won't last a whole season.

Teeth and the distance between threads define a screw's function. The screws from every manufacturer employ teeth beveled on the inside to force ice into the core rather than displacing it outward. The distance between threads determines how deep the screw cuts with each revolution. Finer threads translate to less depth gained per revolution, but they require less energy per turn. A great distance between threads can make a screw almost impossible to turn, especially if the screw is aluminum, which generates more friction than steel. Large tube circumference adds surface area and increases friction. A fatter tube offers more shear resistance, but the difficulty in placing the screw probably outweighs this advantage.

Placing an ice screw

Allan Bradley's partners watched his twenty-four sketching crampon points 35 feet off the belay in the exit cracks of the Eigerwand and heard his shout, "I'd kill for a pizza." His partners figured he was a real hard case. In reality Allan actually whimpered, "I'd kill for a piece of pro," but the wind snatched away the last syllable. Someday you too will beg the universe for a good screw placement.

Now it's your turn. Imagine yourself on a vertical pillar, whining and imploring. You find a solid apron at the base of a little column and decide it's now or never. Climb up until the proposed placement site is at waist level and sink the tool of your weak hand so you trust it totally. Say goodbye to that hand, because it'll be cold and pumped and useless by the time you finish.

With your free hand and tool, clear away as much rotten ice as possible. The better the placement is prepared beforehand, the more efficient placing the screw will be. Sink your strong-side tool and free your hand from it. Don't use a detachable wrist leash—a stupid joke in the mountains because it will cause you to lose a tool someday. Loosen the leash enough to free your hand while leaving the mitten threaded through the leash. Bare hands manipulate gear almost twice as fast as mittened hands, and you're far less likely to drop something.

Unclip the screw from your rack with your strong hand, and stab it into the ice at your waist. Use your body weight to push on it, an impossibility if the screw is any higher. Don't even think about placing one over your head.

If you've done a good job of clearing ice away, you will not have to grab the tool and remove any recalcitrant bubbles or mushrooms after stabbing the screw into the ice, thereby saving time and energy. Once the screw is in halfway, grab it with your strong hand periodically to unweight your failing weak hand. When the eye of the screw touches ice, clip a shock-absorbing quickdraw to the screw and to the rope. Slip your hand back into your mitten on the strong-side tool, hang from the tool, then unstick the weak-side tool and drop that hand below your waist, where blood, warmth, and salvation can flow into it. When strength and feeling return, resume climbing.

Rules of thumb for ice screws

Rack about five or six screws for most routes. Save them for the pure ice pitches, and place pieces of rock protection at the edges of the ice when you can. Even though a screw in good ice will hold 2,500 pounds, rock gear is far more reliable.

The old school taught us to place a screw more than perpendicular to the surface of the ice, 10 degrees in favor of the opposite direction of a potential load. Thus climbers usually tilted the screw a bit uphill. Tests, however, have proved that a screw placed perpendicular to the surface of the ice holds best.

Manipulating gear with bare hands is faster and you're less likely to drop something. Leave the mitten twisted securely into the ice tool leash. Mark Twight in the first rock band during the first ascent of Deprivation on the North Buttress of Mount Hunter, Alaska. *Photo: © Scott Backes*

Equalize screws at the belay. Place one above the other rather than two side by side because it's a stronger configuration (see the description in Chapter 12, Going Up, on how to equalize anchors). Don't hesitate to equalize pieces in the middle of a pitch, especially on thin, unreliable ice or when facing a long runout with a high probability of falling off.

Clean the cores of the screws immediately upon removal so the ice has no chance to freeze solid inside and render the screw useless. To do this, tap the head (hanger end) of the screw against rock, ice, or an ice tool (tapping the threads against rock would damage them and degrade their cutting ability). If the screw is reluctant to give up the frozen core, blow into each end alternately or warm the whole thing inside your jacket. Spraying the insides with WD-40 or silicone before heading up a route will help, but the treatment won't last long.

Drive-in screws

Back when threaded screws were nearly impossible to place, drive-in Snargs became the rage. They went in quickly, could be hammered in place between thin columns with no excavation necessary, and generally seemed like a good idea. But consider this: Hammering in a screw uses the same muscles and movements as excavating rotten ice or planting the ice tools, so putting in a Snarg gives the leader no rest. And because the Snargs were hammered in for placement but twisted out for removal, the leader and follower faced different problems. The follower often squandered time clearing around the eye before being able to twist the Snarg out, cursing the leader all the while.

In the end, Snargs proved no faster for the team, and they created stress between partners—even though alpine doctrine states that leaders can do whatever they want to do for protection and that followers have no grounds for complaint because they have the security of a top rope. Today's twist-in screws work so well that placing and removing them is more efficient than any drive-in screw.

Thin ice

Arguments rage over how to protect thin ice. The old school advocated placing the screw as deeply as possible and then tying it off next to the ice with a sling, to reduce leverage, as with a rock piton. Bad idea. Tests by manufacturers and by the ENSA (French guides school) discovered that tie-off slings may flatten the screw tube under massive impact, causing stress risers to propagate along it. The stress travels to where the exterior threads of a screw reinforce the tube, and the screw usually snaps there. The same problem is true of a long screw placed to the eye but connected to the rope with a tie-off instead of clipped through the hanger. Screws have broken at the threads, deep inside the ice, due to stress risers. So *never* tie off a screw except in dire straits.

When equalizing two ice screws, place them one above the other rather than side by side. Reducing the angle between the two strands of the equalizing sling spreads the impact force evenly between each screw and reduces the force to each by as much as 50 percent. *Photo: © James Martin*

Carry stubby screws for thin ice. They are stronger than a tied-off screw or an ice hook such as the Black Diamond Spectre or Grivel Pit Stop. But if all you have is a screw that is longer than the ice is thick, go ahead and place it. If less than 2 inches of tube are visible between the ice surface and the hanger, clip into the hanger. If more than 2 inches are showing, tie it off. But be aware that under impact, if rotten surface ice fails, the screw will start to shear. Once the tube points slightly downward, the tie-off will slide to the hanger, where it may slip off or be sliced by the hanger.

Ice hooks

These drive-in, chop-out, steel hooks can work extremely well in the right situation. They provide the only option for thin cracks stuffed with ice, where an untoothed piton won't hold, and in normal cracks when the pin supply runs out. Some climbers use them for thin ice, but a stubby screw has greater holding power in thin, uniform ice. On pure ice, placing and chopping out hooks wastes energy, and they demand more experience to place properly than does a good screw.

Grivel named its hook the Pit Stop because the company viewed it as a quick, easy piece for protecting the leader in desperate situations. Suppose you're on a steep pillar, 20 feet out and dying for a screw placement. To protect yourself while removing rotten ice and placing the screw, tap a Pit Stop or Black Diamond Spectre into your last tool placement and clip in. It won't hold the whipper fall, but it adds the reassurance you need to take the time to place the screw securely. Once you're clipped to the screw, pull the hook and take it with you for the next screw placement.

While a hook feels more like a harpoon clipped to your harness, it can prove handy on certain alpine routes. Because of their weight, hooks suit roadside mixed routes and day climbs with short approaches where extra weight doesn't matter. I leave them behind when I go alpine climbing.

Carabiners

Again, light is right. Five or six years ago, when wire-gate biners were still a fantasy, climbers trying to manipulate the gear used large carabiners: Blue Water Vipers, Black Diamond Big Easys, and so on. These weighed up to 57 grams each (over 6 pounds for fifty biners). When manufacturers of climbing gear adapted wire gates from the sailing industry, full-strength carabiners dropped to around 45 grams each (5 pounds for fifty biners), and every rack became lighter.

The lower mass of a lighter gate prevents whiplash openings, too. Solid gates can open and close rapidly from rope oscillation during a fall, which means the moment of impact could hit with the carabiner gate open. Not so with wires. Wire gates don't freeze up readily, either, and their flat profile makes them easy to handle and open with cold hands. Some climbers rack ice screws on conventional large biners with a deep pocket below the nose to prevent one screw slipping out of the biner when unclipping another (using the system described in the section on racks, later in this chapter).

Rack wired nuts on carabiners with a keylock system between gate and nose. The nose is smooth. With no hook to snag cables, nuts slide on and off easily. Petzl, Kong, New Alp, and Simond make keylock carabiners.

Carry a couple of locking carabiners on the rack, one for each belay anchor. They allay any paranoid fears about equalizing pieces with a double-length sling or cordelette and clipping the whole system into a single biner. Back everything up, of course, but the margin of safety built into locking carabiners is huge.

Slings

Connecting the protection gear to the rope is relatively simple. Use either a short sling or a long sling between biners. Most alpine routes call for seven to ten shoulder-length slings (24 inches long when doubled, or 48 inches total) for protection placements and two double-length slings (48 inches long when doubled, or 96 inches total) to equalize each belay anchor or tie off big flakes. Cordelettes—big slings of Spectra cord, measuring 8 or 9 feet when doubled—can serve the same purpose as double-length slings. Carry the double-lengths in a pocket to keep them from getting tangled. Slings don't weigh much, so you can carry several extras for the same weight as an additional piece of protection, and they'll be far more useful. Sewn slings are lighter, stronger, and less bulky than tied slings.

The best strength-to-weight ratio for sling material (and also the most expensive) is found in Spectra, which is lighter and more abrasion resistant than nylon and is stronger over an edge. Since Spectra slings don't absorb much water, they don't freeze solid when they get wet. Spectra slings break-test at 5,000 to 6,000 pounds, making them considerably stronger than nylon slings, especially when the nylon is saturated. Spectra enjoys low friction properties, so mustn't be tied when failure would be fatal because the knot can slip. Spectra slings are all sewn. Compare the weight of ten shoulder-length, half-inch-wide Spectra slings (9 ounces) to ten slings made from nylon webbing nine-sixteenths of an inch wide (13.2 ounces). The 4-ounce savings could allow you to carry and eat an extra 400 calories.

Because Spectra slings are expensive and because, being sewn, they can't be untied for use as rappel slings, many people refuse to use them. But the strength and durability gains and the weight savings are worth the price (check Chapter 14, Going Down, for rappel sling alternatives). For those who insist on tied slings: Be vigilant about the knots you use to tie them and always check them on a route. This concern doesn't apply with sewn slings, giving you one less thing to worry about.

Short slings, or quickdraws, work in the mountains as well as on sport routes. For ice screws or bomber pitons with little chance of rope movement affecting them, a quickdraw with a carabiner at each end is a safer connection to the rope than two carabiners in series. Plus they are easy to handle.

Carry five or six quickdraws on the rack, with three of them featuring a shock-absorbing design. Yates, Wild Things, and others manufacture such load limiters. They restrict the impact force on any one piece of protection with a system of stitching that begins to rip at 500 pounds of force and continues to rip as long as more than 500 pounds is applied. When fully ripped, the sling will still hold 4,000 pounds. To our knowledge no one has fully ripped a load limiter in the mountains (or if they have, they didn't live to tell).

A load-limiting sling may keep the force of a fall low enough to prevent a suspect piece from pulling out. When used in the belay system, a fall directly onto the belay anchor probably won't rip it. A follower pushed off the belay by an avalanche probably wouldn't pull the belay either. That's why the magic number of load-limiters to carry is three: one for a suspect piece and one for each belay. The manyfold increase in security for the rope team fully justifies their extra weight.

In the old days, Bill Forrest made slings he called Rabbit Runners—single strands of sling material with full-strength loops sewn into each end. To wear the sling, you clipped the loops at each end to a single carabiner and carried the sling normally over one shoulder. In practice, Rabbit Runners performed as either a single-length sling when used in a closed configuration or as a double-length runner when opened. Today, climbers praise this design because to remove a runner from the body one simply unclips the biner and pulls, which gives access to a runner even when it's slung over an arm attached to an ice tool sunk in the ice. At my behest, Blue Water is now making these commercially available.

Remember to carry a chicken sling—a daisy chain of Spectra or nylon with one end girth-hitched through a tie-in loop on your harness and the other end clipped to a locking carabiner. The daisy chain configuration allows quick changing of the sling's length. Use the sling to clip into the belay anchor before shouting "Off belay," pulling up the slack in the ropes, or backing up the anchor. Use it to clip in to the rappel anchor before untying and threading the ropes through it. Use it to clip in to your ascenders, to the anchor at your bivouac, or to your tools when soloing. When not in use, simply wrap the chicken sling around your waist and clip it to itself. You'll never have to poach slings or quickdraws off the rack, which should be as anorexic as it can be.

Racks

The old days of a wide, cotton gear sling embroidered with flowered patterns are gratefully gone, along with Jerry. For the mountains, where weight is a consideration and slings tend to absorb water, there are few racking options. Comfort isn't an issue. Forget about a padded gear sling because clothes act as padding; an alpinist should be tough enough to endure a little discomfort. Choose a light, full-strength sling made from nine-sixteenths-inch nylon webbing or from Spectra, which can serve as a regular sling if needed. If the rack gets too big to be endured, go to a 1-inch-wide sling, but no more.

Most alpine racks are too heavy and bulky to rack on one sling or on a harness. A rack slung over one shoulder always works its way forward and hangs at the crotch. It drapes over the legs when you climb and blocks the view of your feet. Racking on the harness pulls the harness down and necessitates handing off pieces one at a time when changing leads, which increases the chance of dropping something.

The answer is to rack all the quickdraws and free carabiners on the gear loops of your harness and to leave the hardware racked on the sling. This way, less gear wraps around your legs, and biners or draws are handy for no-look grabs. Rack ice screws on a harness gear loop or to a gear loop added to the pack's shoulder strap on your dominant side. Clip the screws to a biner, with the gate out and the opening down for easy unclipping with one hand. Slide the hanger up onto the gate, push it open, and slide the screw down the gate until it's free. Trango, Simond, and Grivel make screw-racking clips and holsters, but these gizmos serve a single purpose and add too much weight to carry in the mountains.

A huge alpine rock route or a sick-fest like the Wall of Shadows on Mount Hunter require carrying a double set of everything and loads of quickdraws and biners. In gruesome places like this, wear a gear-racking vest made for big-wall climbing. The vest features a full-size gear sling for each side of you, plus several mini-slings for clipping the panic pieces you think you'll need next. It's easy to change over the whole rack without fumbling too many pieces. The weight of a gear vest and the necessity of taking off your pack to remove it renders the vest unsuitable for most alpine terrain. However, if you're on a route steep enough for hauling, where the leader will climb packless, comfort and convenience may counter these objections.

Ropes

In selecting a rope for the mountains, you've got a short list of critical things to consider. Most importantly, look for a rope and a rope system that's safe and appropriate for the climbing you plan to do. For instance, don't select a superlight Twin rope designed for pure ice routes for a climb littered with loose rock and chopper flakes. Check the guidelines in Chapter 12, Going Up, on rope systems and their appropriateness for different terrain and styles of ascent.

Next, consider the weight of the rope. Then look into the efficacy of the rope's dry treatment. Finally, determine the rope's durability. Durability (defined in terms of the sheath and the number of falls it will hold) is fourth in line in the list of things to consider, because you will want to retire the rope early, anyway. Perhaps it will hold a big fall and both you and it will retire, or it will be stepped on by a great number of crampons, or you'll jumar on it a lot, or rockfall may chop it, or rapping will grind enough grit into it to persuade you to toss it. It's not going to last long in any case. Color and price are at the bottom of the list of considerations for the rational climber, though they seem to be first in the minds of most climbers.

Rope weight

Different brands of rope may vary in weight for the same-size rope due to different core and sheath components, design goals, and so on. Example: the Blue Water Ice Floss is designed as a pure ice rope, so less durability was built into the sheath than for most rock ropes, but more fall-absorbing strands were added to the core. Spend the time it takes to find the lightest rope appropriate for the style of your targeted routes. Carrying 50 to 180 meters of rope means you will definitely feel the difference between 43 grams per meter and 48 grams per meter.

Dry treatment

Some ropes stay drier than others. Treatments differ, so performance varies wildly. The cheapest dry ropes are dipped into a waterproofing solution, which wears off quickly. The driest ropes are yarn-coated. Each individual strand is waterproofed and then woven together to make a rope. This technique ensures that the rope remains dry until you rap through the slush on it—a condition where nothing stays dry.

The durability and efficiency of the dry treatment on a rope relate directly to its weight—not the weight in the store but the weight under climbing conditions. A poor dry treatment on the loosely woven sheath of an 8.5-millimeter rope can result in the rope absorbing enough water to more than double its weight. Should such a rope freeze after soaking, it will be unmanageable and virtually impossible to climb on. A dry rope is stronger than a saturated rope, too. Check the facts of manufacture before you buy.

I asked a manufacturer to conduct drop tests on saturated ropes. The results were sobering. It turns out that a saturated dynamic rope can be expected to lose half of its ability to perform—that is, its ability to hold a fall. This sharp decline in performance may be due to increased friction between strands in the core, which impairs elongation and thus shock absorption. While not scientifically valid, these preliminary results should inspire alpine climbers to buy the ropes featuring the best dry treatment available.

Durability

To help in gauging durability of a rope's sheath, check to see if it is of double-pick or single-pick construction. Double-pick sheaths are less expensive and less complicated to manufacture. Virtually all rock climbing, cragging, and big-wall ropes employ double-pick construction. Dry treatment tends to wear off double-pick sheaths faster than single-pick sheaths, apparently because looser construction (resulting in the softer rope some people equate with better handling characteristics) allows individual picks to "float." The fibers rub against each other as well as against the rock. The dry treatment soon wears off all sides of the yarn, not just off the external fibers. The soft double-pick ropes drape on less-than-vertical terrain, causing rope drag and wear-and-tear on the sheath. Double-pick ropes often become furry after a little use.

Ropes of single-pick sheath construction offer a tighter exterior so the picks can't rub against each other. The dry treatment wears off only the exterior yarn. Single-pick sheaths are quite smooth. The ropes are stiff, so they don't drag so much on easier terrain. Despite the lack of quantifiable test data, experience indicates that single-pick sheaths last longer than double-pick sheaths.

You can also check to see if a rope uses four-ply or three-ply yarns. Four-ply yarns (more strands of nylon) increase a sheath's durability and abrasion resistance, while three-ply yarns make a rope lighter.

Sheath construction, however, has little to do with a rope's ability to absorb repeated falls—which is how the UIAA and the European Community test ropes. If the choice is between a rope rated at eleven falls and a rope rated at eight falls, simply choose the lighter rope. The difference in the rating is not as important, because durability is more a question of what a rope goes through in the mountains than how it performs in a lab test. Take care of it up there.

Try to avoid stepping on the rope with your crampons. But know that you will, and your

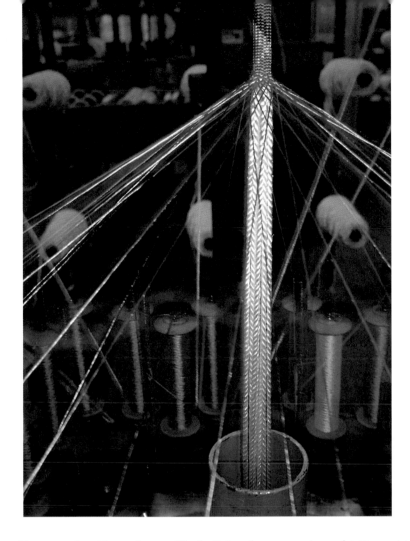

partner will, too, and neither of you will admit it unless you get caught. Try not to jug on a rope bent over an edge. But know that you will eventually do so. Protect the rope from rock and ice fall. Usually if a rope suffers enough damage to be suspect, that damage will be visible. Check the rope as you belay. Feel the rope as it passes through your hands, and search for the flat spot in the core that indicates some injury. Still, even the most rigorous monitoring will not reveal every insult the rope has suffered.

A good rule of thumb is to retire any ropes 9 millimeters and thinner after four hard routes in the mountains—not hard in terms of how difficult you found them, but hard conditions for the ropes. Abuse from mechanical ascenders, a big fall, rappels, hauling through wet and gritty debris, rock fall, ice fall, and errant crampons all add up. If you can't afford to replace your lifelines this frequently, buy a rope scrubber, wash the ropes, and check them with discipline. You'll live a lot longer.

Rope weaving machinery at the Blue Water factory in Carrollton, Georgia. An 8.5-millimeter Excellence Half Rope is being made. *Photo: © Mark Twight*

PART IV
TECHNIQUE

staying alive 10

Alpine climbing is unsafe and no rationalizations can change that. It's a game of survival. Dying, or even getting hurt, means you lost. Whatever safety exists in the mountains derives less from proper technique than from awareness. All action and technique spring from mindfulness.

Safety

Mountains are lovely on postcards, and beautiful when viewed from the valley, but some have teeth. Although climbers die in high places, we who remain go there to live life. What's up there? Virtue and competence, self-knowledge and suffering. Dougal Haston named it "overcoming and watching others overcoming." I cannot say it better.

As an alpinist who carries a long list of dead friends and partners, I approach the mountains differently than most. I go to them intending to survive, which I define as success. A new route or the summit is a bonus. Because my will to survive is strong, climbing as safely as possible without compromising my ethics colors every action. Although the confidence needed to tread the fine line between success and failure or life and death in the mountains demands some machismo, concern with safety doesn't indicate masculine shortcomings, as some French alpinists appear to believe. Constant vigilance keeps people alive. This vigilance may seem paranoid to some, but there is no shame in it.

Climbing difficult and dangerous routes safely requires balance. The climber compromises between preparing for every eventuality, melding tactics with equipment, and climbing practically naked, relying solely on technical skill, the ability to forecast weather and conditions, and the capacity to climb fast enough to be up and off the mountain before danger has an opportunity to coalesce. It is impossible to avoid exposure. But a combination of knowledge and awareness, speed and technique, maturity and utter abandon has allowed me to enter the dragon's lair, tug on its tail, and get away clean.

Interest and inquisitiveness, when combined with a concern for safety, prompt questions that contribute to survival. Awareness and curiosity lead to self-regulating actions too. Good alpinists become automatically hypersensitive to changes in the weather, they belay barehanded to check the condition of the rope, they periodically recheck their tie-in knot and their partner's, and so on. They question everything. And they understand that safety is a relative term.

Speed

Speed equals safety. One season in the Alps fixes this understanding deep in the bones. When I first climbed in Chamonix in 1984, I could not believe how fast alpinists completed

Pages 136–137: **Jeff Lowe on the South Pillar of Nuptse during our first attempt in April 1996. Despite eight attempts on this route it remains unclimbed as of 1999.** *Photo: © Mark Twight*

routes. Climbs that I considered two-day affairs routinely fell to weekend climbers in 12 hours, and the best teams raced up in as little as 3 hours. Neither could I believe the speed with which I accepted and adopted the practice.

It makes perfect sense: the faster climber spends less time exposed to danger. Approaching routes as "day climbs" simplifies virtually every aspect of planning and execution. The 24-hour nonstop blitz is simple compared with the 72-hour effort where sleeping, eating, rehydration, and all the attendant equipment burdens the climbers. A high level of physical fitness, combined with an open mind, allows climbers to move very fast, which proves much safer than taking a slow, measured approach. Speed results from fitness and knowledge, and the efficient application of both.

That first season in the Alps changed me forever. I had all of the technical skills, and I proved it by soloing routes like the Super Couloir on Mont Blanc du Tacul, the Swiss Route on Les Courtes, and the direct north face of the Grands Charmoz. However, these technical skills were virtually negated by the deliberateness I learned in the United States. American mountaineers carry huge loads and breathe once per step because that's how we are taught. When I arrived in Chamonix I was slow, and I didn't know how to think about climbing routes as big and hard as those I aspired to, but being a good mimic, I quickly learned.

I carried less, thus climbed faster, but it took many seasons to learn how to really move on moderate terrain, which is the most important tool for eating up huge amounts of altitude on big routes. I added security to soloing ice routes by testing each ice tool placement with my body weight before committing solely to it, before removing the other tool. I tested each granite edge and every hand jam the same way to determine its solidity. Over the years I learned other techniques to improve safety. I placed my hands and feet precisely, eliminating the possibility of knocking off loose rock or ice that might injure my partner or chop the ropes. More importantly, I learned the art of placing gear to protect myself. I can frig it in anywhere. I will spend whatever time it takes to judiciously protect a pitch. The confidence that any fall will be short allows me to climb closer to my limit, whether it means climbing harder or climbing faster.

Maturity

Age and experience synthesized into maturity for me. I began approaching danger less impetuously than when I was younger. My various mentors (who were always older and mostly wiser) taught that the mature climber refuses anything less than the total application of all his knowledge and skill. Physical and psychological laziness burned him in the past. The mature climber gives 100 percent of himself, 100 percent of the time. He never coasts content with the knowledge that he can turn up the volume when it appears necessary. This does not mean he applys 100 percent of his total power all of the time; it means he gives 100 percent of his attention, even to resting when it's time to rest.

Watching the scene around me when I lived in Chamonix and reading climbing publications from many countries convinced me that wisdom and maturity are more important than technical skill and ambition. History confirms that many of the greatest alpine climbing achievements were realized by climbers in their mid-thirties: Voytek Kurtyka and

Robert Schauer on Gasherbrum IV, Mugs Stump on Mounts Tyree and Gardener in Anarctica, as well as his fast solo of the Cassin Ridge on Denali, Stevie Haston soloing the Walker Spur on the Grandes Jorasses during winter in 17 hours (8 hours of climbing) when he was thirty-five.

To be sure, extremely young (and inexperienced) climbers have accomplished fine routes in good style, but it is the rare alpine climber who gets away with difficult and dangerous routes on a regular basis when young. Either the risk catches up with them and they get chopped, or they begin to recognize their mortality and moderate their behavior.

Swiss alpinist Erhard Loretan is a fine example of a climber who boldly succeeded on many hard routes when he was young and who matured into an even more accomplished climber. He climbed eight 8,000-meter peaks before he was thirty, including Everest's north face, which he soloed simultaneously with Jean Troillet in 43 hours round-trip. In his fourth decade he climbed new routes in single-push efforts on Cho Oyu (27 hours) and Shishapangma (19 hours), only fourteen days apart, as well as climbing Makalu, Kanchenjunga, and Lhotse in alpine style. On the other hand, Fred Vimal, a brilliant young climber active in Chamonix—with an enchainment of the Walker Spur (4 hours, 30 minutes) and Integral Peuterey Ridge (total time for both, round-trip Chamonix to Chamonix, 40 hours), solo of course—was killed soloing on the Grand Capucin. He was just twenty-six years old.

Wisdom and age create a certain composure and the ability to deal with the stress of difficult and dangerous routes for longer periods of time. This really amounts to tolerance, something missing in most young climbers. Walter Bonatti said, "Tolerance is a legacy from an earlier age," and I agree: We can't learn the virtue of tolerance from society. Alpinism, however, teaches it well.

The mature climber knows how to fear that which should be feared and runs away when appropriate. He easily accepts the presence of fear and the stress it implies. He may attain a state of egolessness in which he understands that chaos rules. Upon recognizing his powerlessness over the environment, the mature climber understands the value of spiritual development and the necessity of fostering a connection between himself and the mountain. When this connection occurs—when a climber first becomes what he or she is doing and eventually becomes the mountain as well—he understands the mountain and is constantly aware of danger resulting from his actions, as well as danger arising from changing conditions on the mountain itself. This intuition results from working toward the development of awareness. Finally, he exercises the self-discipline required to heed the messages awareness delivers.

When Andy Parkin and Francois Marsigny were caught by a storm twenty-three pitches up their new route on Cerro Torre, their combined experience (more than forty years between them) of hard alpine routes done in summer and in winter, with partners and alone, in the Alps and the Himalayas—and the psychological maturity that came with it—allowed

Avalanche off the south face of Peak Chapayev, Tien Shan mountains of Kazhakstan. *Photo: © Mark Twight*

them to survive. They began rappelling but couldn't return the way they had come because the objective danger had grown too great. Instead of descending east toward civilization and sanctuary, they were forced west onto the ice cap. They hoped to recross the range toward the east and regain their base camp, but they missed the crucial col in a whiteout.

So they kept hiking, and sometimes crawling, to the south, finally leaving the ice cap after surviving without food for six days. They ate berries and plants once they reached lower altitude. After nine days away from base camp, they stumbled onto an estancia, where they were treated like kings. They ate like gluttons, too, before returning to their camp below the mountain that Reinhold Messner described as "a shriek turned to stone." Both Andy and Francois returned to Patagonia several times, indicating that this particular experience did little to affect their taste for hard climbing, that it was merely another test, another tempering of their already steely composure.

Many individual characteristics can lead to greater safety in the mountains but none more than the cultivation of a high level of awareness. Awareness and experience lead to good judgment. Knowing this does little to help the inexperienced climber. However, there is one rule of thumb to apply to all situations requiring a judgment call. Rely on your own judgment, because only you have the intuition or intellect to determine which action is best for you. Expectations or peer pressure may influence your judgment. Your partner may think you lame for wanting to turn back. Let him think it. You know what is appropriate for you. Honor it.

Good judgment can't be bought or learned from books. People aren't born with it, and it isn't taught in school. Only self-awareness and vast knowledge of circumstances, the environment, and potentialities, when combined with personal experience, result in good judgment. Mentors can speed the process, supplying information and even experience through the artfully told story. Otherwise, the burned hand teaches best.

Good judgment is the result of experience, while an "experience" is the result of poor judgment.

Vigilance

Trouble visits those who relax their vigilance. Imagine approaching a route, a low-intensity situation. Some folks blindly follow another party's tracks. It's easy to fall into the trap of following tracks headed in the correct direction, but doing so presupposes that the track-makers are as smart as, or smarter than, you are. Why allow a stranger to make a judgment about routefinding when you would never allow this person to decide any other safety issue?

Philippe Mohr and I were approaching the Shroud on the Grandes Jorasses in late September 1989. Two Germans had awakened earlier and left the Leschaux Hut an hour before us. This was fine with us because it meant they would have to deal with the breakable crust. Their speed indicated to us that they knew what they were doing and where they were going, so we followed their tracks into the icefall below the Walker Spur. We hiked by headlamp in the predawn darkness, so it was a surprise to come to a crevasse the

Germans had leapt. It was a short hop so we followed suit. But the next jump set my bowels quivering. The leader had jumped down eight feet and across six to a two-foot-wide fin of ice surrounded by nothing but abyss, then jumped another five or so feet onto a 65- to 70-degree ice slope, climbed up it, and then belayed his partner.

Philippe and I were stunned. We'd never seen anything like it, and I certainly wasn't going to do it. We retraced our steps and found our own way, perhaps losing an hour or so in the process. After I finished directing my anger at the Germans instead of rightfully aiming it at myself, I grasped the lesson about blindly following others. We laughed our asses off, though, when we noted later that the Germans were climbing slowly and would have to bivouac on the Walker while we simul-sooled the Shroud and the Arête des Hirondelles in 7 hours. In fact, after descending the Italian side, we caught a bus through the tunnel and were back in Chamonix for a warm dinner with our women. A reward like that could easily prevent the lesson from being learned.

Exercise your own judgment at all times. Be vigilant rather than lazy. You will live longer.

Relying on equipment can lead to trouble just as easily as depending on other people's judgment. Man-made mechanical devices fail on their own and when misused. We implicitly trust gear: an untested fixed piton carelessly clipped on the lead, an ice-tool pick weakened from inappropriate use, or a tattered, oft-used rappel anchor. Test everything and trust nothing. If in doubt, back it up. As the saying goes, "If there is any doubt, then there is no doubt," meaning that if you are uncertain about whether an anchor is safe, behave as though you are certain it isn't. Be vigilant.

Self-rescue

In the event of trouble on a route, knowing self-rescue techniques will come in handy. More than technique, self-rescue is an attitude you carry into every situation. You either accept responsibility for your safety and for the resolution of any crisis, or you don't. Otherwise the burden falls on others. Choose routes that are not only within your limits, but also within your capacities for self-rescue in case the most heinous imaginable accident comes to pass.

In February 1989 I tried to traverse the Mont Blanc Massif alone, without mechanical assistance. I moved from north to south, climbing whatever mountains were in the way. After soloing three north faces (Aiguille du Chardonnet, Les Courtes, and the Aiguille du Midi), I was attempting to cross the Col de la Fourche when I tapped a huge block of snow/ice sitting on the lower lip of the bergschrund to test its solidity. It fell on me, breaking apart on the 40-degree slope. I tumbled a hundred feet with the debris. The fall knocked the wind out of me and it was a long time before I could breathe. My jaw was dislocated, and the ice tool had gone through my cheek. There was blood everywhere. I wedged two fingers behind my lower teeth and yanked my jaw forward and fainted from the pain.

When I came to, I was lying in the snow. I walked my fingers up the right side of my chest. When I got to the squishy section, I figured I'd broken some ribs. My walkie-talkie had broken in the fall. I put my head down and limped back across the Vallée Blanche. Several hours later I staggered up the arête to the cable car station. My yellow pullover

was saturated with blood, and the crowds of skiers parted before me like water. I didn't pay for the ride down. In the emergency room I waited for over an hour for treatment, but I didn't care because I knew things weren't going to get any worse. I even allowed myself a light pat on the back for having gotten out of the mountains more or less on my own.

Numerous alpinists have rescued themselves and their partners from dire situations. Chris Bonington helped Doug Scott crawl and cry and rappel his way down the Ogre in Pakistan after Doug broke both legs in a swinging fall. Joe Simpson dragged himself off Siula Grande with a broken leg. During an early attempt on the Isis Face of Denali, Ken Currens fell more than 200 feet, fracturing his femur. His partner, Jack Tackle, lowered him to an ice cave, downclimbed, and skied out to round up a rescue team. Back at the route, he climbed up to the cave and lowered Currens to the glacier and a waiting helicopter. Rescuing oneself takes imagination and ego and an immense reserve of will, but when these are insufficient or when the task is too great for the survivor, the cavalry must be called.

Competent rescue services exist in few mountain ranges. Throughout most of North America, the county sheriff, the National Park Service, or the four-wheel-drive and snow-mobile clubs handle mountain rescue. Usually these guys can't get close to technical terrain. Most national parks, with the exception of Yosemite, are inadequately staffed with technical climbers to respond to accidents on steep terrain. Despite the enthusiasm exhibited by National Park Service staff and volunteers in Denali National Park, rescues of injured climbers from genuinely technical terrain are virtually impossible with the available assets. You are on your own.

By contrast, in Europe, well-trained climbers and helicopter pilots perform rescues in the wildest terrain. Their equipment and wages are paid by the state or through a comprehensive insurance program readily available to climbers, hikers, skiers, and paraglider pilots. With certain radio frequencies monitored around the clock, the injured climber may enter the ER within hours or even minutes of a fall. On the other hand, relying on the competence of others encourages overreaching.

If you require rescue by professional or volunteer personnel, expect a huge invoice covering the costs of the operation. In some countries, rescue insurance covers 100 percent of the rescue for a paltry sum. In the United States, however, insurance companies don't like the odds. Rescue insurance, although available, offers fairly limited coverage. Some plans exclude snow and ice, others cover any terrain up to a certain altitude and charge an additional weekly fee for higher altitude. Another plan offers coverage with a cap on the total payout, which may leave you with a sizable bill.

Nonetheless, rescue insurance is worth having, and it may be wise to subscribe to several different policies depending on the type and location of the routes. (See additional information under "Rescue Insurance," at the end of Appendix 2, Suggested Reading.) Paying extra premiums for coverage at higher altitudes also may be worth it, but don't count on it. Most rescue services don't operate above certain altitudes, and unacclimatized nonprofessionals

Philippe Mohr high on the Arête des Hirondelles of the Grandes Jorasses after simul-soloing The Shroud, Chamonix, France. Photo: © Mark Twight

may be unable to help you whether you have insurance or not. The desire to help is often confused with the ability to do so. Self-rescue is the only sure way to get the job done.

First Aid

Learn how to respond to a leader fall that results in injury or unconsciousness. Traveling as a team of two across a glacier implies that the climber who falls into a crevasse must rescue himself. If the team goes light and fast, there is no way to carry enough equipment to place anchors for escaping the system and setting up a 3-to-1 hauling system to extract the fallen climber. Sign up for classes teaching self-rescue techniques and for advanced first-aid classes as well. Proper first aid may mean the difference between life and death to an injured climber. Other books cover this subject comprehensively, but there are a few concepts specific to extreme alpinism that ought to be addressed.

Because safety in the mountains depends on speed and mobility, weight limits rule. Climbers often trim the first-aid kit. Most light and fast climbers don't carry much more than a roll of cloth tape and some painkillers on a route, though base camp may be very well stocked. No first-aid kit is big enough to address a serious injury like a compound fracture of the femur on technical terrain. If the victim has broken his femur and punctured the femoral artery, he'll bleed out within minutes so you may as well say your good-byes and prepare for a body recovery.

Based on statistics, though, catastrophic accidents rarely happen to wise, talented climb-

Competent rescue services in the Alps require the extensive use of helicopters. Here, a team exits from an Air Glaciers Lama onto the miniscule summit of the Clocher du Portalet in Switzerland. *Photo: © Twight Collection*

ers who undertake technical routes in alpine style. This is not to say they are immune. Instead, they are lucky, and their experience and wisdom steer them away from situations with a big accident potential. Falls rarely occur, and then predominantly on overhanging terrain. If an injury happens, it will either be total and fatal or it will be relatively benign. A broken ankle is easy to handle on steep terrain since rappelling on one leg isn't so difficult. In 1985 John Stoddard fell and ripped out a piece of protection on the seventeenth pitch of the Rooster Comb's north buttress, in the Alaska Range. He broke his ankle. He rappelled where he could, and I lowered him where necessary. Once on the glacier he crawled back to base camp.

While an arm broken by rockfall may be more complicated than a broken ankle, it is certainly no cause to call in the choppers. The serious injuries in the mountains consist of blows to the head or heavy bleeding. Head injuries result from falling objects or falling climbers, and grave consequences may be avoided by wearing a good-quality helmet all the time. A concussion or a fractured skull on a route may result in death if conditions pin the party down and prevent retreat or if the victim is too damaged to participate in the rescue. Imagine trying to lower an unconscious victim twenty pitches. Heavily bleeding lacerations cause problems. Although continuous pressure may stop the bleeding initially, the movement and increase in blood pressure associated with the self-rescue may start the bleeding again. Judicious application of pressure bandages (perhaps made from spare socks or a balaclava) held in place by cloth or duct tape will go a long way.

The minimum first aid kit for a technical route attempted in a light/fast style will be an individual choice, one I hesitate to list as it may be taken as a recommendation. Base any first aid response on the same theory as your climbing response, which emphasizes speed and mobility. You cannot carry enough gear to deal with a serious injury and hope to continue upward. Any injury compromising the possibility of efficient and safe ascent dictates retreat. So follow your ABCs, then drug the victim enough to get through the pain but not so much that he cannot safely descend under his own power, if possible. Hustle down toward the larger first aid kit, warmer clothes, shelter, and evacuation.

Acclimatization

Rather than recipes for acclimatizing, I offer theory and practical examples. High altitude is the great leveler. It can slap down climbers who acclimatized easily on prior ascents. Because each individual adapts to altitude at different rates and to varying degrees of total acclimatization and since one's psychological state may influence physiological changes, no hard and fast rules apply.

High altitude imposes certain drugs on the first aid kit, especially if the team plans to move up and down quickly. Drugs can help when there's no opportunity to acclimatize above a certain altitude. Suppose you are well acclimatized to 6,000 meters but must climb to 8,000 meters and back without stopping. Certain drugs such as Diamox (brand name for acetazolamide) aid acclimatization by helping prevent high-altitude illness. Take this drug before sleeping because it boosts the respiration and circulation rate by approximately 30 percent, close to the same percentage of decline associated with sleep. Some climbers report good results using Diamox to help them acclimatize, but I prefer not to use it. It is a diuretic, which will create greater demand for stove fuel to supply water to replace fluids lost through all the peeing. The frequent need to urinate also interrupts sleep and limits vital rest. Other side-effects exist as well, although none worse than annoying.

Try to acclimatize to high altitude without using drugs, to avoid becoming physically or psychologically dependent. Then it won't matter when they run out. Be smart, spend the time it takes to acclimatize, and drink a lot of water. Certain herbs (see the section in Chapter 6, Nutrition, on the supplement Eleutherococcus senticosus) aid in acclimatization, but try to assist the process as naturally as possible, using good judgment regarding the speed of ascent and the amount of rest required.

When you do go for a high-altitude route, always carry dexamethasone. This steroid reduces cranial swelling and can give the climber with cerebral edema 24 to 36 hours of leeway for getting down to lower elevation. Dexamethasone may be injected into a muscle or taken orally. Injections take effect more quickly, but needles are tough to use sometimes. I carry both types when playing high-altitude roulette. Dexamethasone can mean the difference between flying home coach-class or arriving there by freight.

Each individual's physiology responds to acclimatization differently, and no amount of physical fitness or technical climbing ability can speed the process. On Everest in 1988, Barry Blanchard and I acclimatized at wildly different rates. My mutant genetic code gave me a green light to attempt the summit after a mere three weeks spent between 16,000 and 21,000 feet. Not wishing to hold me back, Barry agreed to go for it. Our second and third attempts were turned back at 24,500 feet and 26,500 feet by Barry's pulmonary edema and cerebral edema, respectively. However, after full recovery, six weeks into the trip, Barry was stronger than I was on our last try, during which we reached 27,500 feet. Clearly, Barry needed more time to acclimatize initially than I did. His subsequent trips to high altitude indicate that he needs a minimum of four weeks, and five is better if he wants to go high without oxygen. The difference between team members must be addressed. Were Barry and I to attempt a high-altitude route together again, I would travel to base camp two weeks after him to align our acclimatization trajectories.

While recovering between climbs in Lukla, Nepal, in 1991, I met a guided team returning from Mera Peak. Many of the clients had run marathons and completed triathlons, so they were above average in fitness by most standards. None of these climbers summited. Of the eleven members, two guys topped out; both smokers. One roofed houses and the other ran a store that handles occult supplies. They barely nodded in the general direction of training before the trip.

These low-key climbers were my heroes. One had long hair and was covered with tattoos. Neither postured nor went on about how great the route had been; it was just another experience among many, their minds open to all ideas. The businessmen-athletes were falling over themselves to forward excuses or were genuinely shocked at the turn of events. Physical fitness means something at altitude, but not everything. And an easygoing, open attitude works better than a regimented, goal-oriented, summit-at-all-costs, self-aggrandizing approach.

One of the greatest high-altitude climbing achievements in history is Erhard Loretan and Jean Troillet's astonishingly fast 43-hour round-trip ascent of Everest's north face by the Japanese and Hornbein Couloirs in August 1986. Carrying little more than a stove, shovel, and light sleeping bag, the pair climbed over 9,000 vertical feet without climbing rope, fixed rope, or supplementary oxygen. They began climbing at 11:00 P.M., climbed through the night, rested and hydrated during the day, then continued climbing the following evening as the temperature  dropped. At 2:30 P.M. they summited, stayed for over an hour, and glissaded down in 3 hours.

Many factors contributed to their success, but their method of acclimatization had the greatest effect. The team spent five weeks at the 18,500-foot advanced base camp, reading, hiking easily, but never stressing their metabolic systems. The high altitude stressed them enough. Prior to the attempt, they climbed to 22,000 feet twice but did not sleep there. The long period at 18,500 feet allowed them to acclimatize fully to that altitude without tiring themselves. The trips to 22,000 tested their readiness. This schedule agrees with recent research demonstrating that a person may acclimatize fully to as high as 18,000 or 19,000 feet. Above this altitude, human physiology declines. So if you wish to recover from one high-altitude attempt before trying another, descend to 18,000 feet, or better yet 14,000.

Loretan and Troillet began climbing in a rested state with their full reserves of physical and psychological energy topped off. Their confidently executed glissade descent shows how much they still had available after the climb. In the words of Stephen Venables, writing in *Himalaya Alpine Style,* "they took nothing and left nothing."

Their method of acclimatization contradicts the accepted style. Generally, the body can adjust to a 1,000-foot gain in altitude per day (more if there is little physical stress involved, less if those thousand feet are hard-fought). Many climbers, acclimatized to the height of their base camp, simply get on routes and limit their climbing to roughly 1,000 feet per day, guaranteeing a tedious, drawn-out effort that will expose them to danger and weather variables for long periods. Others rehearse the lower sections of their route to acclimatize, but if the route poses objective hazards, this exposes the team to them more often than necessary. I prefer to acclimatize elsewhere at as high an altitude as possible prior to attempting my chosen route. Once on the route, I expect my acclimatization to allow me to

Alex Lowe (aka The Lung with Legs) carrying an injured Spaniard at 19,300 feet on Denali, Alaska. A U.S. Army Chinook landed Alex, Scott Backes, and Mark Twight on the Football Field just below the summit to carry out the rescue. In doing so pilot Bill Barker set a high altitude record for that model of helicopter. *Photo: © Mark Twight*

go as fast as I want without worrying about holding back to adapt to increasing altitude on the route itself.

When I go north to Denali now, I spend a few days prior to the trip climbing between 11,000 and 14,000 feet in Colorado. My experience shows me that if I spend three days at 14,000 and then descend, I have roughly three days to return to that elevation without losing the acclimatization I developed. I then fly into Anchorage and get onto Denali as fast as possible.

Once on the glacier (7,200 feet), I'll climb to 11,000 feet on Denali the first day and 14,000 the next. After spending two nights and a day resting at 14,000, I proceed to 17,000 and return to 14,000 in a quick 6- to 7-hour trip. After another night or perhaps two at 14,000, I jet to the top (20,320 feet) and back in a one-day push. This schedule has worked for me three times. After visiting the summit and spending a total of five or six days above 14,000 feet, I feel confident attempting fast, single-push ascents via technical routes to the top.

Death . . . and Survival

Most mountain climbers and those who love them avoid thinking about and dealing with the consequences of alpinism. The constant threat of injury or death plays a huge role in why people climb the high mountains, in the way they climb, and why some of them eventually quit. Alpinism often means high risk and the loss of life. It is about your friends dying up in the clouds. Swept away by avalanches or cowering under a volley of stones. Perhaps freezing to death alone at the bottom of a deep, dark crevasse. Or just sitting down to take a rest and never getting up again—taking the longest fall, where the sky is rose and the mountains have never been as beautiful as they are today. The head injury, and life bleeding away unnoticed. It's about climbers dying doing what they love and spectators speculating, judging, and maybe having the last word. This is about people and the risks they take: the risks they are equal to, the ones they barely get away with, and the ones that kill them. This is about obsession, the addiction of going harder, higher, for longer. About the times you got away with it and survived when others did not. Death in the mountains can be as ugly as a falling stone surprising an innocent hiker on the trail. Or it can be as beautiful as seven men struggling through a storm day after day, giving everything they have to life and living it. But one by one they die. Slowly. From cold, from exhaustion, from having fought so hard. Until only two remain.

I say this is beautiful because the greatest human act is the act of survival.

The climbers' cemetery in Argentière, France. *Photo: © Mark Twight*

partNeRS

11

The partnership is sacred to alpine climbing. Success and survival depend on an intimate understanding of one another. The sum of two partners' energy, wisdom, and strength of will—when those partners are well adapted to each other after years of stress and adventure—is far greater than their individual power and spirit. It's equally true that two partners who needle each other, who are not aligned in their ambitions or talents, are collectively weaker than they would be on their own. Well-adapted partners see through the other's eyes. They imagine accomplishing a particular task and then execute it in roughly the same way. Trust in each other's ability and judgment is total. Ultimately they become each other.

A solid partnership is not only more efficient and productive, it is also much safer. Similar attitudes and levels of ability permit the responsibilities of leader and second to transfer back and forth easily and naturally. Communication becomes effortless. Because each climber commits equally to safety, they waste less energy worrying about anchors the other guy places, so less time is spent triple and quadruple checking each other's actions.

Communication between partners is essential for efficient movement and energy use, but this occurs only when each climber understands how the other thinks, and the two (or sometimes three) have agreed on basic operating procedure. With similar goals and ideals, you won't ever be surprised by your partner's admission fourteen pitches up that he's there to free the climb while you simply want to get up it as fast as possible by any means. He'll bivouac warmer knowing he successfully achieved his purpose, while each minute drags slowly for you. You failed in your own goal, and something akin to hate for your partner simmers as you blame him.

Finding a partner with similar talents and attitude, comparable goals in the mountains, and a similar level of commitment is not easy. The most productive partnerships develop over many years of climbing and experience. Walter Bonatti and Toni Gobbi, Reinhold Messner and Peter Habeler, Erhard Loretan and Jean Troillet, and Erhard Loretan and Norbert Joos forged history-changing partnerships.

However, dramatic exceptions occur to the general rule that good partnerships are a long time coming. Erhard Loretan and Voytek Kurtyka climbed a new route on Nameless Tower in the Karakoram Range, and they had never climbed together before. The climb forged a partnership between them, and they went on to make two more great Himalayan ascents together. But don't plan on hitting it off right away with any new partner, and don't attempt any genuinely difficult, ability-stretching routes together until you both sort out your prejudices regarding style, food, and gear. Even after many years of climbing together, the partnership will experience conflict in the mountains. It's the nature of the stress involved, where skin wears thin and souls are bared.

You chose your partner. He is someone you care about. Don't ruin a route by hating him for going slow or for slurping his soup. Good and bad vibes run up and down the rope.

Remember, he's not trying to piss you off. He's doing his best, and if he climbs slowly there's a reason. He will be there at the unforeseen bivy with you, sharing the suffering, no matter who caused it.

A few simple rules of thumb go a long way toward maintaining smooth flow and preventing conflict, chief among them being tolerance. Of course he slurps his soup, and his feet stink, or perhaps you fear his inattention to detail, but if you are a tolerant person who recognizes the triviality of these things compared to the immensity of the task at hand, they will disappear. After all, the climbing is the most important thing.

Talk about what you cannot abide. Don't hesitate to criticize any action that jeopardizes either life or success on the climb, and be prepared to accept all criticism with a thank you. The team is there to climb. Accept any advice or criticism that improves efficiency or prevents an accident as a gift.

The free exchange of ideas under the normal circumstances of everyday living promotes better communication in times of stress. Scott Backes and I developed a form of verbal shorthand based on song lyrics and lines from films. We use it to lighten things up when the tension is thick. However, as fatigue and fear work their dark magic on the human mind, those affected tend to become more introverted and communicate less.

Despite the comfort derived from our verbal shorthand, Scott and I had the worst fight I've ever had with anyone in the mountains as darkness fell 2,000 feet up a new route on the north face of the Aiguille Sans Nom above Chamonix. He'd just led a desperate and dangerous pitch, starting in the half-light of dusk and finishing by headlamp. We were low on food and anxious about whether the route would go and where we might find a ledge big enough to sleep on. He shouted "Off belay." I replied weakly so he didn't hear. When I reached his belay, he began shouting about how I'd better answer when he said something to me.

We exploded furiously at each other. I wanted to throw him off. I wanted to untie and continue alone. I wanted to crawl under a stone. Scott had just hung it out there. A couple of placements had moved under his weight, including the ice-tool adze hammered into a bottoming flare. A fall would have sent him onto a six-foot granite spike sticking out of the ice and killed him. But there we were, shouting schoolyard taunts helmet to helmet in the dying light. Gosh, won't it be great when we're in eighth grade next year?

Fatigue clouds the ability to make correct choices quickly and to recognize potential danger. Unless each partner stays vigilant and helps the other remain aware, the safety and productivity of the team declines drastically. The weakest link in any team is the weakest climber, whether physically or psychologically.

Conversation can allay fear, prop up weakness, and motivate a flagging will. Near the summit of Mount Hunter, Scott bonked hard, and his will to speed faded into memory. I cajoled him, tugged on the rope, and laughed when he begged to rest. Thus our team maintained its pace and upward momentum. Three hours later, when I went down the same black hole of motivation-crushing exhaustion, Scott was there, propping me up, taunting me when I deserved it, leading the way. And on we charged, inexorably.

Confrontation will occur in the mountains, often as a result of differing perceptions of

an event experienced by two climbers. This separation of experience springs from each climber's predisposition to a particular response to a stimulus. Rockfall may freak out one climber, for example, while the other may suffer from a phobia about climbing at night and therefore feel pressured toward the end of the day.

Barry Blanchard, one of the most experienced climbers in the world, grew up dodging missiles in the Canadian Rockies, which are not known for being particularly solid. When we climbed together in the Alps, the whine of falling stones did little to faze him, while I cowered at the mere thought, considering retreat. On the other hand, I learned to climb through the night in the Alps and never bivouacked. When we reached the summit of Les Droites after climbing our new route, Richard Cranium Memorial, on the northwest face, it was dark and Barry began clearing a flat spot to bivouac. The descents in the Rockies are

Jonny Blitz and Steve House on The Gift That Keeps on Giving on Mount Bradley's south face, Alaska. Trust between partners is total, the connection surprisingly strong. *Photo: © Mark Twight*

often too complicated to undertake by night. I loathed the idea of sleeping out, especially when I knew the Couvercle Hut was a mere 3,500 feet below us, and I had done the descent once before in the daylight. Down we went. On both these occasions there was no conflict because we each fed off the other's experience and level of comfort.

Circumstances will cast each climber in the role of leader or follower, not just on the rope but politically as well. The role of each climber can change according to the situation, based on fatigue, ability on given terrain, and so on. Learn to recognize who's who and act with the appropriate amount of responsibility. The perceived leader at any given moment is responsible for the security and upward progress of the team as well as bearing the primary burden of routefinding and tactical decisions. While democracy is attractive, it is unwieldy and slow in times of crisis. Better that one climber should just take over, make the decisions, and take the responsibility than to let the team pause for discussion, votes, and confrontation.

One climber may not have the skill to climb a pitch quickly and efficiently. If lacking in communication skills, too, he relieves his own self-imposed stress by arguing over petty issues with his partner. More often, though, he simply maintains residence in the land of denial. I climbed with Jeff Lowe on the South Pillar of Nuptse in Nepal in 1986. I was far from confident in my own ability and lived in my own private hell every hour of every day. We switched leads on every pitch. I never admitted to any misgiving or reticence regarding a particular pitch. I refused to back off. I climbed slowly on terrain I should have sprinted up, terrain Jeff could have sprinted up. I couldn't 'fess up to my discomfort or recognize my tortoise pace. Jeff did. But six months later, when he had the opportunity to attempt the route again, Jeff was loyal to our prior effort and invited me to return with him despite my shortcomings as a climber. It was more than I had a right to expect from the partnership.

I behave differently these days. Scott Backes has far more big-wall experience than I do, and I willingly concede any aid pitch we come across to him because I know he will climb faster. We don't even need to discuss it. But when steps need to be kicked, or when the rope must be quickly run out on 60-degree ice, I always take the lead. We know each other inside and out, and years of talking—on the ground and on the mountains—has taken us to a point where we don't need to say it aloud any longer.

The trust between partners must be total. You cannot afford to have any reservations compromising the commitment you give to the route or to your partner. Trust is built over the years, through a progression of hard routes or training or simply by hanging out and learning to love and respect the climbing partner you choose. At some point during your career, you will have to rely on your partner's judgment and actions absolutely without second-guessing him. It is this trust and belief that creates a foundation of power, that elevates a partnership into something more than two climbers joined by a rope. The partnership between two alpine climbers is sacred, a living entity with dominion over life and death; the source of success, failure, and redemption.

KHAN TENGRI PARTNER: A CAUTIONARY TALE

In December 1990 I traveled to Kazakhstan, in what was then still the USSR, with a partner after soloing in the Pamirs during the summer. Michel Fauquet and I made up the climbing team, while Ace Kvale and John Falkiner came along to support us and take pictures. This region of the Tien Shan mountains on the border with China had been visited by climbers once before in winter, and during that expedition twelve of the fifteen members went home with frostbite. We targeted the south face of Khan Tengri, the northernmost 7,000-meter peak in the world. The average temperature during our four-week stay was minus 27 degrees Fahrenheit in base camp, with the mercury dropping to minus 53 at our high point of 6,300 meters.

I had invited Michel—whose nickname was Tchouky—to go with me because we had similar climbing résumés, had visited the same ranges, and had attempted similar routes. But we had never climbed together. I assumed our similarities indicated that our motivations and methods would be alike as well. But we all know the old wordplay: that to "assume" something makes an "ass" out of "u" and "me" both. I knew it then, but the adventure held my attention. With the potential for such a fantastic new route in view, I ignored an obvious red flag.

From the start Tchouky and I did not get along well enough to attempt so large and involved an objective. He was technically competent and extremely fast, but he wasn't safe by my standards and exhibited a very cavalier attitude toward death. On a training route, he failed to protect one belay because the ice was so easy, but higher up it became quite difficult, with no possibility of placing any gear. He was looking at an 80-footer onto the single No. 1 Camalot belay anchor—the only thing available. I hated him for that.

The frigid temperatures and the isolation (150 miles to the nearest village) compounded every risk, making it far greater than it might be in another mountain range. Dropping a mitten while climbing through the night could mean losing all one's fingers rather than the inconvenience of a little frostnip. An injury requiring hospitalization might be life-threatening, as we had no radio contact with the outside world, only an agreement that our helicopter pilot would return February 1. I was being very careful, aware enough to avoid any mistakes, never committing my full reserves, always holding something back just in case. Tchouky wasn't. He played for all the marbles at every throw. I didn't like it.

When the weather and our acclimatization finally offered the possibility of attempting the route, I went along, but we played without the highest commitment. Unwilling to take the risk of the lightest-weight tactics, we burdened ourselves with just enough gear to prevent us from going fast, but not enough to permit a protracted effort. We never tied in to the rope, and covered over 4,000 vertical feet of climbing in just over 7 hours. Seracs above and to the left of our route, which we considered benign, calved off three times during the

night, twice falling within 100 feet of us. We cowered in the darkness, hope our only ally. At 3 A.M. we pulled the plug. We wouldn't be high enough by the time the sun came up to be safe from avalanches, the wind was too strong, and the temperature had already forced us into all of our clothes, denying us the possibility of stopping to brew up. We could only remain warm through movement. It was too dangerous.

Retreat was dangerous as well because we would not willingly traverse on 50-degree ice below the seracs again. We blindly descended into an icefall, guided by Ace and John over the walkie-talkie as they tracked our progress through a spotting scope. It ended well in that we lived. Tchouky and I never climbed together again.

Khan Tengri's massive south face rising off the south Inylchek Glacier, Tien Shan range, Kazhakstan. *Photo: © Mark Twight*

Michel Fauquet on the north face of Trident Peak in the Tien Shan range, Kazhakstan, during an attempt on a "training route." *Photo: © Mark Twight*

going up

12

Once on the route, the game is to move quickly and safely, using every trick in the book to get up and off fast. The talents of the climbers and difficulty of the route determine the style and equipment of the ascent.

The Rope System

The decision on which rope system to use for a particular route depends on the terrain and the team's ability. There's no single answer to rope system questions, but here are guidelines that work most of the time.

No rope

Before deciding which rope system suits a route, consider whether to use a rope at all. While electing to leave the rope behind may kill you, climbing unroped is the fastest way to climb anywhere, anytime. Using a rope to belay a route or pitch always takes at least three times as long as climbing the same terrain unroped. Unroped climbing is incredibly dangerous, but it is a useful and necessary skill for situations where speed is safer than the usual precautions.

For example: Racing ropeless up easy but exposed terrain ahead of the coming night, or beneath a serac, or across avalanche-prone slopes, or while traversing a rockfall-strafed couloir beats roped climbing if you don't push your technical ability. In these situations the speed, mobility, and self-determination offered by unroped movement provides more security than tying into a rope, even with rockfall danger. If you can scoot out of danger quickly, you probably won't be hit. A rope may hinder moving out of the way.

I'll use Slipstream, the 3,000-foot engagement Grade VI, technical Grade 4 + waterfall on the east face of Snowdome in the Canadian Rockies, to illustrate the pros and cons of unroped climbing. Seracs always, and a cornice sometimes, threaten the route. The first ascent took two days, but climbers all agree climbing the route faster is safer. Jay Smith and Craig Reason simul-soloed Slipstream in 5 hours in 1985, Ward Robinson climbed it alone in 4 hours, Randy Rackliff soloed it in 3 hours, 20 minutes, and I climbed it in 2 hours, 4 minutes. Of all the ascents, roped or unroped, I believe mine was the safest because I spent the least time under the threat. One mistake would have killed me, but I would rather depend upon my awareness and physical skills than upon an unpredictably changing environment. The example of Alan Dean, who was killed soloing on this climb, argues against my position. No one knows for sure, but most believe icefall knocked him off the climb, not faulty technique. A partner and a rope may or may not have saved him.

On the other hand, three roped climbers were killed on this route when they attempted it in heavy snow conditions. They understood they'd be under threat for a long time. Mark Bebie, one of the victims in this story, was a very experienced climber but not particularly fast, and he never consented to climbing unroped. Even if they made a moderately fast 12-

hour ascent, the team was destined to spend at least 36 man-hours climbing and belaying in the danger zone. Compared to the ideal of 2 to 8 hours, this is unacceptable. Period.

Think about objective dangers in terms of man-hours, because these dangers threaten each climber at the same time. The longer one stays in danger, the more depends on luck, not skill. On the other hand, some routes, even when threatened by seracs, are safer to climb belayed. Routes with loose rock or thin, poorly attached ice may require a rope. I say "may" because, depending on talent and risk tolerance, these factors may not pose serious problems. Almost everything you can imagine climbing has been soloed. The potential is limitless for the climber with an open mind who does not strictly adhere to another's precepts of safety or possibility.

Loose rock is an unpredictable hazard, to say the least. It can defeat the soloist before he gets off the ground and complicate life dramatically for a rope team. Placing protec-

tion in loose rock requires ingenuity, nerves, and a very big rack because there's no telling if pieces will hold. Back them up, string them in series, equalize them. This will eat even the fattest rack on a long pitch. Add the probability of the leader dropping rocks on the belayer and of the rope flipping pieces into space or being cut by falling debris.

View thin ice skeptically, whether it's adhering to limestone or granite. It demands careful attention and, more often than not, a rope and belay. More technical terrain will necessitate use of the rope as well, because falls are more likely, packs may need hauling, and so on.

Once you decide to use the rope on a route, choose the best method from the systems available. Twin-rope, Double-rope, and Single-rope systems offer both advantages and disadvantages that you need to assess for your project.

Twin ropes

Twin ropes are drop-tested using an 80-kilogram weight that loads both ropes simultaneously. The two strands together must survive twelve test falls. Twin-rope technique,

The east face of Snowdome in the Canadian Rockies. Slipstream is the right-hand ice flow. It features 3,000 feet of climbing up to 80 degrees, with huge exposure to falling seracs and cornices. Mark Twight soloed this route in 2 hours 4 minutes in February 1988. Photo: © Mark Twight

when used properly, offers the highest margin of safety in the event of a fall.

The climbers use two ropes of 8 millimeter to 8.5 millimeter diameter, always clipping both ropes to each carabiner connected to a point of protection. Because there will never be an equal amount of each rope available and because each will have slightly different elongation characteristics, each rope won't receive exactly the same amount of impact force in a fall. This is good, because if the ropes drape over an edge, the one receiving the higher impact force may fail while the other survives.

Even the lightest ropes available (such as the Blue Water Ice Floss, at 40.5 grams per meter) will hold seventeen UIAA falls, which makes these very trustworthy indeed. There has never been a total rope system failure using Twin-rope technique.

Using the lightest Twin rope you can find will allow carrying longer ropes for the same weight as thicker, shorter ropes. Sixty meters of rope that weighs only 41 grams per meter add up to 2,460 grams (5.5 pounds)—just a few ounces more than only 50 meters of an 8.8-millimeter rope that weighs in at 47 grams per meter. On a 3,000-foot route, the longer ropes will eliminate at least three belays, and the same number of rappel anchors when rapping the route.

Terrain
Twin ropes shine on terrain of moderate difficulty. Moderate terrain is difficult enough for roping up, but usually not vertical enough to call for following on ascenders or for hauling packs.

Above: Twin ropes must both be clipped to the same point of protection for them to be effective. Mark Twight in the first rock band during the first ascent of Deprivation on the North Buttress of Mount Hunter, Alaska. *Photo: © Mark Twight*

Right: Mark Twight on the lower east face of Long's Peak, Colorado. *Photo: © Cathy Beloeil*

Routes where Twin-rope technique would work include the north face of Les Droites in the French Alps, the Lowe-Kennedy route on Mount Hunter or the Colton-Leach route on Mount Huntington in Alaska, the north face of the Eiger in the Swiss Alps, and Polar Circus in the Canadian Rockies. These are routes moderate enough for both leader and follower to climb classically. They are 80 to 100 percent ice and don't involve intricate routefinding that might require Double-rope technique (discussed later in this chapter) to reduce rope drag. Consider Twin ropes for use on similar climbs with few killer edges.

Technique

Twin ropes require extra care. They are thin and can be easily cut if loaded over an edge. The lightest ones suit pure ice routes, as in waterfall climbing where edges are few. Although Twin ropes have the highest fall rating of any system, the lightest models were never intended to hold many falls, especially in the mountains. (The guy who takes the big screamer off ice will probably be hospitalized and quit climbing.) Remember that the small diameter of Twin ropes means they move a lot faster through rappel devices than thicker ropes.

Since the leader clips both ropes to every piece of protection, hauling packs would be difficult (though not impossible). The climbers should carry their packs at all times. On day routes, the pack of both the leader and the second should weigh roughly the same—that is, virtually nothing.

On a multiday route this system demands a light leader's pack and a heavier second's pack. The leader's pack should hold a belay jacket, food and water for the day, a headlamp, spare gloves, and a sleeping bag. In short, limit the load to the day's necessities plus some light, bulky items. Jam all the heavy gear (stove, food, bivy tent, and so on) into the second's larger pack. No matter how you break up the pitches, the leader and follower switch packs depending on their job. It helps when both climbers are about the same size.

Half ropes (Double-rope technique)

The light ropes known as Half ropes are used in Double-rope technique. A Half rope must hold five drops of a 55-kilogram weight on a single strand. These ropes for Double-rope technique can be as thin as 8.5 millimeters and still meet UIAA standards; none are larger than 9 millimeters because of the weight. (And Single ropes exist that are only 9.1 millimeter diameter.) Any of these ropes can serve as a Single climbing rope if the fall factor (discussed later in this chapter) will be less than 1. But if a serious fall is

When using Double-rope technique, each rope is clipped to alternate protection points; this reduces rope drag and the impact force of a potential fall. In this picture both ropes are clipped to the same piece directly above the belay because a fall occurring right above the belay must be absorbed by a short amount of available rope, and the force may be too great for a single strand of Half rope. This may burn the sheaths a bit if the leader does fall but that's better than breaking a rope altogether. Nancy Feagin belaying Mark Twight on the north face of the Aiguille du Midi, Chamonix, France. *Photo: © James Martin*

a possibility, only using both will achieve an acceptable level of safety.

Unlike Twin ropes, the leader clips each Half rope to separate, usually alternate, pieces of protection—essentially providing two Single ropes. This system is very reliable, providing the greatest security against total system failure. Alternate clipping protects a wandering or traversing pitch without inducing undue rope drag compared with a Twin-rope or Single-rope system. You can jug on one of the two ropes if necessary, but don't make it a common practice.

Terrain

The Double-rope setup suits alpine terrain where both leader and follower intend to climb pitches classically, a route that can be climbed mostly free. Mechanical ascenders may be carried for hauling and for following a pitch occasionally. Examples of suitable Half-rope routes are Deprivation on the North Buttress of Mount Hunter in Alaska, the east face of Mount Babel in the Canadian Rockies, and the Colton-McIntyre route on the north face of the Grandes Jorasses in the French Alps.

Technique

Build belays with both ropes clipped to the anchor. If the terrain is moderate, lead wearing your pack. The same principles regarding packs on day versus multiday routes apply to both Twin-rope and Double-rope technique. On pitches where leading with a pack compromises balance or requires too many mental gymnastics, leave it below and haul it later.

Protect the belay by placing protection directly above it. If the pieces are close enough to the anchor, clip both ropes through one carabiner. Higher still, clip each rope to alternate pieces of protection to eliminate rope drag, or clip both ropes to each piece on pure ice pitches where drag isn't a problem. Two different-sounding colors will decrease confusion when calling for slack on a single line to clip it. It's hard to confuse the two-syllable "yellow" with the single-syllable "blue."

If the leader arrives at the belay without a pack, it's time to haul. On a straight up-and-down pitch, pull one line through the gear and toss an end down to the belayer. This is the ideal solution. Otherwise, haul "through" the gear, meaning the leader belays the second on one rope while hauling on the other at the same time. Pull the bag up to the piece of gear above your partner. When the second climbs to it and unclips the carabiner, haul the pack to the next piece—with luck, before the second arrives. This so-called system drains the leader psychically and physically because the rope passing through the carabiners adds a huge amount of friction. But if it's got to be done, suck it up, do it, and don't complain.

If the pitch can't be followed classically, the second uses mechanical ascenders on one of the ropes. Jugging on one of these thin lines over a big void can be a bowel-emptying experience (something you wouldn't want to do on an 8-millimeter Twin rope). The massive stretch in the system pushes the imagination into high gear. The more exposure, the thinner the rope looks. It's disagreeable, but it works. Again, if the pitch is straight up and down, once the leader has hauled, he can toss a free end down to belay the second as he jugs. This is a rare luxury, however.

Single rope with a haul line

A Single rope must hold a minimum of five test falls with an 80-kilogram weight. The leader clips the single strand to every point of protection. While not ideal on an indirect pitch when rope drag poses a problem, a fat rope inspires confidence when looking at the possibility of a way whipper.

Choose a Single rope with the lowest impact-force rating available to reduce the force transmitted to the gear—essential when dealing with less than ideal points of protection. Impact force reflects the maximum load transmitted to the climber and to the protection, and is an accurate indication of how much force a rope can sustain. The lower the impact-force number, the better. UIAA tests allow a rope to stretch up to 45 percent of its total length to absorb this force.

Single ropes should have a minimum diameter of 9.1 millimeters and a maximum of 10.5 millimeters. Weight is, as usual, a factor. Consider that 60 meters of 9.1-millimeter rope at 53 grams per meter weighs 7.1 pounds, while the same length of 10.5-millimeter at 65 grams per meter weighs 8.7 pounds—roughly a pound and a half difference. This is the equivalent of twenty-two packages of GU—about 2,200 calories. Which would you rather carry?

Terrain

Single-rope technique suits routes where the climbing is difficult enough that falling is likely or where it's faster and more efficient to follow using mechanical ascenders on steep, technical routes. In the mountains, the Single-rope system only works when matched with a

Scott Backes jugging on a 10-millimeter Single rope during the first ascent of Birthright on the west face of the Grands Charmoz, Chamonix, France. He is following wearing a "second's pack," trailing the haul line because the pitch was not steep enough to haul. *Photo: © Mark Twight*

7-millimeter haul line, which allows the leader to haul his pack and doubles the length of any rappels.

The exception could include steep, technical routes doable in a single push with a casual walk-off descent so that no rappels are needed. For example, Steve House and Joe Josephson carried one 9.1-millimeter Single rope (and no haul line, since their packs weighed a scant 15 pounds each) on their new route Call of the Wild on King Peak in the Saint Elias Range.

Other good Single-rope routes include Beyond Good and Evil on the Aiguille des Pelerins in the French Alps, the Moonflower Buttress of Mount Hunter in Alaska, the Fowler-Watts route on Tallaraju in Peru, or the Blanchard-Cheesmond route on the north face of North Twin in the Canadian Rockies.

Technique

The leader climbs with or without a pack. The team's packs can be similar in size and weight or they can be set up as leader's and follower's packs, with the follower packing most of the weight. The leader climbs on the fat rope and trails the 7-millimeter line, with the opposite end clipped to the belay anchors below.

The leader builds a belay, clips into it, and fixes the fat rope. If the second follows with ascenders, the leader can haul one pack or both packs. Hauling up the second's pack allows him to follow the pitch faster. Laid-back terrain makes hauling inefficient, so both should climb wearing a pack. Multiple pitches without hauling calls for stashing the 7-millimeter rope in a pack to simplify the process of climbing, belaying, and keeping control of the cords.

On longer routes, with lots of jugging, the rope will often by loaded over an edge. The teeth on ascenders also thrash the rope. Obtain some peace of mind by belaying the second on the haul line while he's jugging if the fat rope shows signs of wear. Use an 8-millimeter or 9-millimeter dynamic rope as the haul line. You can skip backing up the ascenders with a figure-8 knot (a time-consuming process) when jugging while on belay; daring climbers can just let the free end of the fat rope dangle. Once you've completed the climb and rappelled off the face, finish the descent using just the 8-millimeter haul line for glacier travel and stash the 10-millimeter climbing rope in a pack—or in a crevasse if it and you are totally exhausted.

Count on getting only one or two hard routes out of a Single rope. Imagine the wear from loading over edges, jugging, stepping on the rope with crampons (you can't prevent it, so don't worry about it), icefall, and rockfall. Lead ropes age prematurely. Retire them before you harbor doubts.

Rope Tricks

Thinner rope

Most of the ropes UIAA-rated for use as Half ropes will hold one Single-rope fall (with an 80-kilogram weight). Usually they fail on the second drop, and these tests are not done with the rope over an edge. Loaded on an edge, Half ropes fail the Single-rope test fall. But if you want to save weight, climbing on just one 8.8-millimeter or 9-millimeter rope can be a viable solution.

Sport climbers often use these thinner ropes for red-point ascents where a fall is unlikely and will be clean if it happens. The waterfall route, Slipstream, in the Canadian Rockies is an example of a climb that can be suitable for a single thinner rope. There is no documented case of one of these ropes failing from the impact of a falling climber—unless the rope was loaded over an edge—so try not to be the first. Always use a new rope.

Longer rope

For years the standard length of a rope was 50 meters, or 165 feet—usually long enough and rarely too long. As sport climbers began demanding longer Single ropes so a pitch needn't arbitrarily end after 80 feet (so they could lower off on the same rope), longer ropes became available. On extended alpine routes where a long rope reduces the number of pitches and belays, a 60-meter rope makes sense. The team gains an extra pitch for every five pitches climbed, or about five pitches for every twenty climbed. This also means fewer rappel anchors on a retreat.

Some climbers argue that a longer rope requires more gear on the rack to protect longer pitches; that you can get along with smaller racks if you use shorter ropes. But the rack ought to be about the same no matter the length of the rope, because you need to cover all crack sizes (up to 3 inches) with both passive and active pieces of rock and ice protection. While longer ropes are heavier, more difficult to keep organized, and tougher to deal with in the wind, climbers must keep their options many and open. With 60 meters you can go farther up or down. If you run out of rappel slings, you can cut more from the rope. After eight rappels, each time cutting a rappel sling from the climbing rope, you'd still have two 50-meter ropes left. These slings could give you an extra 900 feet of descent.

Anne Smith in the Chere Couloir on the north face of the Aiguille du Midi, Chamonix, France. In the interest of saving weight we climbed on a single strand of an 8.5-millimeter Half rope. *Photo: © Mark Twight*

Leading in blocks

Don't automatically change leads after every pitch. While each climber leads the same number of pitches by changing after each one, it may not be the most efficient method either psychologically or physically. Changing leads every pitch obliges each climber to stand still for two full pitches at a time.

If, instead, the team changes jobs after every three pitches (or every six pitches, or every day), the leader stays psyched to lead while the second enjoys a genuine psychological rest. By leading in blocks this way, the leader can dress in a very light clothing system, enough to keep warm while moving and for one pitch of waiting instead of two. The second can dress lighter as well, layering a big belay jacket to belay, then stripping it off to follow. Neither climber ever sits for longer than the time it takes to lead or follow one pitch.

The disadvantages of leading in blocks are few. The rope must be restacked at each belay. You'll still have to exchange the rack, so it won't save much time, but it will ultimately increase efficiency in terms of the total weight carried (that is, lighter clothing) and each climber's psychological state. As Rob Newsom, aka The Reverend Hotrod, noted, "This system leaves you dying to lead when it's your turn, no matter how awful the pitch looks."

Team Configuration

The climbing team may consist of one to four people. Obviously, one climber alone will be the fastest and four will be the slowest, in most instances. In general, a team of two makes the most sense. A team this size moves quickly and efficiently, divides weight and responsibility evenly, and offers a rough democracy in the decision-making process.

On routes of great difficulty—technical and psychological—or when requiring a wider margin of safety, a team of three works well without compromising too much speed. A team of three climbed The Weeping Pillar, a 1,000-foot Grade IV, 6 waterfall route, in 6 hours round-trip. Both ascents of The Wild Thing, a 5,000-foot Grade VI alpine route on the east face of Mount Chephren in the Canadian Rockies, were made by teams of three.

In fact, if all climbers are of equal ability and know what they're doing, a team of three moves no slower than two. Each climber will do one-third of the work rather than half. When not leading, one climber can "draft," let go of the stress, recover, eat and drink, and then start psyching up to lead when the time comes.

With three climbers, the leader carries a small pack and leads on Half ropes. Once the leader sets a belay, the second climber begins following classically, climbing ten feet ahead of the third, who also follows classically. The two clean alternate pieces of gear or alternate halves of the pitch. Each carries a "second's pack" with both individual and group gear inside. Or both can follow with mechanical ascenders on their respective ropes.

Consider a team of four on a big Alaskan or Himalayan face where the climbing is moderate and each pair can operate independently. This style has been used successfully in both ranges. Barry Blanchard, Kevin Doyle, Ward Robinson, and I climbed as two autonomous teams of two on the Rupal Face of Nanga Parbat. Doing so adds an extra margin of safety. When belaying pitches, gang the ropes and gear together. Everyone gets off with

a little less weight because the two teams can split the rack between them and each team has to carry only one of the two 60-meter Half ropes. If either team retreats due to illness, gear failure, or terror, both teams should descend—because it is really a single team of four.

Belay Anchors

Build a good one. At some point each belay becomes the party's sole connection to the mountain. Use whatever gear is needed to feel certain the belay will hold a fall or support the second while jugging on it. Building a good anchor requires knowledge seasoned with some paranoia. A cavalier attitude will kill you. The '60s dictum "If it feels good, do it" usually ensures a solid anchor.

Common practice suggests placing at least two pieces, but be ready to adapt to conditions. On granite, live by the maxim "One piece may fail, two probably won't, and three never will." But on the shale, limestone, and quartzite of the Canadian Rockies, use more care and more gear because the rock is untrustworthy.

In the Mont Blanc Massif, a route graded TD (a North American Grade V or so) without fixed gear undertaken by a competent team should require a rack of four or five springloaded cams, nine wired nuts, two ice screws, four pitons, twenty carabiners (nine for racking gear and eleven free), two locking carabiners (one for each belay station), eight standard-length slings, and two double-length slings. In the Canadian Rockies for a route of the same grade, double the cams; dump the wired nuts (they won't work in smooth, parallel-sided cracks) and replace them with Tri Cams and TCUs, and add more pitons. Creating a reassuring belay anchor may take five pieces.

Imagine you've just led a pitch and arrived at a good stance. You've used at least 90 percent of the rope. It's time to build a belay station.

Place pieces in separate cracks if possible. Alternatively, put two pieces in one crack and equalize them to build the primary anchor. (The next section tells how to do it.) Then back those up with a piece in another crack or with an ice screw. Don't believe an ice tool pounded in to back up the anchor has any value. Tests prove that ice hooks like Spectres don't hold falls consistently, so why would an ice tool, which is essentially the same thing?

Conserve gear if possible so there's something left for leading. Check out the next pitch and try to imagine what the leader will need. Don't use the only No. 2 cam you have at the belay if the next pitch starts with a thin-hands crack without other evident ways to protect it. Look for inventive ways to use slings. They are the lightest pieces of protection, so carry a lot of them, especially on granite where horns and flakes for tying off abound.

Always clip into the primary anchor using the rope and a locking carabiner; carry two lockers on the rack for this purpose. When on a ledge, allow enough slack to permit moving to avoid falling debris. Set the stance far enough below the equalized point of

With a team of three, both climbers may follow the pitches at the same time. Steve House and Jonny Blitz following the sixth pitch of The Gift That Keeps on Giving on Mount Bradley's south face, Alaska. Photo: © Mark Twight

the anchor to allow belaying up through it. If the second falls, the tension will pull you up instead of down, adding some dynamism to the system. True paranoids belay through a load limiter, a sling with stitching that tears on impact to absorb shock and limit the impact force on the anchor from any fall to 500 pounds.

How to equalize anchors

Always equalize anchors to distribute impact force evenly among the component pieces. It's easier to equalize two pieces and back them up with another piece than to try to equalize three separate pieces.

Tests show that joining two anchors together using one sling with the load falling on a single point (that is, a carabiner) between the pieces reduces the load on each piece and distributes it equally only when the angle is less than 25 degrees between each "leg" of the equalizing sling.

Imagine a 1,000-pound load distributed between two anchors through a sling. If the slings are short and the angle obtained between them equals 120 degrees, each piece will receive 1,000 pounds. This attempt at equalization gains nothing.

On the opposite end of the scale, two pieces placed one above the other, aligned with the direction of pull and equalized with a sling, would produce an angle of 0 to 5 degrees between the slings. Each piece would absorb half of the load, or 500 pounds. Done right, equalizing pieces in your anchor spreads out impact force and greatly reduces the risk of any single piece ripping.

Some anchors automatically equalize the load and self-adjust to any variations in the direction of pull. This system employs what John Long, in his book *Climbing Anchors* (see Appendix 2, Suggested Reading), refers to as a "sliding knot" on the sling. It is nothing more than a twist in the sling held in place by the load-bearing carabiner. This twist ensures equal load distribution to every piece while preventing total system failure should one component fail. However, if a piece fails, the resulting slack in the system must be absorbed, thus shock-loading the remaining piece or pieces with a "fall" of several feet. Can each component of your anchor sustain this? You must decide.

Mark Twight equalizing an anchor near the top of the Frendo Spur on the north face of the Aiguille du Midi, Chamonix, France. Two pieces are equalized with one double-length sling, a third piece backs up the main anchor. Clip a locking carabiner to the "power point" for the maximum margin of safety. *Photo: © James Martin*

If unsure, build a static equalizing system. The static system will distribute equal force when loaded in one particular direction of pull. It cannot self-adjust because a knot is tied at the apex of the sling (called the power point) where the load-bearing carabiner is clipped. However, this knot prevents shock-loading of individual pieces should one fail.

To facilitate equalizing three or more pieces, carry a cordelette, which is a 16- to 20-foot-long piece of 5.5- to 6-millimeter Spectra cord tied into a sling. Using this in place of a double-length runner allows clipping more pieces into the system without wasting quickdraws and carabiners. Although this sounds convenient, and it will become necessary at some point, trying to equalize multiple suspect pieces to form one solid anchor consumes both time and gear. Sometimes it's better to keep going even if it means simul-climbing.

Off belay

After building the primary anchor and clipping into it with a chicken sling, shout "Off belay" so the second can get ready to climb. When the second takes you off, pull up all the remaining slack and tie it into the primary anchor. Shout that the "rope is fixed." Now your partner knows he is tied off safely, effectively on belay, which leaves him free to dismantle his anchor while you begin to back up your primary anchor, eat, or pull on some warm clothes.

If the second is using ascenders, pull up all the slack and fix it before he jugs so the extra rope won't loop around a flake or get chopped by rockfall. This guarantees that some of the rope will survive if something goes wrong.

Following the Pitch

Once the station is secure, with the second either on belay or clear to follow with ascenders, inform the second. When the second starts up, keep control of the rope. Never, never let slack rope hang down the pitch after reeling it in. Rope can jam behind a flake, get wrapped around an icicle, knock loose rock down on your partner, or worse.

If you're on a ledge, stack the rope on it. If hanging, butterfly it back and forth across your leg or tie-in rope. Better yet, employ a solution big-wall climbers hit upon long ago. They use a nylon rope bucket, essentially a hanging funnel-shaped stuff sack. No company makes a bucket light enough for alpine climbing. Make your own; such a rope bucket helps organize long, skinny ropes, makes belaying and throwing rappel ropes easier, and keeps them out of harm's way.

During the first ascent of the Whymper Spur of the Grandes Jorasses, Walter Bonatti and Michel Vaucher's ropes got chopped by rockfall on the first bivouac. When the avalanche subsided, their longest usable section was 40 feet. With rappelling out of the question, the pair had no choice but to continue up even when the weather turned bad. So keep your ropes protected. They are both lifeline and link to the ground.

The second must climb as fast as possible. To speed up while seconding, make it a practice to follow pitches belayed on a tight rope. On ice don't worry too much about the quality of ice-tool placements. Hook sections instead of swinging. Make dynamic moves that

would be unthinkable with slack in the rope. Constant tension from above makes wearing a big pack feel less cumbersome and you will climb faster. If following with ascenders but not hauling, and using Double-rope technique, the leader can provide a tight belay on one line as the second jugs on the other. The second won't have to stop to back himself up every 10 meters, so he can race on the jugs.

The second must clean every piece. When carrying minimum gear, losing any piece can end a climb. Learn from René Desmaison and Serge Gosseault on their attempt of a direct route on the Grandes Jorasses in the winter of 1971. Gosseault suffered from a chemical deficiency and grew weaker each day, too weak to clean all the gear as he followed. The pair then didn't have enough gear to retreat when a storm hit 300 feet from the top of the 4,000-foot route. Trapped, without food and water, they slowly lost strength. Gosseault died, and Desmaison was rescued just a few hours before total renal failure after fifteen days on the wall.

The second needs to organize the cleaned gear to efficiently transfer it back to the leader's gear sling or for his sling to quickly become the leader's sling. The only way to transfer gear quickly at the belay is for both climbers to know what the rack will look like when complete. Every climber brings different racking preferences to the partnership, so sort this out on the ground. Create a plan, know it, and use it.

When tired or distracted, discipline yourselves to maintain verbal signals when exchanging gear (or anything else) at the belays. Say "got it" when you have control of something handed to you. This speeds things up and establishes responsibility if something is dropped. You *will* drop gear during your career, but try to make it the unimportant stuff. I failed to follow this advice when I dropped my jumars and my figure-8 belay/rappel device off the South Pillar of Nuptse in Nepal during a winter attempt with Jeff Lowe. The jumars were irreplaceable, but ever resourceful, I used a No. 5 Tri Cam as a belay device for the next few days, and eventually made forty-eight rappels with it to get off the route.

Even if it's cold, do all the fine, skilled gear manipulation with bare hands or liner gloves. The work goes almost twice as fast compared with wearing mittens or "warm" gloves, and your chances of dropping something plummet.

Protect the Belay

After exchanging the gear at the belay, it's time to continue up. It's written above, but it cannot be stressed enough: The leader *must* protect the belay by placing protection directly above the belay anchor. Nothing is more frightening than having the leader fall and hit a suspect belay anchor with a Factor 2 fall while hanging a dozen pitches up (the fall factor is discussed in the next section).

Stack the ropes neatly as the second follows the pitch, otherwise the rope may hang up on flakes or icicles below, or it could be chopped by falling stones or ice. Mark Twight belaying Nancy Feagin on the north face of the Aiguille du Midi, Chamonix, France. *Photo: © James Martin*

During the first ascent of Beyond Good and Evil on the north face of the Aiguille des Pelerins above Chamonix, Andy Parkin lost his hammer while jumaring the twelfth pitch. Removing pitons with the adze of a Barracuda was fairly ridiculous, but placing them was harder and he couldn't get them in very far. As he started the thirteenth pitch and reached a point 10 feet above the belay—with no protection placed—he fell. It was a Factor 2 fall, of course, putting max impact on our suspect belay anchors. I had one hand in the pack searching for some food when he came off. I inadvertently gave him a dynamic belay, but that reduced the impact and probably saved us from going to the ground.

Place gear to protect the belay even if you could climb the pitch blindfolded on roller skates. When the climbing is easy, everyone runs it out, so big-fall potential is huge. Fight the impulse to conserve gear for higher up at the cost of protecting the belay. These mistakes can kill both of you.

The fall factor

The fall factor is a theoretical number representing the force applied to the ropes and protection system during a fall. I say theoretical because many variables affect falls and forces in real climbing situations.

To determine the fall factor, you simply divide the distance of the fall by the amount of rope available to absorb it—that is, the length of rope from belayer to climber. The higher the fall factor, the more force is transferred to the falling climber and to the gear that must stop the fall.

For example, say a climber falls from 10 feet above the belayer with no intermediate protection in place. In this case, the force of the fall hits the belay directly. The energy generated by the 20-foot fall must be absorbed by 10 feet of rope, resulting in a fall factor of 2—the harshest possible impact. Most falls develop less devastating forces.

Take another climber, who placed a solid stopper 10 feet out, falling from 20 feet above the belayer. The total fall is 20 feet, absorbed by 20 feet of rope—for a fall factor of 1. A similar 20-foot fall held by 40 feet of rope would generate a fall factor of .5 and place far less impact force on the entire system.

A fall from overhanging terrain develops forces similar to the UIAA methods for testing ropes, but other elements conspire to reduce impact force: a tumbling fall off less than vertical terrain; rope slipping through the belay device; energy absorbed by the belayer's body weight; and so on. However, a Factor 2 fall onto the belay in the mountains may well rip the anchors. This should inspire all climbers to protect the belay with intermediate pieces immediately upon climbing above the anchors.

Protect the belay by placing a piece directly above it no matter how easy the climbing is. Nancy Feagin belaying Mark Twight on the north face of the Aiguille du Midi, Chamonix, France. Photo: © James Martin

Protect yourself

On any pitch, consciously place gear as often as you can whenever you can, no matter how easy it is. Because if the climbing gets hard and fear grips you, you will want the protection but probably won't be able to get it. This is one of God's cruel jokes. If you've followed the rules, you'll have a few pieces between you and the belay, so you won't rip the belay or hit the ground.

KISS (Keep It Simple, Stupid)

Keep rope commands simple. Shout them loud and clear. Inaudible and misunderstood commands waste time and create tension. Simplify and amplify to keep things running smoothly. When taking a long time to lead out of sight, let your belayer know what's going on from time to time.

Gathering Speed

Ultimately the generations of alpine climbers who proclaimed that "speed is safety" were right. Faster climbing exposes the alpinist to less time under the threat of death and serious injury. Whether leading or following, always think "fast."

As terrain becomes easier, consider dispensing with conventional belaying techniques. "Pitching it" takes time because one climber always remains stationary. But if the climbing is well within the team's ability and confidence level, climb simultaneously with the rope strung tight between you—a technique often called a running belay. Keep at least three pieces of solid protection—multiple pieces equalized if necessary—clipped between you at all times. The gear in this running belay may need to hold a huge fall with the weight of both climbers so make it bombproof.

For a running belay, the leader should start with a full rack and keep the lead until out of gear or until the climbing warrants a true belay. On moderate ground a team can eat up altitude this way without the commitment of climbing ropeless. The rope is merely a gesture to fate, though. Each climber must climb like he's soloing because if one falls, he'll drag the other off as well, leaving them both hanging from the protection. It's a team decision to climb this way, a test of trust affecting both climbers.

Cheat by pulling

If you find yourself on a pitch debating with yourself about how to free-climb something, tentatively making moves, backing down and trying something else, get over it. Just put in a piece and pull on it. Unless your goal is to free-climb the route, pulling on pro is the most sensible thing to do. It generates speed.

Keep your eyes open

If pulling down and locking off on one or two pieces won't get you through a hard section, then look around the corner. It's easy to put on blinders and only look up. The key to solving routefinding problems often consists of traversing.

When the view is blocked, place a piece, tension off it, lean out, and search. The old-fashioned tension traverse may save hours of fooling around. Climbing three moderate pitches around a problem often goes faster than confronting the problem head on.

Obey the law of perpetual motion. Psychologically it is more satisfying and energizing to move and gain ground with each movement than to grind to an agonizing halt. After the exhilaration of moving fast and gaining altitude, the psyche wilts when a time-consuming technical pitch slows the team. The leader, absorbed in the task, can occupy his mind, but the belayer suffers. It's difficult to regain the upward flow after a slow pitch. Maintain momentum.

Use alpine aid

If pulling on gear or traversing fails, aid the difficult section—the alpine way. Use three-step aiders. They are lighter than four- and five-step etriers, and every move you make will win ground. Unlike with the larger etriers, you cannot step sideways from one etrier to the other, only up. Every motion must be made with the objective of upward progress.

Some teams carry extra slings, figuring they'll aid with those in a pinch. Bad idea. Slings don't stay open like sewn steps, and if aiding in crampons, the points will punch holes in the slings. Don't rely on punctured slings. A pair of three-step aiders made from half-inch flat webbing weigh about six ounces. Keep a set tucked away in your pack because they'll save a lot of time.

Climb rock in crampons

Learning to climb rock while wearing big boots and crampons is one of the best time-saving skills. Difficult mixed routes change media several times in the course of a pitch. They go much faster if the crampons stay on. "Sport" mixed routes of this era often demand climbing rock at a high standard (5.11 or 5.12) while wearing crampons. It can be done. However, these roadside routes usually exact no penalty for falling, while peeling off the same pitch in the mountains could easily prove fatal.

Crampons possess the advantage of edging better than plain boot soles. However, when overloaded, they tend to pop off rather than to ooze off of small holds like rubber soles do. Their performance is not dramatically inferior to soles unless the terrain turns to pure friction. If you must climb in boot soles and then pull onto an ice feature, you'll have to hang and reapply your crampons. Place a solid piece and hang from it. In the absence of cracks, only a hook will do, such as a Black Diamond Skyhook. On a technical route always carry at least one hook on the rack or stashed in the leader's pack. Combined with three-step aiders, hooks help finesse a blank section faster than any other solution.

More Unconventional Warfare

While equipment manufacturers design hardware for a specific purpose, there's no reason not to press it into service in unconventional ways. For example, ice hooks like the Spectre

were designed as pound-in protection for thin ice. Although they rarely hold falls in this application, they are brilliant as pitons hammered into frozen moss or driven into iced-up cracks where a toothless pin would fall out. The spare pick for your ice tool will work well here, too.

As last-ditch ice pro, ice hooks can work; stories with happy outcomes abound. But a short screw will always hold better in thin ice. That same ice screw can act as a nut in thin ice. Punch a small hole through the curtain of ice, feed the screw (with a sling girth-hitched around the middle) through the hole, and turn the screw horizontally to jam it. The fiddling may slow you down, so use it only in extremis. Better yet, slot the screw like a hand-placed piton above a correctly shaped constriction in a deep crack. Tapping on it to wedge it snugly may damage the threads. But this is the mountains: Anything goes, and gear gets trashed. So what.

Eastern Europeans were fond of the jammed knot before metal nuts became available. Again, use this when out of options. Reserve runners for tying off icicles, slinging over horns, wrapping around natural chockstones, threading through the ice, and equalizing the belay.

The last resort

If you've run out of rope on the lead and tried all the conventional and unconventional uses of the gear without being able to create a safe belay anchor, take a deep breath and shout down for your partner to unclip and climb with you. The feasibility of this tactic depends on the terrain. The concept is the same as a running belay with a different psychology, because this is inadvertent simul-climbing. Often the terrain is more technical than that where a running belay would ordinarily be considered acceptable.

The second now strips the belay and moves with the leader, who keeps the rope relatively snug and continues to place intermediate protection to keep them from going to the ground if one of them should fall. While not ideal, this sort of climbing beats the alternative: 45 minutes of wasting time trying to concoct an inadequate anchor. The added risk of this climbing violates the safety ethos of orthodox belaying, but there is still a reasonable margin for a competent team. Don't make a habit of it, and stop at the first opportunity for building a solid belay. Alpinists employ this tactic far more often than most people imagine.

Doing the Right Thing

The "right thing" is what is safe, what is smart, what keeps you alive. We hear discussions about clean climbing, such as using nondestructive methods of protecting oneself, which

Jonny Blitz starting pitch 15 on The Gift That Keeps on Giving on Mount Bradley's south face, Alaska. He's aiding "the alpine way" with three step aiders that force him to move up with every step, never allowing a sideways movement to the other etrier. Every movement you make must gain altitude. *Photo: © Mark Twight*

rules out pitons. Ethical concepts like clean climbing are sound for heavily traveled crag and wall routes where, if everybody used pitons, climbers would destroy the rock. Difficult, dangerous alpine routes don't see heavy traffic, and pitons are often the only protection available. In these cases, "ethics are for the ground."

Don't pay attention to the jeremiads of nonparticipants. If only direct aid will let you maintain a comfortable margin of safety, use it. If only pounding pitons will protect the team, go ahead and weld them. You are there, you make the decisions, and they don't affect anyone but you and your ropemate. Don't allow the herd to make judgments for you.

I don't place bolts. The routes of the future may well require the tactic of drilling bolts into the rock, but I know that the most desperate of alpine routes have been done without resorting to making permanent anchors. Reinhold Messner said the practice of carrying bolt kits, for upward progress or possible retreat, equaled "carrying one's courage in his rucksack." If you don't have bolts, you find a way to do without them, or you fail. At least you won't permanently scar the mountain. You don't leave trash behind, do you?

As long as climbers try to resolve conflicting ethical issues presented by alpinism honestly, no gross transgressions will occur. In the end, only the climbers will have to live with any particular action. My ethic has been to climb the biggest objective with the least amount of gear and to do it as fast as possible. Follow your own lights.

Learning to climb rock well and confidently wearing crampons is an essential skill which translates to more speed. Mark Twight belayed by Nancy Feagin on the Aiguille du Midi, Chamonix, France. *Photo: © Mark Twight*

RESOURCEFULNESS

During the winter of 1989-90, I lived in Chamonix and spent a lot of time around the east face of Mont Maudit. Both Alain Ghersen and I wanted to climb DOM, one of the hardest routes on the face, named in memory of Dominique Radigue, who died climbing the south face of Aconcagua. The route requires ice to be climbable, and had not come into condition since the first ascent. In March we thought it might be ready, so we went up to the bivouac hut at the Col de la Fourche.

Sunrise revealed no ice on the opening pitches, and it was warming up fast, too warm for the higher waterfall sections even if we fought our way through the lower wall. We spotted what we figured to be a new line to the left, and because it terminated in rock, the warm weather would help. Our rack was anorexic: five cams, six nuts, two pins (an angle and a knifeblade), and two screws. We would have been cutting it close had DOM been in condition.

The opening pitches of our line contained difficult and awkward mixed climbing that ate the rack and yielded inadequate belays after long fights. The first real rock pitch was my lead; I don't climb rock at a high standard so I don't run it out too crazily. By the time I ran out of rope, which coincided with the first real ledge of the pitch, I'd run out of rack too. I was reduced to runners and screws. There were no horns to sling, and only 2 inches of ice for screws. I placed them both and tied them off. Obviously, it wasn't enough. The rock below was too hard to consider simul-climbing. I racked my brain for a solution.

My first partner, Andy Nock, had pounded into me the concept that the best alpinist may not be the best climber, but simply the most resourceful. I remembered his counsel as I shrugged off my pack and pulled out a spare ice-tool pick. The crack in front of me was perfect. I hammered the pick deep, never expecting to get it out. It was the sole piece of the belay with any value and might have to hold us both. Alain followed, and the rest of the pitches flowed beneath our hands and feet, as they can do when the weather is perfect and the route matches the team's ability and ambition. He and I didn't share much common cultural heritage so a clever route name was beyond us. It became the Ghersen-Twight: 700 meters, TD+, 90-degree ice, 5.10.

The east face of Mont Maudit, Mont Blanc Massif, on the Italian side of the range. The Ghersen-Twight route is at the extreme left edge of the photo. *Photo: © Mark Twight*

BIVOUACS

13

Alpine climbers agonize over bivouacs. Even after twenty years' experience, most alpinists still sweat over what to wear and what to sleep in, which stove to trust, which bivy system to use.

Deciding whether to bivouac on a route is the first crucial decision. Planned or unplanned, you'll need to decide sooner or later. My recommendation: Don't stop.

The Unplanned Bivouac

This is something I can do without. On every climb but one in which I've been taken by darkness on a day route, I've kept moving instead of sitting down. By planning to climb continuously instead of "sleeping," my pack is lighter and my head is much clearer throughout the day. I'd rather carry an extra headlamp battery and more water than a bivy sack, stove, and pad. Planning for a winter day route confirms the method's validity. Calculate the weight for the amount of food, insulation, and gas you'd need to stop comfortably for a 14-hour night. Then compare that to the weight of the extra headlamp battery already sitting in your pack.

Open your mind to moving at all hours, in all situations. Don't plan on stopping. Count on climbing through.

Objective danger—the threat of remaining at high altitude too long; the prospect of an incoming storm—is best dealt with by spending as little time in the danger zone as possible. Be fast, move constantly, sleep when safely down. Because movement is my ideal, I never sit down to wait out a storm and I never sleep when I could be climbing. I know that the less time my head is in the noose, the more likely it is I'll survive.

When racing the clock toward the end of the day, people rush. Tension mounts crazily and nerves buzz until it gets too dark to see. Once it does, all you can do is turn on the headlamp, relax, and slow down, because it's going to be a long night.

Climbing or descending through the night depends upon intimate knowledge of the mountain and the route. If you haven't done your homework and memorized the elements of the route, darkness usually will stop you. Routefinding at night is hard enough when you know what you're looking for. If you don't . . . just sit down, tie in, and suffer silently. Misery will instruct you to avoid that mistake in the future.

As a younger climber I rehearsed for unplanned bivouacs, but it didn't seem to do much good. When forced to bivy for real, knowing what's about to happen doesn't make it any less unpleasant. And as a friend of mine once said, "There's no point in practicing for a bad night's sleep." It comes down to carrying enough gear to survive while saving enough energy for climbing the next day, but not so much gear that a bivouac appears inviting. If you slept well, you weren't doing it right.

The Planned Bivouac

A planned bivouac operates in a different paradigm. Multiday routes demand recovery each night so the team can climb strongly the following days. The biggest enemy is fatigue, the thing that prompts stupid decisions, slows the team, and erodes the ability to deal with ballooning risk. Anyone can forgo food without ill effect, but prolonged sleep deprivation kills quickly.

The planned bivy requires meticulous consideration. For example, should the team carry a tent, or bivy sacks? Count on natural ledges or haul a portaledge? Take only one sleeping bag for both climbers? Every choice must be made with an eye toward maximum efficiency.

Use the following list of gear and concepts as you wrestle with decisions regarding spending a night in the open. Don't imagine a romantic night out; prepare for a battle. The gear is listed in order of importance.

Headlamps

Whether climbing through the night or stopping for rest when it gets dark, bring a headlamp. A decade ago lithium battery-powered headlamps won converts because the batteries lasted up to 20 hours without exhibiting any loss of power. On the downside, the light would click off without warning, and the 20-dollar batteries were no bargain.

In a crowded market one product has demonstrated superiority: the Petzl Zoom with a halogen bulb and the Arctic battery pouch. I discovered the Petzl headlamps on my first trip to Europe. I borrowed one after my lithium battery died, and I couldn't find replacements in France, Italy, or Switzerland. The Zoom uses a flat 4.5-volt alkaline battery costing around $8 each or a rechargeable battery. Go alkaline because they last longer. To keep the battery warm, wear the Arctic pouch inside your clothes next to your chest. Expect from 20 to 24 hours per alkaline battery with a normal bulb or about 8 hours with a halogen bulb.

For climbing or skiing at night, nothing beats halogen bulbs. Use standard bulbs for cooking, gearing up, and hiking. Carry a few extra bulbs in the battery pouch so you'll never be caught out.

Stoves

Leave the bivouac stove behind if your route is either totally dry and snowless or running with water. Dry routes demand that you carry liquid. If water's flowing, then stones are probably flying, too. Get the hell off the thing until it freezes. Upon returning, bring a stove to convert ice and snow into water. Carry lighters, lots of them. I stash one with the stove and others in various pockets of my shell, belay coat, and pack. No sense packing a stove you can't light.

After deciding to carry a stove, pick the right one for you. Some lightweight models burn cartridges of pressurized butane, or a propane/butane mixture, which, according to cartridge stove designer Todd Bibler, doesn't perform any better than straight butane. Other stoves burn everything from super-clean white gas to aviation fuel to dry-cleaning fluid.

I liked cartridge stoves for their convenience, the hanging windscreen/pot sets that work

well inside small tents, and, I once believed, their relatively light weight. Today I use an MSR stove that burns white gas. I use it in a tent. I hold it on my lap. I set it on a ledge. I constructed a hanging system for it and mastered the field maintenance these finicky stoves require. The choice hinged on a question of overall efficiency.

Cartridge stoves are simple to light, and several after-market manufacturers offer neat hanging sets to use in portaledges or bivy tents. They emit relatively benign fumes. Once the stove is hanging, one can doze off while the snow melts without fear of catastrophe beyond burning the pan or spilling the contents.

Still, all cartridge stoves require some kind of heat exchanger to keep the gas warm enough to maintain a gaseous state. Remember high school physics? Escaping pressurized gas induces a decrease in temperature, so the cartridge housing cools down; the gas itself cools off, becomes liquid, and no longer jets out of the cartridge. Add freezing air temperatures and you're doomed, although lower atmospheric pressure at high altitude helps counteract cartridge and gas cooling.

The solution is to make a closed-cell-foam sleeve to insulate the fuel cartridge. Leave the bottom open so you can "prime" a frozen cartridge with an open flame from a lighter or another stove. Then hammer a 24-inch length of copper tubing flat and bend it so it lays vertically down one side of the cartridge, across the bottom, and up the other side, terminating with the copper touching the stove's flame. This heat exchanger keeps the stove running in the coldest temperatures.

Warning No. 1: You'll melt a lot of liner gloves by accidentally touching the copper tube.

Warning No. 2: This is a dangerous practice. The stove manufacturers explicitly instruct users not to do it. The safety Nazis agree and obey. But virtually every good alpine climber I know who uses these stoves modifies and uses them in this way, and none of them have suffered an accident, yet. Maybe heating the cartridge in this way ensures that every last bit of gas burns out of the cartridge, reducing the risk of unused vapor leaking out and blowing up during the cartridge-changing procedure. I don't know. Consider the above as information, not a recommendation.

Cartridge stoves perform poorly where they are needed most, converting snow into boiling water. Prior to climbing Mount Hunter, Scott Backes and I tested our new cartridge stove/hanging system in Talkeetna, Alaska (elevation 300 feet). We refrigerated two 1.5-liter bottles of water overnight and then heated them up. With the cartridge stove, burning a propane/butane gas mix, the water took 18 minutes to boil. An MSR stove burning white gas did the same job in 8 minutes, not a surprise given the fact an MSR sounds like a blowtorch compared to a cartridge's gentle whisper. Admittedly the cartridge stove had a small burner head; larger ones available today may produce more heat. Also, the small cartridges had also been exposed to below-freezing temperatures all night, and we did not use a heat exchanger for the test.

A cartridge stove burns at minimum 125 milliliters of gas per person per day—at least 250 milliliters per 24 hours for a two-person team, or 500 milliliters and some extra for a two- to three-day route. Cartridges are available in 250- and 500-milliliter sizes; fuel efficiency can vary wildly, so test your brand and stick to it. The metal cartridges, empty or full, consume space and add weight to the pack, especially noticeable on a multiday route.

There is a risk of the rubber ball-seals or O-rings on the cartridges freezing solid and not sealing properly. Jeff Lowe and I lost a cartridge of fuel on the South Pillar of Nuptse in winter to this problem. Once the cartridge had been punctured and the seal failed, there was nothing to do but let it all go before we could heat up the seal to make it flexible again. We were destined to fail on the route anyway, but it was a hard lesson. If you blow a seal on an MSR bottle or pump, you won't lose all the gas; it's easy to bleed off the pressure and replace any part of the stove, even on a wall.

Although hanging stoves fueled by cartridges need little attention, the awful truth is that they require from 30 to 45 minutes to boil a liter of water from snow. That trans-

lates to between 3 and 5 hours spent awake each night, melting and waiting. An MSR stove requires attention, but it will produce 6 liters of boiling water in 1 hour. Then you can sleep.

With an MSR stove, plan on burning 8 ounces of gas per person per day—16 ounces per 24 hours for a two-person team, or one quart for a two- to three-day route, or two quarts for a four- to six-day route.

Whichever stove type you choose, experiment where results don't matter and record the boiling times and fuel consumption so you can plan your long nights out. Personally, I'll never use a cartridge stove on a route that matters. An MSR is the only stove that yields enough BTUs to produce enough water to stay hydrated during a 24- to 48-hour single-push effort.

Shovels

On any alpine route with snow where the team could stop, either to brew up or bivouac, bring a small aluminum shovel blade. You can use it to fashion a ledge, dig a cave to escape from the wind, serve as a stove platform, climb otherwise unclimbable snow features, etc. Buy one that fits over the end of an ice tool—curved shafts need not apply—so you won't

An MSR XGK is the only stove that yields enough BTUs to produce sufficient water to stay hydrated during a 24-to-48-hour single-push effort. Mark Twight on the North Buttress of Mount Hunter, Alaska. Photo: © Scott Backes

have to carry the handle. Buy aluminum. Lexan and plastic shovels won't move hard snow, and buckle when they hit ice. A good blade can serve as a deadman anchor in deep snow with properly attached slings or cord.

Sleeping Pads

When sitting or lying down in the snow or on hard rocks, a foam pad is the single most effective tool for fighting heat loss. In the mountains, climbers battle four types of heat loss.

Evaporative: When you sweat or as your clothes dry, you cool down.

Conductive: Heat leaves your body when it touches colder objects.

Convective: As cooler air moves over your body, it steals heat.

Radiant: Heat radiates into the sky.

Conductive and evaporative loss are the main worries. A good foam pad thwarts conductive loss better than sitting on the rope, and high-tech clothes go a long way toward stopping evaporative loss. A thoughtfully designed pack will include a removable foam pad. Find one that unfolds to make a square. When you're caught out by surprise and spend the evening sitting rather than lying down, the square shape is ideal. For the planned bivy, add that same square pad to your three-quarter-length sleeping pad to create a full-length insulating surface for sleeping.

I always use a sticky three-eighths-inch, closed-cell-foam sleeping pad—sticky so I don't slide around, closed cell so it doesn't compress. Shop around. Some foam resists compression better than others. Punch a hole near the edge, reinforce it with duct tape, and sling some perlon cord through the hole for clipping the pad on a precarious bivy ledge. It's not something you want to drop.

Inflatable pads are comfortable until they puncture. They will pop on hard routes because there's no safe place to carry them. Sharp objects are a constant threat. Jeff Lowe popped an inflatable pad on the South Pillar of Nuptse, John Bouchard popped his on Cerro Torre, and John Stoddard sliced his open on the north buttress of the Rooster Comb. Three partners have brought them on routes with me, and three partners popped them. Psychologically speaking, a popped pad weighs heavily on the soul. Some guys can shake it off, but I refuse to take the risk.

Bivy Sack, Tent, or Open Sky?

The body experiences a 30 to 40 percent reduction in respiration and circulation, with a concomitant heat loss, during sleep. Even the thinnest shelter can help compensate for that heat loss. The lightest effective shelter is a bivy sack. It'll keep you dry if it snows or there's spindrift. (If it rains, you should just go home.) A bivy sack reduces evaporative heat loss and keeps the wind from removing heat through convection. They can weigh as little as 7 ounces for "disposable" models or up to 28 ounces if equipped with lots of bells, whistles, and reinforcements.

Only waterproof/breathable fabric will do. While Gore-Tex is the most commonly used fabric, Todd Bibler makes bivy sacks from his proprietary Todd-Tex, which works on the same principal, while Wild Things uses a monolithic coating process on their Vapex fabric

to achieve waterproof/breathable performance. Some bivy sacks employ only waterproof/breathable fabric; others use the waterproof/breathable on top and coated fabric underneath. As long as you slide your foam pad inside the sack, you gain no advantage using the full waterproof/breathable model since the pad is impermeable anyway.

Several bivy sacks feature a pole system to keep the fabric off your face while sleeping. This works on flat ground, but not when sitting up on a ledge. Avoid the extra weight.

At high altitude or in cold conditions where wet snow is unlikely, a light bivy sack made from Gore Dryloft, or even silicone-impregnated breathable nylon, will save a lot of weight. These are less waterproof, but are more breathable and work fine in these conditions. Mont Bell used to make disposable Dryloft sacks weighing 7 ounces. Today the only commercially available option is the Outdoor Research Wintersack at 13 ounces.

A small bivy tent is the next step up in comfort and warmth. If it's uncomfortable and weighs less than 4 pounds, it's a bivy tent. Don't exceed a 4-pound limit. Only single-wall tents made from waterproof/breathable fabric can meet that criterion. Such a tent will measure roughly 72 inches by 48 inches and will "fit" two people. Sleep head to toe to avoid squeezing two sets of big climber shoulders across the 48 inches.

The tent should have a small tunnel vent opposite the door. When cooking, face each other with the stove in between. One person can breathe through the door and the other

Mark Twight digging a cave in the Canadian Rockies. Caves are very warm and quiet, but count on getting very wet while digging one. *Photo: © Barry Blanchard*

through the small vent. A bivy tent can forgo pole sleeves. The poles support the tent from the inside. In theory, a fellow could crawl into the tent, zip it shut, and then set it up.

A tent is much warmer than a bivy sack. There's more room for gear, egos, and cooking indoors when the wind is howling. If planning to wait out storms, choose the tent over the sack. The tent's disadvantages show up on a genuinely steep wall where sleeping options consist of either an existing rock ledge or a platform hacked out of a 50-degree ice slope. How many rock ledges will be large enough for the tent? Will ice cover any or all of the ledges? Photos from the ground certainly won't say. If there's a good chance I'll have to chop a ledge, I'll take a bivy sack. Chopping out a long, shallow platform for two people sleeping head to head takes far less energy than chopping out an 80- by 50-inch ledge for a tent. Compare two man-hours versus six to eight man-hours in hard blue ice.

In the right conditions a snow cave beats any sack or tent. The temperature in a correctly built and sealed cave never dips below freezing, which translates to carrying a lighter sleeping bag. Everyone gets soaking wet digging one, so synthetic insulation is a must. Count on about an hour per person for building a decent cave. Each two-person team will carry one small shovel blade between them on any ice and snow route, but to dig a quick cave, you'll need a larger size.

On continuously steep routes, climbers have used portaledges with some success. But a two-person portaledge with a tent weighs 12 pounds or more. Its absurd bulk dictates the style of movement. The extra weight requires hauling on pitches that might otherwise go classically. Slower movement may require fixing some pitches.

Answer these questions before bringing a portaledge: Is the terrain steep enough all the way to the summit? (The ledge will be useless once the wall kicks back.) Are you willing to carry the pig up and over the top, or will you just leave it as litter? What will you use for shelter once the ledge loses its utility?

The hardest routes of the future may require portaledges. But before we allow technology to determine how we climb, let's try to make ourselves equal to the task as climbers and people. For example, Michael Kennedy and Greg Child made an awesome commitment and succeeded on one of the finest routes in the world when they climbed the Wall of Shadows on Hunter. They fixed pitches, hauled a haul bag, and slept on a portaledge. Perhaps a repeat ascent can refine the style. If a team could climb sixteen pitches on the same route on their first day, they'd reach a decent bivy ledge. Thereafter the possibilities for chopping a ledge from the ice become more abundant. Someone willing to push the boat way out, someone who could climb really fast, might approach the wall in a different style. Such a task is for the future.

Sleeping Bags

On a multiday route where you want to sleep well enough to recover for the following days, a sleeping bag is essential, especially at high altitude. There are many options to consider, but really only one rational choice for each specific situation.

Insulation choice determines the weight-to-warmth ratio, durability, and resistance to moisture. While many styles of synthetic insulation exist, goose down is the gold standard for natural fills. Down is the most weight-efficient insulator available. A bag weighing as little as 1.5 pounds works to 20 degrees Fahrenheit. But the disadvantages of down erase its usefulness on most routes. Down loses virtually all insulating ability when wet. It's easy to soak a down bag if you're not paying attention every minute of every day, which is too much attention to dedicate to one piece of gear.

Some designs try to improve the down bag's chances in the wild, wet world of alpinism by protecting it with a Gore-Tex or Gore Dryloft shell. These shells offer protection from catastrophic soaking such as spilled soup or an unforeseen night in a snow cave. Sadly, a semipermeable shell reduces the bag's overall breathability, so moisture coming from your body or from wet clothes won't pass through the insulation quickly. The bag still wilts. A vapor-barrier liner (see next section) inside the bag will protect the down, but it prevents your clothes from drying. To sleep efficiently and without worry, use synthetic insulation.

The many forms of synthetic insulation won't absorb water, and they remain "warm when wet"—in quotes because there is no such thing. When wet, synthetics remain warmer than natural fibers, but they are by no means cozy. They have drawbacks. Synthetics are heavier than down for a given warmth, and they are not as compressible so they make a bulkier package. But they cost less, about half the price of a comparable down bag. Best of all for the exhausted climber, synthetics are virtually idiot-proof. The climber doesn't need to think about them or care for them.

Trying to differentiate between synthetics lands you in a quagmire of statistics and superlatives. When it comes to the action, though, only a few materials work in sleeping bags. Stay away from short-staple fibers. These filaments, while acting more like down than other man-made fibers, require stabilization to prevent them from clumping. The stabilizing scrims add weight to the product and don't contribute to warmth. Besides, of all the short-staple fibers my partners and I tested, none stood up to the abuses of stuffing, soaking, freezing, and washing as well as long, continuous fibers.

The old standard was a 3.5-pound Polarguard bag rated to 20 degrees Fahrenheit. I used one on the South Pillar of Nuptse in both spring and winter of 1986. Today's Polarguard 3D bags achieve equal warmth with a 12-ounce weight savings. A similar insulation called Exccloft electronically bonds short-staple fibers to a continuous long fiber. I used this to good effect in a 20-degree bag on Mount Hunter, but it didn't withstand repeated stuffing as well as the Polarguard 3D.

If you expect temperatures down to minus 20 degrees at night, is there any reason to carry a bag rated to minus 20 or colder? No. Climbers already carry insulation to stay warm during the day in their outer shells, pile clothes, and belay jacket. By sleeping in clothes at night, a lighter bag will suffice, and the clothes will dry out over the course of the evening. The total insulation load will contribute warmth all the time. Wear the belay coat over the shell and get into the bag. Upon waking there is no need to dress.

For a synthetic bag, find one with a simple breathable covering. A totally breathable shell doesn't hinder efficient moisture transport. To protect the bag from spindrift or water, put a bivy sack over it. The moisture evaporating through the sleeping bag will either pass through the bivy sack or condense and freeze on the inside of it. When that happens, turn the bivy sack inside out and shake it, or scrape the ice off with a gloved hand. It's much easier than wringing out a wet sleeping bag.

Both Gore-Tex fabric and Gore Dryloft are among the coverings available. As with down bags, while the shell increases the bag's warmth without adding significant weight, it limits vapor transmission and slows the drying of wet gear in the bag.

Vapor-barrier Liners

The genuine vapor-barrier liner is a complex issue to say the least. The advantages of the vapor-barrier liner are many, but first the theory. The vapor-barrier liner is an impermeable bag (or shirt, socks, or pants) worn close to the skin to stop evaporation. You can imagine how sweaty and gross this would be if your body didn't stop sweating once the humidity next to your skin reaches a certain level—but it does.

Stopping evaporation from your body through a sleeping bag radically increases the bag's heat efficiency. A vapor-barrier liner will generally increase a sleeping bag's advertised warmth rating by 20 degrees or more. This could allow a substantial savings of weight by permitting you to use a lighter bag. The vapor-barrier liner will eliminate the danger of moisture soaking your bag from within, which means the insulation in a bag covered by a Gore-Tex shell would probably remain dry through repeated bivouacs. And a vapor-barrier liner will keep you from losing as much fluid as usual, which translates into drinking less, thus melting less snow and carrying less fuel to do it.

However, the disadvantages outweigh the plusses. You cannot sleep wearing more than your long underwear, so the weight of your clothes won't work for you at night. Gloves and socks won't dry inside the bag at night, nor will boot liners. Worst of all, you will have to pee more frequently through the night, which interrupts sleep.

Most vapor-barrier liners are cut "efficiently," meaning low volume. They can feel a bit claustrophobic, especially when tightly sealed around your neck, which is the only way to stop evaporation out of the hole. For me, the concept works in shirts and socks, but I never sleep in a vapor-barrier liner.

Warmth

When bivouacking, I fill my two-liter Dromedary or CamelBak water bladder with very hot water and stuff it into my sleeping bag before retiring. Bingo! I've just increased the temperature differential between the inside and outside of my bag, and according to the laws of physics, this differential pushes any moisture out through the bag. Not only am I warmer instantly, meaning I can get away with a lighter bag, but my clothes dry out over the course of the night.

To maintain circulation to your feet, never sleep with your feet higher than your heart. To keep feet warm, always remove wet socks and put them against the skin of your torso. The socks won't dry out on your feet because the extremities don't produce enough heat. But you'll barely notice them on your torso, and they'll be dry by morning. Put dry socks or down socks on your feet.

Adding one Shake-n-Warm to each dry sock generates heat. Shake-n-Warms are packages of organic materials (iron, water, cellulose, vermiculite, activated carbon, and salt) that produce heat when exposed to the air. These amazing devices work for about 7 hours. Get a few extra hours out of them once they cool by kneading them with your fingers to expose unused crystals to air.

One beautiful thing about a bivy tent is that you virtually sleep on top of your partner so both of you need less insulation to stay warm. If it gets too cold, however, partners should not hesitate to hug each other for warmth, or to sleep spoon-fashion if it helps. Do whatever it takes to get a little rest so you won't be wasted the next morning.

The Pee Bottle

To keep your bladder from repeatedly ruining an otherwise decent sleep, pee into a bottle while remaining in your sleeping bag. Peeing "in" and then pouring the bottle out doesn't catapult you into full wakefulness; crawling out of the bag and tent every time the body remembers it's well hydrated will.

Use a wide-mouth bottle with a good seal on it. Cap the thing to avoid accidental spills. This bottle must hold at least one liter. Mark the bottle clearly with a skull and crossbones so no one confuses it with a beverage, although urine won't hurt you a bit. The weight-conscious will share one bottle. Etiquette demands that one empty the bottle and let it cool off before handing it over to your partner.

This whole action is definitely friendlier to males than females. Women need to carry an adapter. Even with it they won't be able to pee lying down with confidence. However, kneeling to pee in a tent beats having to go outside to squat.

Sleeping Pills

Proper sleep is essential on a multiday climb. Sleep deprivation kills. On stressful routes, and all meaningful ones are, it may be impossible to fall asleep or remain asleep. Sleeping pills can have unwanted side effects, so choosing a depressant wisely is essential. Halcyon induces sleep and comes doctor-recommended for climbers because it is not a respiratory depressant. Also, it doesn't produce much of a hangover with the proper dose. However, a few chronic users have come unglued and killed their loved ones. Calms Forte is a homeopathic remedy for insomnia, but it causes sluggishness the morning after.

The captain of the modern sleep-inducing team these days is melatonin, a hormone sold over the counter in health food stores. One to three milligrams under the tongue goes straight into the bloodstream. (Experiment with dosage at home.) It metabolizes quickly and induces sleep gently. If you must react in the night (to an avalanche, a sick partner, or whatever), you can shake it off easily. Most people experience no morning hangover using dosages of less than four or five milligrams. Daily use of melatonin for months on end slowed reaction times in test subjects, especially athletes, but short-term use appears safe.

To illustrate the dangers of sleeping pills in heavy doses, Michael Kennedy told me a story about his route on the northeast face of Ama Dablam, undertaken with Carlos Buhler

in 1985. Several bivouacs up the climb, Carlos, who was using Halcyon, rolled over to pee in his bottle, but fell back to sleep before capping it. Hydrated as he was, it turned into quite a mess, for both him and Michael.

Climbers who train with hemispheric synchronization tools can learn to induce a sleeping state without herbs or drugs in times of stress. (See "Brain Synchronization" in Chapter 2.)

Tying In

OK, you're stopped, you're insulated and prepared to sleep. How are you going to stay on the ledge if you toss and turn?

Tying in isn't simple because little of the gear on the market is made for technical use. Tents and bivy sacks need modification. Staying tied in to a tent requires snaking the rope out the door to the anchors or modifying the tent by sewing a quickdraw through a floor seam or the roof. Seam-seal generously.

While sitting down, brewing up, and getting ready to sleep or move, stay tied in by clipping an ascender or prusik to the rope fixed above. This will allow movement around the bivy. For sleeping, however, don't trust anything other than a knot. On some bivvies, you'll have to tie in tight to eliminate the chance of sliding off a sloping ledge or because the rope alone keeps you on the ledge.

If you have anchors, use them, and make sure all your gear is clipped, too. I met a guy in the Alps who was famous for having dropped his boot from a bivy on the north face of Les Droites in winter. Another fellow did the same thing off Meru Peak in the Garwhal of India. Happily, both climbers had plenty of extra socks, but the losses led to retreat and failure.

Final Details

When a bivy is a possibility, the environment determines how much gear to bring. Obviously Alaska demands more than the Alps, the Himalayas more than the Andes. Learn to think conceptually about the problems involved in climbing the route. Perhaps it will be faster and more efficient to take breaks to rest, eat, and hydrate whenever necessary, without ever stopping to sleep.

On the other hand, there may be no way in hell to do the route without sleeping on it. If that's the case, live with the minimum. Do not pursue comfort. Aim for success only. On a one-bivy route, don't plan on a good night's sleep. Never take a cup and a bowl. The water bottle and the pan for the stove will do. Each climber may carry a spoon—that's it. Forget your manners. Forget the Ten Essentials. No matter how long the intended route, carry only the genuinely essential.

Don't forget to bring a watch. You'll need it to wake up on time, and also to play "the watch game" during bivvies. Here's how to play. One guy asks, "How long do you think it has been?" The other climber answers. The answer is always wrong.

Nancy Feagin and Mark Twight preparing for a bad night on a bad (small) ledge. Mont Blanc Massif, France. Photo: © James Martin

ORDEAL ON EVEREST

In October 1988, when Barry Blanchard and I attempted a new route on Everest, the climb followed a system of gullies between the northeast ridge and the north ridge. We carried no ropes, fixed none, and used no supplementary oxygen. We proposed climbing through the night, using motion to stay warm, then bivouacking and rehydrating during the day when the sun would make stopping comfortable.

On our first two attempts, which ended at 23,000 feet and 24,500 feet due to cold feet and pulmonary edema, respectively, we didn't carry sleeping bags or a tent. By our third attempt, temperatures plunged and the forecast predicted wind, so we compromised by taking a 4-pound bivy tent and one foam pad.

We left our advanced base camp at 21,000 feet at 10 P.M. and climbed to 25,000 feet by 7 A.M., where we stopped, pitched the "coffin," and brewed up for 6 hours—toasty in the tent from the sun beating down and our stove roaring, though temperatures outside were about 10 degrees Fahrenheit. At 5 P.M. we reached 26,500 feet, where Barry began exhibiting signs of cerebral edema. We spoke by radio with a doctor, who insisted on descent.

Our route was too steep to downclimb, and we had no rope for rappels. Barry chased 10 milligrams of dexamethasone (a steroid that reduces cranial swelling) with two quarts of liquid. We traversed easy terrain to the north ridge. At the north col we poached a bottle of oxygen from another team, and Barry sprinted down their fixed ropes to relative safety and full recovery.

For our fourth attempt we switched to an easier route, the line Messner soloed. It required less commitment, but we were the only two climbers remaining on the north side of the mountain. The colder temperatures of late October compelled us to take the tent, two pads, and one sleeping bag. Fifty hours after leaving base camp at 15,800 feet, we turned back at 27,500 feet. I was afraid of losing hands and feet I could no longer feel, and Barry wasn't willing to die for the summit.

Barry Blanchard at 25,000 feet while attempting a new route on the north face of the northeast ridge of Mount Everest. A few hours after this was taken, Barry was almost overcome by cerebral edema, forcing us to traverse to the north ridge (visible in background) and descend to the North Col, where we poached a bottle of oxygen from a team camped there and then rapped their fixed lines back to relative safety. *Photo: © Mark Twight*

A LOWE NIGHT

I have suffered through only one unplanned bivouac in my entire climbing career, and I once maintained it was not my fault. Actually, every climber involved in an unforeseen bivouac shares equal blame for the event. You choose your partner knowing his capabilities, and he does the same with you. One may be faster than the other, but partners are bound together by the rope for better and for worse.

Now more than a decade after the unplanned bivy I forgive my partner for the night out. We were on the Bonatti Route on the east face of the Grand Capucin above Chamonix. My partner, Jeff Lowe, wanted to climb it free. I wanted to climb with him, and although I preferred ice to rock, conditions were against me. Rock climbing we went.

Some guys had done the route free at about 5.12a/b, and Jeff figured he could work it out. Even though I didn't climb very fast, I was on a speed trip at the time, mostly doing day routes, and I was fairly "ethics free," meaning I'd pull on gear if it would make the route go quicker. I didn't care about free climbing.

The crux took Jeff over 3 hours to do free, with many retreats to rest without hanging on gear and only one fall. I knew I was watching an impressive trad effort, but I couldn't resist stealing glances at my watch. When my turn came, I pulled through on the quickdraws and fixed pins, then swung the lead up a 40-meter-long corner where I could clip, pull, lock off, and reach the next piton without using aiders. I still wasn't fast enough, and nightfall caught us one pitch below the summit. We hadn't learned enough about the terrain to climb through the night. Although we had headlamps, we sat down to suffer.

It was late September, and we were sitting still at around 13,000 feet. I hadn't foreseen a night out so I was wearing tights, a tank top, and a fleece pullover. Jeff had about the same. We flipped for it: He got to sit on the ropes; I got to put my feet in the pack. It was cold and windy and neither of us slept. We told stories and rubbed our limbs.

Happily, the thing was east-facing, so the sun hit us early. We split, astonished and irritated by the easy third-class terrain but later mollified by the fact that the rap anchors were difficult to find. Walking back I noted how one night out wasted me. I felt relieved that I only needed to descend. Later I spent many nights on mountains with Jeff but none as "memorable" as that first bivy on the Grand Cap.

The Grand Capucin—its east face lit by the morning sun—Chamonix, France. *Photo: © Mark Twight*

A 43-HOUR-DAY: MOUNT HUNTER: MAY 17–19, 1994

We climbed 2,500 vertical feet and started chopping our ledge at 7 P.M. We chopped it long and shallow, just enough for the two of us to sleep head to head in our bivy sacks. We didn't bring a tent. We set the MSR stove on our shovel blade, melted water, and changed into dry socks. The socks and some delicious halva were our luxuries. We had calculated everything in terms of speed and efficiency. Our bivy sacks weighed 7 ounces each, so fragile we knew we'd throw them away after this route. Our packs, without the rope and rack, weighed 27 pounds each when we started up the route, absolutely naked for the Alaska Range.

We didn't start climbing until 10 A.M. the next day, preferring to spend the extra hours resting and replacing the liquid and calories we had burned. Staying strong was more important than getting an early start. Once moving, we climbed as fast as possible, simul-climbing terrain where we felt competent. The time saved was well worth the risk.

By sundown we climbed through the fourth and final rock band. The temperature started dropping, and we thought about the storm forecast for the following afternoon. It was a race, and we felt continuous movement was safer than sleep. We climbed through the night, watching dumbly as the carabiners froze shut and cores froze inside the ice screws. There was nothing to do about the gear, so we concentrated on keeping our toes warm and relaxing our calves so they wouldn't explode on the 55-degree rock-hard ice. We moved steadily rather than quickly.

At 5 A.M. we tunneled through the cornice at the top of the North Buttress of Mount Hunter, out of the shadows and into the sun. We shoveled out a platform, got in our sleeping bags, and started brewing up, agreeing to stay until we had each consumed three liters of Cytomax and eaten breakfast as well as the dinner we had deferred the previous night.

By 9 A.M. we were simul-climbing across the top of the buttress, through a couple of seracs, one of which kicked up to about 80 degrees. We didn't belay, understanding full well a fall would kill us both, but we knew we had transcended the making of mistakes. Trust was total.

Just 150 feet below the summit we looked at each other and with few words skirted the left side. The summit rose between us and the west ridge descent route, but standing on the summit wasn't necessary for either of us. We were racing the clock and wanted to get as far down as possible before the storm hit. Summiting would have cost us time.

Bad weather caught us halfway down the west ridge, and whiteout conditions stopped us temporarily. Scott fell in five crevasses, once in over his head. I punched through into

Jeff Lowe free climbing on the east face of the Grand Capucin, Chamonix, France. Photo: © Mark Twight

three but never past the waist. At an impasse, we called Steve Mascioli on our walkie-talkie to ask for directions. He'd done the route and quickly sorted out where we were. Following his directions, we rappelled and traversed toward the northwest basin.

The basin is a deadly place, threatened on three sides by big seracs. Above the seracs we rested for twenty minutes, ate some GU, and drank the last of our water. Our plan was simple: Run, don't walk. For that we needed to rest and eat. We sprinted through the danger zone in just over twenty minutes, not enough time for anything to fall on us. Dusk came again. We staggered under the effects of the previous sleepless night, but there was nothing to do except to press on.

Out on the Kahiltna Glacier I saw four black dots moving toward us, and within half an hour we met Michael Kennedy, Greg Child, Joe Josephson, and Ken Wiley. They had gone up to our cache below the North Buttress to pick up our skis and bring them to us. It meant we wouldn't have to wallow the last miles back to base camp. They plied us with hot tea, snacks, and much-needed moral support. At camp a huge meal awaited us. We drank some wine, ate incredible spaghetti, and finally sank into oblivion after battling for 43 hours straight.

Scott Backes and Mark Twight in the middle of the 43-hour day, seen here below the west ridge of Mount Hunter after being on the move for 39 hours. *Photo: © Michael Kennedy*

going DOWN

14

Nothing grinds on a climbing team more than trying to descend safely. Exhausted, impatient, and often battling bad weather while trying to decode unfamiliar terrain, climbers often make fatal errors. Descending is a time for discipline.

Psychologically, descending can be the most demanding aspect of alpine climbing and one of the most dangerous. Climbers train and plan for a difficult climb, but most devote an inordinate amount of energy to going up, and little to the descent or retreat. Think about any climb in toto from safe haven to safe haven. Planning for the descent, in any conditions, is essential.

Consider how the route will affect the mind and body. If the route will stretch the team's limits, then count on being exhausted and mentally fried. Is this any condition in which to undertake a complicated and dangerous descent or a traverse of the mountain? Sometimes it's part of the package.

The west ridge of Mount Hunter is a horrific descent route. As a climb it earns an Alaskan Grade of 3 +, featuring extensive cornicing and ice climbing up to 70 degrees. It rises 8,000 vertical feet in five miles. If the ascent route of Hunter involves an Alaskan Grade 6—such as the North Buttress or southeast spur, which require from four to fourteen days to complete—the climbers must approach descending the long, involved, and technical west ridge with discipline.

After a week or so on the mountain, the brain goes on life support. Unanticipated conditions, foul weather, routefinding difficulty, evil snow conditions, avalanche danger, lack of food and fuel, dropped gear, lost goggles, and the ever-increasing effort required to move at all exponentially increase the problems one faces in the best-case scenario. Plan on being wasted. Plan on inadequate food and fuel. Plan on losing some gear. If these conditions are virtually guaranteed, success and survival depend on training, psychological preparation, and experience.

Although training for a bad night's sleep appears foolish, knowing how one responds to exhaustion and lack of food is useful. Try this exercise. Continue a regular training program over a period of 48 hours without eating and with only minimal water intake while sleeping normally. On the morning of the third day go climbing all day on something long and easy. Note how difficult every little bit of uphill becomes, how every decision takes twice the usual time, and how coordination suffers. This reflects how one feels after hanging it out on a hard route. Train for it. Address it in the planning stage.

Technical preparation may involve marking compass bearings on the map at points where changes in direction must be made. (Bring a compass.) Indicate approximate altitudes where a rappel may be required or where you need to start looking for the entrance to a couloir. (Carry an altimeter.) Use the altitude alarm function on your high-tech altimeter watch. Do not trust your memory, trust notes. If planning to descend the ascent route, do not expect your tracks to show the way down. If the terrain is convoluted—and

all terrain *is*, once it gets dark—a Global Positioning System unit will come in very handy. GPS units work for navigating in a total whiteout, useful for getting off Denali or a similar peak provided you log key waypoints into the system during the ascent.

Downclimbing

Downclimbing is both the best and the worst way to descend. If the terrain allows it, downclimbing is much, much faster than rappelling because one never stops moving and thus loses no time searching for a crack in the rock or thick patch of ice for establishing an anchor. Both climbers can move at the same time. A competent climber can descend an incredible amount of altitude in a very sort time.

Safe downclimbing depends on technical ability and psychological state. Practice it whenever possible in the mountains. There are no tricks or mysteries. Downclimbing simply reverses climbing motions. However, routefinding becomes more problematic, especially at night. The difference between a superb and an average alpinist often consists of the ability to downclimb quickly and efficiently.

Rappelling

More climbers are killed descending than ascending. More climbers are killed rappelling than downclimbing. Rappelling is arguably the most dangerous aspect of alpine climbing because the climber depends on the anchor 100 percent. Many anchors are hand-placed, often in a suspect medium (loose rock or bad ice). Pay attention. Never consider this activity "fun."

Rappel-station etiquette

After deciding to rappel, set an anchor (see the details later in this chapter). Use a daisy chain girth-hitched to your harness for clipping into the anchor. Call the daisy chain by its real name—a chicken sling—which implies that the climber isn't brave enough to just stand there holding the anchor or the ropes while waiting to rappel. All it takes is one falling rock to ruin your day; a small one will do. (See "Slings" in Chapter 9 for details on the chicken sling.) Without the chicken sling, you'll have to poach a sling from the rack, reducing by one the number of anchors or equalizing slings.

This anchor will be the sole point of attachment and everyone may be hanging or partially hanging, so a locking carabiner on the chicken sling makes sense. Two reversed carabiners will suffice if a locker isn't available, but they are more difficult to manipulate with gloves on, take up more space at the "power point" of an equalized anchor, and are less reliable.

One law of rap station manners defies normal safety procedures. If you're certain you can downclimb, even if difficult, unclip from the anchor while others are rappelling. Then

Michel Fauquet rapping from a natural ice feature on the south face of Khan Tengri, Tien Shan range, Kazhakstan. We have no idea how this icicle got here. *Photo: © Mark Twight*

if the anchor fails, it won't drag you down with it. If it's impossible to downclimb and you cannot climb back up and descend another way, remain clipped to the station while others rappel. If the anchor fails, you will die quickly, which is better than slowly freezing to death or dying from renal failure once you dehydrate.

Rappel anchor rules and practice

To stay alive, follow the rules. Ideally, back up everything, and don't rappel off of a single piece. Equalize the components of the anchor system. Use a knot at the power point of the equalized anchor to eliminate the possibility of one piece being shock-loaded after another piece fails, as would happen if a sliding power point was used. (See the information on how to equalize anchors in Chapter 12, Going Up.)

Recognize that rapping off multipiece anchors will consume the entire rack long before the ground is reached. Thus, despite all warnings about the very real dangers, in practice one must rap off single pieces when necessary. Ninety-five percent of my rappel anchors have been single pieces.

Here's one way to consider doing it. After placing a single piece to serve as the primary anchor, back it up with one or more pieces. Use a shock-absorbing quickdraw to clip the backup anchor to the rappel ropes, but don't allow the backup to be weighted. It prevents total system failure should the primary anchor fail. If the primary piece pulls, the shock-absorbing sling will limit the impact force on the backup anchor to 500 pounds so it will probably hold, although nothing is certain.

Now test the primary anchor before relying on it 100 percent by persuading the heaviest climber to rappel while the anchor stays backed up. If there is no difference in weight between climbers, the first guy down can carry the heavier pack or both packs. The test driver should bounce on the ropes after rappelling a short distance. The shock-loading will test the piece with greater force than the second, lighter climber can generate. If the primary piece holds, the second may calculate the risk of removing the backup pieces and then rap off the single-piece primary anchor. Whatever the last climber down decides, it is ultimately that person's own choice. Criticism is out of bounds if he leaves the backup intact.

Anchor tricks

There are few hard and fast rules to building rappel anchors, as long as the pieces are solid. Configuration is limited only by the imagination. People tend to leave the least expensive pieces behind. Some days the weather will be good, time plentiful, and the team can indulge in a search for the best value-for-the-money anchor. Other times, nightfall and an approaching storm will render rapping off a 70-dollar cam attractive.

Be creative when searching for anchors. Use the terrain when possible. Sling horns, tie

The heaviest climber rappels first to test the anchor while the back-up piece is in place. The first one down may also carry the heavier pack or both packs. Nancy Feagin and Mark Twight rapping off the Aiguille du Midi, Chamonix, France. Photo: © James Martin

off natural chockstones, find the optimum bottleneck for placing a nut, leave pitons (they're not cheap, but they do give feedback regarding the quality of the placement that a cam never offers), make threads or bollards in the ice (described below), do whatever it takes while remaining safe and maintaining speed.

Carry sling material to avoid sacrificing lightweight and expensive sewn Spectra slings off the rack. Six-millimeter suffices for most rappelling. Cheaper and lighter yet, pull the core out of your old 9-millimeter or 11-millimeter ropes, and use the sheath as sling material for rap anchors. Double it if concerned about strength. Some people precut the sling material to 6 or 8 feet, lengths that work in most situations. Ideally, leave the material intact, and carry a knife hanging from the rack to cut it to the right size for each anchor.

Whatever you do, leave behind the least gear possible, preserving the maximum amount for the balance of the descent. Remain open to leaving expensive pieces when necessary. Do not assume silly, avoidable risks in order to save a few dollars. If rapping the ascent route with a good topo, you will have enough information to predict how many raps will be required and what stations are in place. However, do not count on finding existing anchors, as ice and snow cover varies from season to season.

If rapping a first-ascent route, base your assessment of the number of anchors needed on the height of the route, the type of rock (granite offers more horns and flakes than limestone), and the type of terrain. When plenty of ice covers the route, count on a free ride down by rapping off ice threads.

Ice threads

Ice threads (Abalakov threads) are lightweight rappel anchors created in hard ice. Tests conducted at the University of Calgary, Canada, found that in a correctly crafted Abalakov in dry, cold ice, a 7-millimeter rappel sling breaks at a force of 1,500 to 2,000 kilograms before the ice fails. Similar tests in wet ice, with a large content of actual liquid, broke the ice around the anchor at approximately 300 kilograms. The system is designed for use as a rappel anchor, not as a primary belay point, and should be backed up with an ice screw and tested before relying on it. If the anchor tests OK, you can remove the screw and take it with you.

Here's what you'll need for creating an ice-thread rappel anchor: Two ice screws, each 17 to 21 centimeters long (though you can make an ice thread using only one screw); 1 meter of 6- or 7-millimeter perlon cord or eleven-sixteenths sling material; and one thread hook to feed and retrieve the cord. Several companies make hooks, although a coat hanger works just as well. The cable of a wired nut works in a pinch. The screws and the hook are just tools; the only thing you'll leave behind when you rappel is the piece of cord.

After selecting your spot and clearing away any rotten ice, place the first screw 45 degrees off perpendicular in the ice. Place the second screw at a 90-degree angle to the first, to form a rough V shape. The first screw may be backed out several turns, but left in place to serve as a "sighting line" for the second screw. When the two screws meet, remove them and blow out any powdered ice obstructing the tunnel. (If they don't meet, choose another site at least one meter from the first and start over.)

Now insert one end of the cord in one hole and the thread hook into the other. The end of the cord should be cut and melted for best penetration, although frayed ends are easier to hook. Hook the end of the cord, coax it around the corner inside the tunnel, and pull it out the other hole. Tie the cord ends together around the rappel rope with an overhand, double fisherman's, or water knot. Slide the knot out of the way of the rappel ropes. Depending on the temperature and exposure to sun of the site, the threaded tunnel will last anywhere from ten minutes to the entire winter season.

Although wet ice offers far less integrity, threads work in this soft ice with acceptable security. With wet ice use only the longest screws for excavation so the holes are as deep as possible, increasing their strength and life expectancy. For maximum security, make two or more threaded Vs, with equalizing slings between them.

Some may argue for use of the bollard as a practical and inexpensive anchor in ice. Since the bollard is basically a mound or broad pillar created by trenching around it, the bollard requires nothing more than an ice tool to make. The rappel sling is then looped over the bollard. However, they are physically brutal to construct in ice, and tired climbers tend to quit cutting before making the groove around the mushroom-shaped feature deep enough for a safe rappel.

Bollards have a place as rappel anchors in snow where a thread won't hold, a picket will pull, or you're not willing to leave behind a helmet or shovel blade as a deadman anchor. In soft snow, where you can't downclimb (as in passing the overhanging lip of a bergschrund), cutting a bollard makes sense. Learn how to make them. (You'll find a clear description in *Mountaineering: The Freedom of the Hills,* see Appendix 2, Suggested Reading.) If in doubt about the integrity of the snow, make the bollard bigger.

Rope management

When tying the two rappel ropes together, one knot jams less frequently than all others: the overhand knot. Single and double fisherman's knots and figure-8 knots are strong, but

When making an Abalakov "ice thread," once the two holes drilled by ice screws meet, use a thread hook or coat hanger to retrieve the cord and feed it through the V. Then tie the ends around one strand of the rappel rope. Back up any ice thread and test it before fully committing to it. *Photo: © James Martin*

they tend to jam in cracks. The ubiquitous overhand knot, however, also strong and UIAA approved, rarely jams because it tends to face outward when under a load, which prevents it from sneaking into cracks. Simply take both rope ends in one hand and make an overhand knot in both ropes simultaneously. Under a load the knot self-tightens. Be aware that it's tougher to untie after loading compared with a figure-8 knot.

Tossing the rappel ropes down the cliff without their hanging up is an art. The best advice: Never throw the whole thing at the same time. Starting from the anchor or from the ends, make two separate coils and throw each individually. Some climbers prefer to throw the middle coil first while retaining control of the ends, but that tactic prevents throwing the rope far, since the ends of the ropes remain in your hands. Instead, throw the ends of the rope—knotted together to keep you from rapping off the end—as far away from the face as possible. Once the rope uncoils and hangs, feed the remainder without throwing it. The weight of the rope below will pull the rest of the rope down smoothly.

A knot in the end of the ropes won't always stop an uncontrolled descent. The knot can blast right through the rappel device. It's safer to tie in to the ends of the rope. This technique maintains control of the ropes better than tossing them.

By using a prusik sling, you can safeguard yourself against loss of control in case you're hit by a stone or pass out from fatigue while rappelling. After clipping into the rappel descender, unclip the prusik sling from your harness (always carry one there to permit you to get out of the belay system in case your partner falls) and clip it to your strong-side leg loop with a carabiner. Wrap it two or three times around the rappel ropes below the descender and clip it back into the carabiner. While rappelling, grip the prusik knot loosely to keep it from jamming on the main ropes as you descend. Letting go of the knot causes the prusik to grip the rope, allowing you to stop and hang, hands free, to untangle the ropes, build the next station, or find the way. If you lose control, the prusik knot will automatically lock.

Never toss the entire rope all at once before rappelling. Throw the ends and half of the coils, then let the rope's weight feed the rest of it through your hands. Nancy Feagin and Mark Twight above Chamonix. Photo: © James Martin

Keeping control of the ropes is vital in windy conditions. Beware of tossing the ropes to the fury of the wind only to have them hang up on a flake, requiring climbing to recover them or hanging them up irretrievably. You can clip a pack to the end of the rappel ropes in order to weight them and lower the pack down. This requires relatively steep terrain, and the first climber down must then fight to feed rope through the descender because of tension from the weight of the pack below.

The most reliable way to control the ropes is for one climber to lower the other. The climber's weight on the ropes prevents the wind from snatching them. If communication could be difficult, the first climber can be lowered on a single rope while using the second rope to communicate through a series of previously arranged tugging commands (two tugs means stop, three means resume lowering, etc.).

As soon as the first climber down sets up a new anchor, the rappel ropes must be attached to it. This ensures that the ropes stay in control, unaffected by wind, and offers some hope that the second won't ground out if the anchor above fails as he raps off it.

It's imperative that the first climber test-pull the ropes before the second starts rappelling. The test will identify the friction points and indicate how to arrange the ropes to make them pull easier. This is the last chance the team will have to make changes to the rappel anchor easily or to modify how the ropes hang.

As the second descends, the first should keep hands lightly on the ropes, ready in case the rappeller loses control of the descent. Pulling on the ropes from below will jam the second's descender and hold him in place. If the second is knocked unconscious, the climber below can regulate his descent by judiciously applying tension to the ropes. This presupposes terrain steep enough so that the victim will not hang up.

If you rappelled in windy conditions on one fat rope (10 or 10.5 millimeters) and one thin rope (6 or 7 millimeters), always pull on the thin rope. The thin rope will be harder to grip, and you'll be fighting the friction of the fat rope, but the wind will affect the fat rope less as it falls. In calm conditions, you can take the easier way, pulling instead on the fat rope.

In the unfortunate but not uncommon event of a hung rappel rope, do not act too hastily. If in control of both ends, try to untwist them if they appear to be wound around each other. If the strand you are pulling stops moving, try pulling on the other strand to unwedge it. Flip the ropes to send a loop of slack up them in hopes of flipping them over a horn or out of a crack. Try the same with a loop of slack even if you only have one end. If all this fails, use a jumar to get a better grip on the rope, clip into it, and use body weight to pull. Try applying the weight of both climbers. If the rope dislodges suddenly, duck for cover, as the rope may pull off some loose rock.

Attempt to climb back up to recover the rope only as a last resort. It will be completely obvious when the time comes to follow this course of action. Climb back up placing gear while being belayed, even if it is on just one strand of a Half or Twin rope. A belay on a rope that may fail is better than no belay at all. This situation probably won't develop in daylight, so practice by headlamp.

ALONE ON THE CHARMOZ

On my birthday in 1984, I decided to treat myself to a last big route for the season. I'd just spent two weeks furiously soloing routes during the best ice conditions I have ever seen in Chamonix. My knuckles were permanently bruised, my hands shaped into the curve of an ice-tool shaft by the swelling. But the month-long high pressure I had enjoyed was predicted to move on within the next two days. I wanted to take advantage of what might be the last good weather of the year.

I chose the north face of the Grands Charmoz with the Heckmair-Kroner Direct Finish. The length and difficulty matched my desire and ability, and the wall was quite beautiful, with easy access from the Montenvers train. I knew the route by heart from having stared at it so often, but I needed some information about the descent. Since I spoke no French at the time, my sources were limited. I happened to run into expatriate Brit Jules Mills, who'd done the route, on Rue Paccard after buying groceries. He claimed it had an easy, obvious descent. "Just look over the ridge and you'll see a couloir. Drop into it, make a couple of raps, and it'll all become clear."

Early the next morning I started climbing, linking narrow runnels together to reach the 50-degree snowfield that divides the two steep sections of the face. I was climbing quite fast, but the approaching storm was moving faster, 12 to 24 hours ahead of schedule. It caught me on steep ice a couple of hundred feet below the summit ridge.

The ice at my feet peeled off the rock and one tool ripped, leaving me hanging by the other. Once I reestablished myself on lower-angled ice, fear overruled rational thought, and my mind narrowed down to a beam tightly focused on getting down. I sped to the ridge crest enveloped by clouds and blowing snow. From the crest I glimpsed a couloir through the murk and convinced myself it was the couloir I wanted.

I downclimbed into it. The clouds obscured all reference points, but it didn't matter because fight-or-flight pointed down. When I couldn't downclimb, I played for the highest stakes by rapping off single pieces to preserve the remains of my puny rack. I had brought a 50-meter, 7-millimeter rope on the climb, plus ten slings, six wired nuts, four pitons, one ice screw, and a No. 2 Friend.

After descending more than a thousand feet with no friendly ground in sight, I concluded I had taken the wrong gully. Night fell. The spindrift avalanches grew bigger but ran with enough regularity to predict respites. I sped from one sheltered stance to the next. Another 1,800 feet of descent brought me to within sight of a hut that was marked on my

The north face of the Grands Charmoz above the Mer de Glace, Chamonix, France. Seen in summer. *Photo: © Mark Twight*

map. I discovered that by not following the summit ridge to the actual top of the Charmoz, I had missed the west-facing descent gully completely and dropped down the massive east face instead.

Using markers painted on the slabs and boulders, I made my way down to the Mer de Glace where, still in a whiteout, I used the echo of my own shouts to find the big rock wall below the Montenvers train station. I had missed the last train down, of course, but the long, lonely hike home gave me plenty of time to appreciate what I had just survived.

Now every time I ski down the Vallée Blanche or find myself with a view of the east face of the Grepon-Charmoz massif, I marvel at my own folly and luck. I didn't deserve to get away with such inattention. To this day I have never heard of anyone descending this face, in storm or otherwise.

ANNAPURNA EPIC

In October 1992, Jean-Christophe Lafaille and Pierre Beghin attempted a new route on the enormous south face of Annapurna (8,091 meters). After three days of hard climbing, night caught them out at 7,300 meters as they searched for a ledge visible in the photos. Instead, they found a 70-degree slope of dense, black ice. They couldn't chop a platform for the tent and had to bivouac hanging in their harnesses. Unable to fire up the stove because of the wind, the night trudged by slowly, foodless and bitter.

The next morning they climbed to within 150 meters of the easy terrain. But a storm developed, and spindrift stopped further ascent. They headed down. Wasted and slightly out of control, the pair took huge risks on every rappel. At one point Pierre was willing to rap off a single tied-off ice screw, but Jean-Christophe insisted on hammering in one of his tools to back it up.

Two rappels lower, Pierre set the anchor that would allow them to reach lower-angled terrain and arranged the gear over his shoulder. Holstering both ax and hammer was too complicated, and, annoyed, he handed his ax down to Jean-Christophe, who was standing on a small ledge, out of reach of the anchor. His years of experience muddled by fatigue, the confusion of the storm, and the need to get down quickly, Pierre leaned back on a single anchor without any backup. It failed, and he fell 1,500 meters to his death, taking both ropes and the rack with him.

Jean-Christophe watched, sickened, but certain that Pierre could stop himself. "Even though it was so steep, I believed he would self-arrest," Jean-Christophe says. "I won't ever forget thinking that." Suddenly Jean-Christophe was alone on one of the biggest alpine walls in the world with nothing but his nearly empty pack, clothes, and a pair of ice tools, two carabiners, and a sling.

He recognized it would be impossible to go up. He downclimbed through relatively difficult mixed terrain to their last bivouac and 20 meters of rope they had left at 7,000 meters. He spent 48 hours cowering while the storm blew itself out. During intermittent clearings he retreated, using a combination of downclimbing and short rappels. With the 20 meters of rope, he rapped off whatever anchors he could fashion. The tent poles went first, two sections at a time, hammered in as far as they would go.

His crampon bindings had been steadily loosening, but he was too tired to deal with it. One of them popped off and disappeared down the face. He continued down, hopping on one cramponed boot. One hundred and fifty meters lower he miraculously recovered the crampon, which had lodged in soft snow. At 6,600 meters, he reached the top of 150 meters of fixed rope. Only a hundred meters lower was a cache of extra food and fuel. Before he could reach it, a falling stone broke his right arm.

Bivouacked at 6,500 meters, he considered rolling over in his sleeping bag and ending the struggle once and for all with a long fall of his own. Primitive man prevailed: "I had a little bit left, and I figured I should at least give everything I had."

From 6,500 meters he rapped for 200 meters and then left the ropes because they were too hard to pull down with only one hand and his mouth. He downclimbed 55-degree ice using a single ax. The rope they had left to get back over the bergschrund was frozen, and no amount of yanking and chopping and biting would loosen it.

On the morning of the fifth day after the accident, his eighth on the wall, Jean-Christophe downclimbed into the bergschrund. Sheltered from stonefall by the overhanging lip, and not far from base camp, he relaxed. After unfastening his helmet he threw his pack off and lay down for thirty minutes, saying over and over, "I will never, ever go into the mountains again in my life."

After nearly two years of rest and therapy, Lafaille began climbing again, with a vengeance. He climbed Shishapangma in 1994, and made a solo traverse of Gasherbrum I and II in three days round-trip in 1996. Active in the Alps as well, he has established several difficult waterfall and roadside mixed routes, and continues to teach at the French guides school in Chamonix.

Jean-Christophe Lafaille attempting a new route on the north face of the Grandes Jorasses, Chamonix, France. *Photo: © Mark Twight*

DOWN THE RUPAL FACE

During my alpine-style attempt on the Rupal Face of Nanga Parbat with Barry Blanchard, Kevin Doyle, and Ward Robinson in 1988, things spun out of control. After climbing over 13,000 vertical feet in five days, we were tired. The climbing absorbed us so totally that no one noticed the clouds.

My first clue that a storm had broken was an avalanche of spindrift that forced me back down to the belay. We'd reached 25,800 feet, having surmounted all of the technical problems. There remained 1,200 feet of comparatively easy snow between us and the summit. But because of the storm and our thin margin of safety, there was only one way out, down, either the fast way or the slow way.

Snow collected in the bowl above, and the wind spit it down the gully. Lightning flashed across the ridge every two minutes. We heard no explosive punctuation of thunder, just the uninterrupted sound of something tearing. I was strung so tightly I burned. Beside me, Ward was slowly dying—the altitude was killing him—and hypothermia worked its foul magic. I watched him fighting to keep his soul from leaving his body. The avalanches were waist-deep and washed down the face constantly.

Barry went first to set up the rappels, Kevin next to chop stances, then Ward. Being the lightest, I went last. It was my job to pull the backup anchors. Halfway through the second rappel a surge in the avalanche flow flipped me upside down. My goggles were ripped from my face, and my hood filled with debris.

At the bottom of the third rap, we all clipped into an eleven-sixteenths sewn sling girth-hitched through the eye of a Snarg. Just as we pulled the ropes, the bowls above emptied tons of snow into the gully all at once. It hit us like an express train and swept us off the 60-degree ice. I choked on my heart. I could not force my hand up through the maelstrom to the screw or even get a tool off my harness. I knew I had to unweight the Snarg.

My imagination was going wild. I could see the screw pop or the runner fail and the four of us dumped into a Himalayan-scale Cuisinart. Eight ice tools, eight cramponed boots, four packs, and four bodies chewed up, spewed out, dead in a hole. I didn't want to die like that, but I was in no position to choose.

When the avalanche subsided, we noticed Ward's face was aimed up into the void. It was streaked with snot, and his eyes were frozen shut. Without inflection he said, "I was just going to unclip and get it over with."

When we reached the icefield at 9 P.M. it felt like we still had a grip on the controls. I started digging a ledge where we could get Ward into his sleeping bag and fire up the stoves.

Barry and Kevin were cleaning the last of the seven rappels. Barry was at the top of the

Nanga Parbat (8,125 meters), Pakistan. The Rupal Face is the highest precipice in the world, almost 15,000 vertical feet. *Photo: © Mark Twight*

final rappel, planning to downclimb because he worried that the ropes could jam if we pulled them diagonally from below across an intervening rock arête.

"Kevin, I'm letting go of the ropes," Barry shouted down.

"OK. I let go," answered Kevin.

I suppose that's when we finally lost control, along with our only two ropes. Kevin thought Barry had pulled them up. Barry believed Kevin still had his hands on the ends. Both were wrong, though no one realized it at the time.

Barry and I downclimbed to our last bivouac at 23,000 feet. Kevin took care of Ward. They would join us later.

Forcing a pole into one of our Gore-Tex tents, I accidentally pushed the tent off the ledge. I listened dumbly to the fabric slithering away. I didn't jump on it or chase it. Instead, I threw the pole off after it, thinking, "Well, I don't have to carry that anymore."

I started digging a snow cave and finished just as the others arrived. The storm kept up through the night. Daylight brought little promise of improvement. We had to get off the face, haunted as we were by one of Reinhold Messner's remarks, "It is impossible to descend the face in a storm so keep the high camps well stocked." We ran out of food that morning.

Packing up, Ward asked about the ropes. We stared horrified at him, at each other, and all sank into the snow weighed down by the realization. Twelve thousand feet up the biggest wall in the world without any ropes. I looked into the three other sets of knowing eyes and wondered which of us would survive.

We figured there was enough old fixed rope strung in the Welzenbach Couloir that we could tie together a section long enough to rap on. One by one I watched the blue and yellow suits disappear into the storm. A team to be sure, but of lone animals, each fighting for survival. We climbed straight down a windslab because we couldn't avoid it. "What's the difference?" I thought. "I die in this avalanche or I die when the four-

Barry Blanchard and Ward Robinson near 22,000 feet at the top of the Welzenbach Couloir, on the Rupal Face of Nanga Parbat. *Photo: © Mark Twight*

year-old fixed rope breaks, or I just sit down too exhausted to go on. What's it matter?"

We discovered an old, tattered pack with Japanese characters written on it, clipped to some pitons at 22,000 feet. We cut it open without expectation—idle curiosity. We could not contain ourselves. First sixty pitons spilled out, then a dozen ice screws, then chocolate bars. At the bottom Barry found two new 50-meter ropes. It was Bastille Day and we'd just escaped the guillotine. At 6 P.M. the next day we walked into base camp.

Later, during the Ministry of Tourism debriefing, an official asked how we enjoyed our expedition to Nanga Parbat. Barry answered, "It was like having sex with death."

Kevin Doyle descending into the avalanche-scoured Merkl Gully at 25,100 feet on Nanga Parbat's Rupal Face. *Photo: © Mark Twight*

APOLOGIA

I learned a lot during the course of writing this book. I had been retired from alpine climbing for a year before I began typing. But during the process I realized how much I know about alpinism and how much I love/hate doing it. I became excited enough about climbing to postpone writing about it and spend a few months in Alaska actually doing it. I managed one new route on Mount Bradley with Steve House and Jonny Blitz, then 22-hours round-trip on the west face of Mount Huntington (7 hours too long by my estimation) with Bill Belcourt. All in the name of research . . .

These climbs, coupled with the usual hours of introspection, allowed me to understand some things about my career as a climber. In the beginning I was drawn to climbing and climbing hard because I was angry—with the world, my family, and with my future. I chose climbing as self-expression because I needed to feel superior. Soloing hard routes definitely placed me a cut above the rest, in my opinion. The need for superiority conditioned me to desire adulation. I didn't do many of my formative climbs for myself, but for an audience, and I wrote articles because I was dependent upon that audience. I wanted to affect them in some way. The more I did, the happier I was. These actions imposed the great responsibility of living up to my ranting and posturing. No man wants to be found out or proven transparent and irrelevant. I worked hard to live into the personality I created, to live up to his strong beliefs and confrontational attitude.

Through dedication, and effort piled on top of effort, I used the mountains to transform myself. They kept me honest. They threatened me with dire consequences for failure, so I learned to be 100 percent present in every moment I spent among them. I used the mountains to test myself, and when I came up wanting, I trained even harder and studied more. I tried many different forms of climbing over the years, but nothing engaged me like alpine climbing, no other form required the psychological commitment alpinism demanded. So, to me, all other forms became pointless except as training.

Through the testing and training, I developed my own style of active meditation. On certain routes I achieved a mind/no-mind state of mystical connection to the mountain so powerful I knew I could not fall or make mistakes. I could read my partner's mind. I was not affected by gravity. I lost myself on those days. I became the mountain. It is when I did my best routes.

The self-destructiveness of my early days evolved into the destruction of "self" I experienced many years later. In the beginning I concentrated on stripping away the characteristics that didn't contribute to the new future I had mapped out for myself. I acquired attributes that might help me. Today, I struggle to maintain balance between the supreme ego required to conceive and undertake the hardest new routes and the longest single-push efforts, and the egolessness required to become a part of the environment where these actions take place, to become what I am doing.

Through this process I learned that the summit is of little relevance to me. I value the experience and the changes in my character that each experience imposes. I used to attempt routes with a difficult grade for the validation that succeeding on those routes bestowed. These days I could care less about the grade of a route or whether I succeed or fail. What takes place in my mind is primary.

Besides, what truthfully determines difficulty? Pure force and technical skill required, length of effort, objective danger, approach, retreat, weather, ease of living on the route, altitude? No isolated aspect of alpine climbing is solely responsible for its difficulty. Instead, the whole package, when added up and carried for hours and days, makes modern alpinism extreme. This is reflected in the ambiguous system of alpine grades, where a couple of letters or a roman numeral are supposed to cover the entire range of problems encountered on a particular route. Be-

cause dramatic changes occur from day to day and season to season, it's impossible to precisely grade a route that involves 2,000 to 10,000 vertical feet of relief. And therein lies the beauty of alpinism. No matter how often the route has been done, you still never know precisely what you are in for, so you must be prepared to deal with absolutely anything.

I believe climbing mountains changed me for the better. Without the influence of the authentic values reinforced by mountains and the many inspiring and commanding personalities I encountered along my path, I don't know who I would have become. I can only imagine where the trends of my adolescence may have led. But climbing itself has no value, and it is only given worth by what each individual is willing to commit to it. Walter Bonatti said, "The value of the high mountains is that of the men who measure themselves against them: otherwise they are no more than heaps of stone." The energy I offered up to the mountains has been returned tenfold. Climbers undertake incredible challenges in the most beautiful and savage places on earth. Those experiences transform us.

Scott Backes moving ropeless, packless, and fast during the first ascent of Fuck 'em, They're All Posers Anyway on Pico del Norte (19,700 feet), Bolivia. We simul-soloed the 2,500-vertical-foot route in 4 hours 8 minutes and graded it 5.8, 90 degree ice, TD. *Photo: © Mark Twight*

Over the years I developed an ethic to aid in the quest for some form of purity in myself. I learned to respect the mountains, not just because they can kill me, but because they are powerful and enduring; they are the Earth. I could use man's technological advances to overpower the mountains, to bring them down to my own level, to satisfy my ambition and to impress anyone benighted enough to care. But whatever I achieve by exploiting technology and permanently altering the mountain is without value. If I want to look at myself in the mirror and respect what I see, I must climb while adhering to one simple premise: I must attempt the biggest possible objective with the least amount of gear. I must move quickly, but in rhythm with the mountain. I must open myself to fresh experience every hour of every day. I'd rather fail than place a bolt. I'd rather fail than use supplemental oxygen. I'd rather fail than siege a route. And I have.

On certain days when my commitment is high, when my partner and I become each other and become the mountain, anything is possible. In July 1996 Scott Backes and I climbed a new route on Pico del Norte in Bolivia. The mountain is over 19,000 feet high, and our route offered 2,500 vertical feet of climbing. We were so well attuned to the mountain that we left everything behind. We each carried a pint of water, ten packages of carbohydrate gel, spare gloves, two ice tools, and a collapsible ski pole. No ropes, no hardware, basically naked. We agreed beforehand to turn back if anything looked too dangerous, or at 3 P.M., whichever came first.

We left our 17,000-foot bivouac at 11 A.M. The difficult climbing lasted for only 1,000 feet. We were too close to the top when the alarm went off to turn around, so at 3:08 P.M. we stood on the summit of the last mountain we would climb together. Later that year Scott retired from alpine climbing. I felt that this route, though it wasn't as difficult or as long as others we had done, expressed and fulfilled our partnership fully. No extraneous gear or expectation had distracted us from the climbing itself. We honored the mountain and our own ethics by playing as fairly as we could while leaving no trace of our passage. Although no rope bound us together, the connection we felt between us was stronger than ever.

This new route—we called it Fuck 'Em, They're All Posers Anyway—was the culmination of many of the teachings of this book, and certainly the full expression of the attitude necessary to climb hard in the high mountains. Just as skiers learn every style of turn to prepare for the day when they will be good enough to do away with turning altogether, alpine climbers must learn all of the skills and attitudes available so that one day they may climb simply, like animals. I hope you can take something of value from this book and use it for climbing mountains or for whatever else you choose to do. But as my good friend and mentor Brian Enos said, "Everything in this book could be wrong." Your sole responsibility is to learn what works best for you. When you copy others, or do what they tell you is best, you are not learning, you are only a monkey. Come down out of the trees.

Remember, it doesn't have to be fun to be "fun."

THANKS

This book is for the mentors and partners who helped me along the way. I attempt to honor my teachers by not remaining a student. I offer heartfelt thanks to Scott Backes, Barry Blanchard, Randy Rackliff, Jonny Blitz, Andy Nock, Jon Krakauer, John Bouchard, Jeff Lowe, Thierry Renault, Andy Parkin, Mathurin Molgat (wherever you are), Brian Enos, Mad Dog, Steve House (the future), Bill Belcourt, Alex Lowe, Dr. Bill Vaughan, Michael Kennedy, Gary Smith (are you alive?), Nancy Feagin, Gioachino Gobbi, Rolando Garibotti, Dr. Zipper, Ward Robinson, and Kevin Doyle.

I also honor those friends and climbing partners who are no longer alive to read this book: Dave Kahn, Philippe Mohr, Fred Vimal, Alison Hargreaves, Mark Sinclair, Trevor Peterson, Steve Mascioli, Mugs Stump, Roger Baxter-Jones, Richard Ouairy, Tahoe Rowland, Mike Vanderbeek, and Eric Escoffier, to name a few. Tell your friends you care about them now, because you never know when the big storm will hit.

And a loud shout of thanks to Jim Martin for convincing me to accept the inevitability of this book, and for all the blood he has put into making it real.

audacity
a personal perspective on the history of alpinism

Historically, the American mountaineering press gave alpinism only passing notice, focusing instead on big-wall and siege climbs. There have been exceptions, of course. Messner's Himalayan exploits received Page 1 treatment, but many of the fast, light successes in the great ranges earned only a few lines of reporting. While not an exhaustive list of advances in alpinism, the events described below influenced the way I approach climbing mountains.

Alpine-style climbing developed into a high art in the 1980s, but it wouldn't have evolved without those visionary climbers who ascended the north faces of the Eiger, Matterhorn, Grandes Jorasses, and other north walls in the Alps in the years before World War II. Climbing these classics today instills generous respect for the alpinists who had the stones to venture onto this unknown terrain with primitive gear.

After the war, new and more difficult lines were stitched in between existing routes on every big face. Walter Bonatti established one of the hardest mixed routes in the Alps on the north face of the Grand Pilier d'Angle on Mont Blanc in 1962. It was an audacious step toward the future, serving as training for the first winter ascent of the Walker Spur in 1963 and his new route on the Whymper Spur of the Grandes Jorasses with Michel Vaucher in 1964.

As talent increased and training techniques improved, routes that once took three days were routinely flashed in one. Reinhold Messner began the trend by soloing the Davaille route on the north face of Les Droites in 9 hours in 1969. At the time, curved picks on short axes had been in use for only three years, reverse-curve picks were a pipe dream, and ice daggers were the customary second tool.

The 1970s saw a host of steep ice climbs established in the Alps and elsewhere, notably the Cecchinel-Nomine routes on the Pilier d'Angle and the Northeast Couloir of Les Drus, as well as the Super Couloir of Mont Blanc du Tacul. Waterfall climbing accelerated in North America. As tools, technique, and knowledge developed, these routes saw quick repeats and ropeless solos.

Because the mountains weren't getting any higher or more difficult, alpinists focused on speed and purity of style. Climbers routinely soloed routes like the north face of Les Droites in 4 to 6 hours. To fill the remaining 18 to 24 hours, they began linking several faces together in a single marathon push. During the winter of 1983 the brilliant French alpinist Christophe Profit climbed the north faces of Les Droites, the Aiguille du Talefre, and the Grandes Jorasses (by the Shroud) in a 21-hour nonstop effort. Patrick Gabarrou traversed the Mont Blanc Massif alone, climbing seven north faces along the way, in 1989.

This era in the Alps of linking climbs—enchainment—climaxed in 1996 with Patrick Berhault and Francois Bibollet combining extremely difficult routes on Les Droites (Colton-Brooks), Grandes Jorasses (Colton-McIntyre), Pilier d'Angle (Cecchinel-Nomine), and the

Francois Marsigny climbing mixed terrain on the Aiguille du Midi, Chamonix, France. Photo: © Mark Twight

Hyper Couloir on the south face of Mont Blanc. While many more enchainments wait in ranges throughout the world, the statement has been made in the Alps, and eyes must look elsewhere for big challenges.

The early 1990s in the Alps saw creation of severely difficult routes that followed ephemeral ice features. Andy Parkin and I established Beyond Good and Evil on the north face of the Aiguille des Pelerins in 1992. Scott Backes and I climbed a new route on the north face of the Aiguille Sans Nom a year later, and graded it harder than Beyond. Andy and Francois Marsigny established several similar routes, the most difficult being Alaskan Freeway on the Dent du Caiman in 1998. Each new route was more committing than the last.

Parallel to these developments in Europe, extreme alpinism evolved elsewhere as well. George Lowe and Chris Jones made a spectacular commitment to the 6,000-foot north face of North Twin in the Canadian Rockies in 1974 and climbed themselves into a predicament from which they could not retreat. With dwindling food and fuel, and gear dropped from an already anorexic rack, it was Lowe's will and Jones's "high survival potential" that allowed them to finish the climb. As the twentieth century drew to a close, this route remained unrepeated. For the most part only North American mountains, not yet overrun by mechanized means of access, demand the commitment required for a route like this.

In 1977 George Lowe partnered with Michael Kennedy to make the first ascent of the Infinite Spur on the south face of Mount Foraker in the Alaska Range. The spur offered 10,000 vertical feet of difficult climbing to a remote 17,000-foot summit with no easy way off. The pair carried only the slightest margin of safety in their packs and operated in total autonomy for eleven days.

Hard technical alpine climbing came to the Alaska Range in March 1981 when Mugs Stump and Jim Bridwell made the first and, as of this writing, only ascent of the east face of Moose's Tooth. This route stretched the imagination of many climbers, myself included, while shattering the egos of others. Mugs quickly followed this with his ascent of the North Buttress of Mount Hunter. He is not generally credited with the first ascent because he did not continue to the summit, but he regarded it as one of his best climbs. He and Paul Aubrey tackled the 4,000-foot buttress with light packs, two bivy sacks, and one hammock between them. The climb is graded 5.9, A3, 90- to 95-degree ice, and no ascent in the range equaled its difficulty for the next thirteen years.

Mugs applied his light-and-fast style all over the world, culminating in his solo ascent of the Cassin Ridge on Denali in 15+ hours in 1991. He proved that a skilled and fit climber with an open mind can climb the biggest routes in a single push. Mugs, the motivator for a whole generation of North American alpine climbers, died in a crevasse fall on Denali in 1992.

Following Mugs's lead, rapid, lightweight ascents of technical routes became more common in the Alaska Range. In 1994 Scott Backes and I put up Deprivation on Mount Hunter's North Buttress in 72 hours round-trip. Steve House and Eli Helmuth followed in 1995 with their ascent of the 6,000-foot route First Born on the Fathers and Sons Wall of Denali in 36 hours round-trip. House soloed a new 7,000-foot route on the northwest face of the West Buttress on Denali, Beauty is a Rare Thing, in 14 hours in July 1996. In 1997, climbing with Steve Swenson, he ascended a 3,000-foot route on Denali's south buttress, which they named Mascioli's Pillar. They completed the climb, graded 5.10, A0, 90-degree ice, in 30 hours round-trip.

Having accumulated enough experience with single-push tactics in the Alaska Range, Steve attempted something a bit bigger, carrying even less equipment. In June 1998, with Joe Josephson, he established a 7,100-foot route to the top of King Peak, a 17,000-foot satellite of Mount Logan in the St. Elias Range. The pair's two packs weighed 30 pounds total. They climbed on a single 9.1-millimeter rope and blasted the face in 35 hours round-trip.

Elsewhere during this period, Rolando Garibotti and Doug Byerly made an alpine-style ascent of the 37-pitch Tehuelche on the north face of Fitzroy in Patagonia. Rolo said a pure alpine-style climb was "a way of being fair and showing respect to such a beautiful face and grandiose peak." The pair climbed from base camp to base camp in 48 hours.

Add the component of high altitude to alpine-style climbing, and it becomes much more complicated. Lightweight tactics had been used on Himalayan giants as early as Alfred Mummery's attempt on Nanga Parbat in 1895. Light expedition-style tactics proved successful during the Austrian ascent of Broad Peak in 1957, when Hermann Buhl and Kurt Diemberger captured the summit.

In 1975, Reinhold Messner and Peter Habeler made the biggest leap in the history of Himalayan climbing by ascending Hidden Peak (also known as Gasherbrum I; 8,068 meters) in three days round-trip, using perfect alpine style. Until then, all other 8,000-meter peaks had been climbed slowly, using a safety chain of fixed ropes and well-stocked camps, so when Messner and Habeler cut the umbilical cord of security, they entered the unknown.

Three years later the pair became the first to climb Everest without supplemental oxygen, albeit as part of a large siege-style expedition. Messner soloed the Diamir Face of Nanga Parbat two months later. Then, in 1980, he soloed Everest without oxygen. He had absolutely no support above base camp for the three days his climb required. Their eyes now opened, alpinists began applying lighter and lighter tactics to the Himalayas, with Europeans dominating the high-altitude alpine-style scene.

In 1982, Doug Scott, Roger Baxter-Jones, and Alex McIntyre walked up to the unclimbed south face of Shishapangma and began climbing. They summited in alpine style after three bivouacs. The torrent was let loose, and speed became the new ethos for high-altitude climbing.

The year 1985 was an amazing one in Himalayan climbing. Benoit Chamoux climbed the Abruzzi Spur of K2 in 23 hours only a couple of days after soloing Broad Peak in 16 hours. Eric Escoffier climbed K2, Hidden Peak (Gasherbrum I), and Gasherbrum II within a one-month period. These were not strictly alpine-style ascents as the climbers benefited from the presence of other climbers' tracks and fixed ropes. Still, every ascent provided more knowledge.

Erhard Loretan climbed with Escoffier on K2. The previous autumn, Loretan had made the first ascent of the east ridge of Annapurna with Norbert Joos. The pair traveled 7.5 kilometers of ridge between 7,000 and 8,000 meters, bivouacked twice above 8,000 meters, and traversed the mountain, descending by the north face. After K2, Loretan finished the year by joining Jean Troillet and Pierre-Alain Steiner on the first winter ascent of the east face of Dhaulagiri, doing it in 36 hours.

On each of these climbs, Loretan pared his gear down more and more until his team climbed packless on Dhaulagiri. This era of what Voytek Kurtyka termed "night naked" climbing peaked in August 1986 with Loretan and Troillet's remarkable 43-hour round-trip ascent of Everest.

In addition to the oxygenless speed ascents, 8,000-meter peaks saw technical ascents as well. In 1984 two Catalonians, Nils Bohigas and Enric Lucas, finished a route attempted by Rene Ghilini and Alex McIntyre on the massive south face of Annapurna I. (McIntyre was killed by stonefall while retreating from the face in 1982.) The extremely bold pair spent six days on the face, with the most difficult climbing at around 7,100 meters (5.9, A2, 80-degree ice). They joined the Polish route up high, and after visiting the summit, rappelled down that route—8,000 vertical feet—to base camp in a single day.

The 2,500-meter west face of Gasherbrum IV (7,925 meters), known as the Shining Wall, saw many attempts during the early '80s. In 1985 Voytek Kurtyka and Robert Schauer climbed the wall in alpine style, but missed the summit by several hundred feet. Trapped by a two-day storm at the top of the face, they ran out of food and water. They began hallucinating. Schauer imagined himself as a big raven, hovering over his own body, waiting to pick the bones clean. Once the storm cleared, they chose descent and survival over the improbability of traversing to the main summit.

One final route on an 8,000-meter peak merits attention because it ushered in a period when Slovenians began to dominate Himalayan climbing. In 1991 two intense and visionary Slovenian climbers, Marko Prezelj and Andrej Stremfelj, climbed the awesome south ridge of Kanchenjunga on-sight and unsupported. Climber and author Stephen Venables calls the ascent "one of the boldest ventures of all time." These three climbs—on Kanchenjunga, the Shining Wall, and the south face of Annapurna—epitomize the commitment and confidence required to climb in alpine style on any mountain.

Prezelj and Stremfelj followed their success on Kanchenjunga with a 53-hour round-trip climb on the extremely dangerous 2,000-meter-high southeast face of Menlungtse (7,181 meters). While not rising to the revered height of 8,000 meters, peaks like Menlungtse have been the scene of much technical development in recent years.

Mick Fowler and Victor Saunders climbed the Golden Pillar of Spantik (7,028 meters) in Pakistan over seven days in 1987 in a futuristic effort. The 2,100-meter-high route on the mountain's northwest pillar featured more than twenty pitches of Scottish Grade V and harder, aid climbing, and dubious points of protection. The poor quality rock and thin ice presented few opportunities for rappel anchors, so the face demanded huge commitment.

The north face of Changabang (6,864 meters) in India, although less committing, is more technically difficult than Spantik, featuring sustained pitches of Scottish Grade IV and V punctuated with several cruxes of VI—described in typical British understatement as "hard." Foul weather and spindrift hampered the ascent, in 1997, of the 1,600-meter face. Mick Fowler and Steve Sustad joined Andy Cave and Brendan Murphy high on Changabang after starting up one day apart. They finished by climbing together following more than a week on the wall. They described many of the bivouacs as "character-building" sit-down affairs exposed to constant spindrift. The descent required another six days, during which Murphy was killed in a fall. Fowler later called the climb "the greatest adventure of my life," but conceded it may have been "a touch too much."

The stories of extreme climbs told on these pages give some idea of the history of modern alpine climbing and a sense of the many possible disciplines within alpine style. All point toward a future when the lines sieged yesterday will fall to single-push, "night naked" ascents undertaken by talented and open-minded alpinists who evolve from the at-once glorious and pitiful efforts of the present.

suggested Reading APPENDIX 2

Bowerman, William J., and William H. Freeman. *High Performance Training for Track and Field.* Champaign, Illinois: Human Kinetics, 1990. Good source for decathlon training tactics.

Buhl, Hermann. *Nanga Parbat Pilgrimage.* Seattle: The Mountaineers, 1998. Reprint of a book written by the climber who put "hard" into the term "hardman." Unbelievable.

Castenada, Carlos. *Tales of Power.* New York: Pocket Books, 1992. Reprint of a book that represents a journey of the mind, pointing to the proper attitude for confronting the problems of climbing and earning psychological strength.

Chouinard, Yvon. *Climbing Ice.* San Francisco: Sierra Club Books, 1978. Chouinard's way of thinking as it applies to alpine climbing is as appropriate and important today as it was when the book was first published.

Colgan, Michael. *Optimum Sports Nutrition.* Ronkonkoma, New York: Advanced Research Press, 1993. Perhaps the best compilation of diet-related material as it applies to athletics.

Desmaison, René. *Total Alpinism.* Translated from the French by Jane Taylor. New York and London: Granada, 1982. A personal account of a situation gone bad, by a climber who had the will to survive.

Gatorade Sports Science Institute. Website: www.gssiweb.com. Test results and position papers regarding hydration and nutrition for athletics.

Graydon, Don, and Kurt Hanson, editors. *Mountaineering: The Freedom of the Hills,* sixth edition. Seattle: The Mountaineers, 1997. The most comprehensive primer on mountaineering.

Haston, Dougal. *In High Places.* Seattle: The Mountaineers, 1997. Reprint of a book by a climber who was the physical and philosophical master of his generation.

Hatfield, Frederick. *Power.* Chicago: Contemporary Books, 1989. The ultimate resource for an athlete who wishes to develop power.

Houston, Charles S. *Going Higher,* fourth edition. Seattle: The Mountaineers, 1998. The definitive study of man at altitude and of acclimatization.

Janssen, Peter G. J. M. *Training Lactate Pulse Rate.* Finland: Polar Electro Oy, 1987. The most scientific book on training heart rates and anaerobic threshold, with training prescriptions and logs. There are more user-friendly books, but none match this one's volume and intensity.

Kammer, Reinhard, and Betty J. Fitzgerald. *The Tengu-Gejitsu-Ron of Chozan Shissai.* Boston and London: Arkana, 1986. One of the best books describing the making of the warrior spirit and how to deal with fear. Translation of *Die Kunst der Bergdämonen.*

Keirsey, David. *Please Understand Me II: Temperament, Character, Intelligence.* Prometheus Nemesis Book Company, 1998. Temperament and character tests; take a test on the Internet at http://keirsey.com.

Krishnamurti. *On Fear.* New York: HarperCollins, 1995. Philosopher's meditation on fear.

Krishnamurti. *Think on These Things.* New York: HarperCollins, 1964. Eastern thought applied to western problems: a great influence on Bruce Lee.

Lansing, Alfred. *Endurance,* second edition. New York: Carroll & Graf, 1999. The ultimate Antarctic survival story.

Lee, Bruce. *The Tao of Jeet Kune Do.* Burbank, California: Ohara Publications, 1975. The teachings of Krishnamurti adapted to personal expression within an athletic discipline; goes a long way toward describing how to approach and resolve problems.

Livingston, Michael K. *Mental Discipline.* Champaign, Illinois: Human Kinetics Books, 1989. A scientific approach to mental conditioning, detailing the physiological mechanisms involved.

Long, John. *Climbing Anchors.* Evergreen, Colorado: Chockstone Press, 1993.

Maffetone, Philip. *Training for Endurance.* Stamford, New York: David Barmore Productions, 1992. An alternative look at training and nutrition for endurance effort, used by world-champion triathletes Mike Pigg and Mark Allen.

McArdle, W. D., F. I. Katch, and V. L. Katch. *Exercise Physiology,* fourth edition. Philadelphia: Williams & Wilkins, 1996. The bible of sports physiology.

Messner, Reinhold. *The Seventh Grade.* New York: Oxford 1982. Basically the training and climbing diary of the man who was the greatest rock climber in the world and then decided to become the greatest ice climber, which he did, and then chose to become the greatest high-altitude climber, which he also did.

Mishima, Yukio. *Sun and Steel.* New York: Grove Press, 1972. Autobiography of the novelist whose personal dedication to physical training and the martial spirit appears to contradict his fiction.

Miyamoto, Musashi. *The Book of Five Rings.* Woodstock, New York: Overlook Press, 1974. About the samurai code and about strategy; climbers may learn how to think about problems of a hard alpine route and how best to apply one's energy.

Monroe, Robert. *Ultimate Journey.* New York: Doubleday, 1994. Personal notes on "out of body experiences" and brain hemisphere synchronization.

Niednagel, Jonathan P. *Choose Your Best Sport & Play It.* Laguna Niguel, California: Laguna Press, 1992. A temperament-typing book, useful for learning a bit about you or your partner's predilections if you can be honest about taking the tests.

Noakes, Timothy. *The Lore of Running.* Champaign, Illinois: Human Kinetics, 1991. Good information on training and exercise physiology.

Pearl, Bill. *Keys to the Inner Universe.* Pasadena, California: Bill Pearl Enterprises, 1979. An encyclopedia of weight-training exercises.

Radcliffe, James, and Robert Farentinos. *Plyometrics.* Champaign, Illinois: Human Kinetics Publishers, 1985. A brief look at the science, techniques, and benefits of ballistic training.

Sears, Barry. *The Zone.* New York: Harper Collins, 1995. A diet-oriented book proselytizing the 40-30-30 diet, which does work, but requires very strict self-discipline.

Tasker, Joe. *Savage Arena.* New York: St. Martins Press, 1983. After each experience described in this book, the normal climber would gladly retire. Tasker didn't. He had an unparalleled will.

Werner, David. *Where There Is No Doctor,* revised edition. Palo Alto, California: The Hesperian Foundation, 1990. Health information on third-world travel, medicines, illness diagnosis.

Wilkerson, James. *Medicine for Mountaineering and Other Wilderness Activities,* fourth edition. Seattle: The Mountaineers, 1992. A standard manual.

Yessis, Michael. *Kinesiology of Exercise.* Indianapolis, Indiana: Masters Press, 1992. Critical analysis of form and style for strength-training exercises; how to do every exercise you can imagine, wnat each does, and how it relates to particular sports.

Rescue Insurance

Air Glaciers S.A.
1951 Sion, Switzerland
Rescue insurance for Western Europe.

American Alpine Club
303-384-0110
www.americanalpineclub.org/
insur.htm
For AAC members only: rescue insurance below certain altitudes, riders available for higher altitudes, a cap on the payout.

Divers Alert Network
800-446-2671, Fax 919-490-6630
Repatriation insurance.

Federation Francaise de la Montagne
8-10 Quai de la Marne, F-75019
Paris, France
33-1-40187550
Rescue insurance for Western Europe.

Brain Synchronization Tools

Human Potential
801-487-0754
E-mail:
humanpotential@compuserve.com
Produces CDs using radio sonic technology; the Deep Sleep product induces sleep. One may learn to access a brain state that will induce sleep when you want, an essential asset for a bivouac or when recovery is essential before climbing the next day.

The Monroe Institute
P.O. Box 505
Lovingston, VA 22949
804-361-1252, Fax: 804-361-1237
E-mail: monroeinst@aol.com
Tapes and CDs featuring sound frequencies corresponding to brain wave activities. The hemispheric synchronization (Hemi-Sync) signals may be buried in music or broadcast alone depending upon the intent of the tape or CD.

Peak Performance Institute
2902 East Campbell Avenue
Phoenix, AZ 85016
Fax: 602-912-9533.
Employs light and sound frequencies to influence brain states. Produces a small, portable device called the Sportslink that features programs that aid visualization, anchoring, precompetition, recovery, sleep, and other areas of importance to athletes.

ABOUT THE AUTHORS

Photo by Lisa Boshard

Mark Twight is one of America's leading alpinists. His routes in Asia, North America, and the Alps have stretched the limits of the possible, and many remain unrepeated. Among his more recent accomplishments are the first telemark ski descent of Pic Fourth and the first solo ascent of the Czech Route on Pic Communism (24,600 feet) in the former Soviet Union (1990); the first ascent (with Scott Backes) of Deprivation on Mount Hunter in Alaska (1994)—a 72-hour marathon that halved the previous fastest time for any route on the North Buttress of this difficult mountain; and the first ascent (again with Backes) of They're All Posers Anyway on Pico del Norte in Bolivia (1996), a minimalist attack undertaken without ropes or packs.

Mark's acerbic writings and vertiginous photographs have appeared in leading climbing magazines around the world. His climbing has been featured in television programs, including ABC's "The Extreme Edge," and he played the lead role in *Pushing the Limits,* a film by Thierry Donard shot on location in France, Switzerland, Bolivia, and Argentina.

James Martin is a freelance writer and photographer whose work has appeared in *Smithsonian, Sports Illustrated, Climbing, Outside, Outdoor Photographer,* and a host of other publications. He is also the author of *North Cascades Crest: Notes & Images,* which showcases seventy-five of his color photographs. He has been climbing since 1966 and established several first ascents in the United States and Canada.

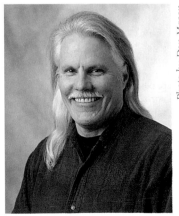

Photo by Don Mason

THE MOUNTAINEERS, founded in 1906, is a nonprofit outdoor activity and conservation club, whose mission is "to explore, study, preserve, and enjoy the natural beauty of the outdoors. . . . " Based in Seattle, Washington, the club is now the third-largest such organization in the United States, with 15,000 members and five branches throughout Washington State.

The Mountaineers sponsors both classes and year-round outdoor activities in the Pacific Northwest, which include hiking, mountain climbing, ski-touring, snowshoeing, bicycling, camping, kayaking and canoeing, nature study, sailing, and adventure travel. The club's conservation division supports environmental causes through educational activities, sponsoring legislation, and presenting informational programs. All club activities are led by skilled, experienced volunteers, who are dedicated to promoting safe and responsible enjoyment and preservation of the outdoors.

If you would like to participate in these organized outdoor activities or the club's programs, consider a membership in The Mountaineers. For information and an application, write or call The Mountaineers, Club Headquarters, 300 Third Avenue West, Seattle, Washington 98119; (206) 284-6310.

The Mountaineers Books, an active, nonprofit publishing program of the club, produces guidebooks, instructional texts, historical works, natural history guides, and works on environmental conservation. All books produced by The Mountaineers are aimed at fulfilling the club's mission.

Send or call for our catalog of more than 300 outdoor titles:

The Mountaineers Books
1001 SW Klickitat Way, Suite 201
Seattle, WA 98134
800-553-4453
mbooks@mountaineers.org
www.mountaineersbooks.org